An Art of Instrumentality

The Landscape Architecture of Richard Weller

ORO Editions
Publishers of Architecture, Art, and Design
Gordon Goff: Publisher

www.oroeditions.com
info@oroeditions.com

Published by ORO Editions.

Copyright © 2023 Richard Weller.

All rights reserved. No part of this book may be reproduced, stored in a retrieval system, or transmitted in any form or by any means, including electronic, mechanical, photocopying of microfilming, recording, or otherwise (except that copying permitted by Sections 107 and 108 of the US Copyright Law and except by reviewers for the public press) without written permission from the publisher.

You must not circulate this book in any other binding or cover and you must impose this same condition on any acquirer.

Author: Richard J. Weller
Editor: Tatum Hands
Book Design: Elliot Bullen
Project Manager: Jake Anderson

10 9 8 7 6 5 4 3 2 1 First Edition

ISBN: 978-1-957183-62-6

Color Separations and Printing: ORO Group Inc.
Printed in China

ORO Editions makes a continuous effort to minimize the overall carbon footprint of its publications. As part of this goal, ORO, in association with Global ReLeaf, arranges to plant trees to replace those used in the manufacturing of the paper produced for its books. Global ReLeaf is an international campaign run by American Forests, one of the world's oldest nonprofit conservation organizations. Global ReLeaf is American Forests' education and action program that helps individuals, organizations, agencies, and corporations improve the local and global environment by planting and caring for trees.

An Art of Instrumentality

The Landscape Architecture of Richard Weller

RICHARD WELLER

Foreword by JILLIAN WALLISS
Afterword by DIRK SIJMONS

ORO EDITIONS
Novato, CA

Richard Weller is the Meyerson Chair of Urbanism and Professor and Chair of Landscape Architecture at the Weitzman School of Design, University of Pennsylvania. Image by Gordon Stillman.

TABLE OF CONTENTS

FOREWORD BY JILLIAN WALLISS

A WIDE OPEN ROAD[1]

Most celebrated designers and academics have a good origin story: graduating from an esteemed design school or scoring a breakthrough moment working in a major designer's office. Richard's career has no such story—a rarity in the design disciplines, where networks and affiliations underpin much individual success. Shaped by a deep interest in design and a dose of serendipity, his career has taken him from Sydney to Berlin, to Perth, and to Philadelphia, with many side trips along the way.

Australians have a strong sense of the periphery and the center. Occupying the center does not come naturally to antipodeans, and risks the dampening of original insights gained from being on the fertile edge. Richard's influential iconoclastic views of landscape architecture in the 1990s and 2000s constructed from Perth—the most isolated capital city in the world—reflect these advantages. Forty years since his first exposure to landscape architecture during his studies at the University of New South Wales,[2] he is now in his final term as Chair of the Department of Landscape Architecture at the University of Pennsylvania, part of an esteemed lineup spanning Ian McHarg, Anne Whiston Spirn, John Dixon Hunt, and James Corner. In this role, Richard has managed to maintain his independence, work ethic, criticality, and Australian accent. Through projects he continues to speculate and provoke, capitalizing on his prominent position to lobby for a globally driven landscape consciousness: a McHargian-influenced visionary with a Bob Geldof presence.[3]

Competitions are the "Arte Povera" of the Periphery[4]

Good design competitions are a mirror to the issues of our times and play a critical role in extending and challenging academia and practice. In many ways, design competitions, rather than formal design education, have shaped Richard's career and craft. Writing in 2005, he commented that "by virtue of anonymity," design competitions "allow one to transcend rank."[5] Competitions helped Richard, a "blow-in" from Australia, to get a foot in the door of Berlin design firm Müller Knippschild Wehberg (now Lützow 7). But even more importantly, the competition format has honed Richard's practice, offering concise provocations to explore via theoretical and creative speculation. Through the strict limitations of the competition, Richard has developed his signature approach—a manifesto-like proposition communicated through a compelling graphic and narrative.

Competition briefs provided Richard with an opportunity to directly engage with the impossibilities of absence in postwar Berlin (explored over a four-year period); the events of 9/11 (which many claim as the end of postmodernism); the experiential potentials of Sydney's postindustrial harbor sites; the enormity of loss inflicted by tsunami; and the culture wars of Australia. He has taken students on this journey using competitions in studio teaching and more recently conceiving competitions for *LA+ Journal*. In this later incarnation, Richard has become the author of angst, challenging academics and practice to grapple with the (im)possibilities of the Anthropocene.

But it is in the story of *The Garden of Australian Dreams* (GOAD) in the National Museum of Australia that the double-edged sword of design competition success becomes evident—the initial accolade is tempered by the challenges and tensions of manifesting speculation into the physical. In this case, construction collided with the heated culture wars of late twentieth-century Australia. Not for the fainthearted, the debates over GOAD crossed national politics, academia, the profession, and the public. Who would have thought representing the "lucky country" could be so fraught? As Australia moved past the limp celebrations of the 1988 Bicentennial to construct a postcolonial identity of multiculturalism and pluralism, it failed to acknowledge its treaty-less foundation. Charged with constructing a new postcolonial national museum in the heart of the nation's capital, Canberra, this collaboration between architects ARM and Room 4.1.3 (Richard's design practice with Vladimir Sitta), pulled off the many band-aids patching up Australia's national identity.

Their design response was not the celebration that conservative politicians and academics had hoped for. Hidden amongst the symbolism employed in the GOAD were high and low cultural references, barbs, and provocations. The incorporation of the word "sorry" expressed in braille on the façade of the museum pushed many over the edge, leading to calls for the redesign of GOAD. This morphed into debates over the moral rights of designers—the first time that Australian landscape architecture had entered this arena.[6] The garden remains intact, although a little worse for wear as its colored-concrete ground surface fades (hopefully) alongside the conservative racial politics of Australia.

Twenty years on, there is a new competition for the heart of Canberra's Parliamentary Zone, to be known as the Ngurra precinct.[7] Conceived against the political backdrop of Reconciliation, the emergence of state-based treaties and rumblings of an Indigenous voice to parliament, this competition represents a national maturing where direct Indigenous representation and input (rather than passive symbolism) will shape the outcome. At the time of writing, the winner is yet to be announced, but given a newly elected Labor government, the process should be somewhat smoother than the controversy surrounding the National Museum of Australia. As the saying goes, "you can't make an omelet without breaking some eggs," and GOAD offered a timely provocation during the uncomfortable process of reconciling Australian national identity with unfinished business.

At a more personal level, Richard acknowledges that such a close collaboration with architect Howard Raggatt (ARM) is a rare experience and served to amplify ideas. The project also garnered international attention, and was a catalyst for the publication of the Room 4.1.3. monograph by Penn Press in 2005. The value of GOAD—and the National Museum of Australia more generally—is far greater than its physical form, inspiring extensive professional, academic, and public discourse crossing Australian history, cultural studies, museum studies, architecture, urban design, and postcolonial theory. Arguably, GOAD might be the most discussed landscape architecture project in Australia in the past fifty years, if not since Walter Burley Griffin's plan for Canberra.

A Designer in Wolf's Clothing

The relationship between planning and design continues to be a source of tension in landscape architecture, splintering landscape praxis into the two camps of repeatable analytical methods and more-creative design speculation. In my conversations with American academics, Richard is often described as a planner. From an Australian perspective this is surprising, given that he is strongly identified as a designer and driven by an equally strong conceptual art practice.[8] This disputed identity is partly driven by the Australian understanding of the term "planning," which conjures up images of imported British town planning ideals guiding the development of our cities and suburbs through green belts, subdivisions, and rational road systems. But when considered against the North American landscape planning tradition, Richard's speculations on urbanism make the description of planner somewhat less design averse.

In 2005, Richard's new role as director of the Australian Urban Design Research Centre (AUDRC) at the University of Western Australia, reoriented his focus toward the slippery challenges of an Australian urbanism. He identifies as part of the early twenty-first-century push toward conceiving a landscape-driven urbanism (although aligned with the North American landscape fraternity rather than the AA parametric flavor). Working within the research context of Australia, where money is tight, and grants are highly competitive, he began with the potentials of Perth's suburban housing. Supported by a modest team of PhD candidates and researchers, Richard spent eight years interrogating Australian urbanism across the scales of the suburb, the city, and the megaregion. Mapping is critical to this practice, and unquestionably Richard loves a map. Historical maps offer a host of cultural and political references, while landscape architecture's beloved GIS provides a comprehensive inventory of spatialized physical and social data. When applied critically and creatively, mapping offers a generative technique for merging planning and design, which Richard and his team used to great effect in their foray into urbanism.

Over time, he managed to wrangle the world of Australian competitive research grants into his preferred mode of design speculation. *Boomtown 2050: Scenarios for a Rapidly Growing City*, funded by a three-year Australian Research Council grant, presents alternative design scenarios for Perth's urban development. Published in 2009, the research aimed to graphically present density speculations with a detached neutrality, hoping to prompt a wider debate engaging politicians, the public, built environment professions, and the media. *Boomtown* morphed into a major communications exercise with Richard delivering up to four lectures a week outlining future scenarios for Perth's urbanism. Here the graphic images count—offering a far more accessible story than conventional planning documents.

However, this urban development story inevitably must include economic growth in its plot. And therein lies the failure of landscape urbanism: its agendas are most easily realized in the excess space of the shrinking city, or alternatively in China, where technically no one owns land, and the government operates as developer and authority. In an Australian urban growth model, where the economy is underpinned by the construction industry, it is extremely challenging to bring questions of biodiversity and ecology into the urbanism equation. No art of instrumentality here—just the blunt instrument of short-term economic growth. Richard's 2008 essay "Landscape (Sub)Urbanism in Theory and Practice" oozes with this frustration, drawing attention to landscape urbanism's lack of engagement with the suburb, including the economic realities "where developers, service providers, and ultimately consumers all operate within narrow financial margins."[9] As Richard reflects, "large-scale urbanism is a fool's game"—as you move away from discrete design projects to the larger scale you inevitably lose control.[10] There is a vast gap between landscape urbanism as a theoretical concept and a constructed reality.

Building Penn's Landscape Legacy

In the world of landscape architecture academia, the chair at the University of Pennsylvania (Penn) is the holy grail. Past chairs have demonstrated Penn's openness to non–North American candidates, as evidenced by Scotsman Ian McHarg and Englishman James Corner. Or have they? This claim is only partially true, given that both McHarg and Corner studied landscape architecture at Harvard and Penn respectively.[11] The appointment of Richard in 2013 was far more of an unknown, gained without the advantages of an East Coast landscape pedigree. His new role came as a surprise in Australia. After decades of importing North American academics and practitioners (with mixed results), this was a major shift in fortunes. In his essay for this book, the significance of this career move barely rates a mention. I pressed him on it.

Richard did not aim to go to North America. He was successful and comfortable in Perth with an off-campus city-based studio, good resources, and access to policy makers and politicians, including the premier of Western Australia. His collaboration with Vladimir Sitta had allowed him to build a practice, continue to operate as an academic, and have ample opportunities to travel and lecture internationally. However, after Boomtown he felt that his urban planning project was done, and he was ready to move on. Whereas some might have chosen the path of comfort, shoring up their expertise and reputation, Richard by his own admission gets bored once a project has played out.

Penn presented the lure of an international platform along with its historical legacy of critical thought and leadership in landscape architecture. Moving countries meant a new academic culture—the public Australian university system, heavily influenced by the United Kingdom, is very different from a private Ivy League university such as Penn.[12] In this new context, the pressure to "talk up" the program and the discipline more generally did not come naturally to Richard, who prefers to have influence through projects rather than rhetoric.

Penn offered resources to seed projects, and over time Richard has become more comfortable asking donors for funds to support initiatives to extend Penn's influence and facilitate his own projects. In his first year he edited *Transects: 100 Years of Landscape Architecture and Regional Planning at the School of Design of the University of Pennsylvania*, and in another nod to legacy, in 2016 he curated the International Festival of Landscape Architecture "Not in My Backyard" in Canberra, celebrating the fiftieth year of the Australian Institute of Landscape Architects. At the same time he led the process of writing the New Landscape Declaration, a statement of the profession's core values by the Landscape Architecture Foundation (LAF) in Washington DC.

Recognizing the absence of theoretically driven landscape journals and landscape critique more generally, in 2015 he established the *LA+ Interdisciplinary Journal of Landscape Architecture* with his partner, Tatum Hands. A trained lawyer and professional editor, Tatum is the Editor in Chief of *LA+* and works closely with Richard on many of his publications. Inspired by *Daidalos*, which Richard read as student, over the past nine years, *LA+* has explored themes as diverse as Wild, Pleasure, Creature, Tyranny, Simulation, Risk, and Interruption, and it is now considered central to disseminating landscape discourse internationally.

Relocating to Penn also meant engaging with the North American landscape agendas dominated by issues of resilience, climate change, and now decarbonization. The establishment of the Ian L. McHarg Center for Urbanism and Ecology as a multidisciplinary research center has provided a major mechanism for Penn's landscape program to focus their work. Marking the fiftieth anniversary of the publication of McHarg's seminal work *Design with Nature*, the center was launched in 2019 with an international symposium, the publication *Design with Nature Now*, and a supporting exhibition. And in a final homage to Penn as his tenure as chair concludes, *The Landscape Project* (2022), coedited by Richard and Tatum, draws together the writings of his colleagues to offer a record of ideas which influence the contemporary project of landscape architecture.

Developed in collaboration with many, these highlighted projects are vehicles for documenting and disseminating *other* people's voices and ideas. Instigating, editing, organizing, framing, hosting, curating—this is work that is taken for granted in the hierarchical academic model that rewards individual success. Richard has done plenty of it in his career. Many students, academics, researchers, and practitioners in Australia, North America, and from wider geographies have been provided opportunities by Richard, me included. Thank you.

A Question of Scale

The climate crisis has reinvigorated landscape architecture internationally. It has, though, been accompanied by two problematic tendencies: first, for the profession to spend considerable energy *describing* the crisis (as if it has gone unnoticed); and second, the declaration of landscape architecture's unique position to address these issues. For example, the recent 2022 IFLA world congress in Korea featured a "motivating" film clip on a loop depicting landscape architecture with almost superhero characteristics. Stewardship on steroids.

Critical of landscape architecture climatic dogma, Richard entered the era of the Anthropocene through his preferred mode of the project. His intentions were not to find a solution but to work with design speculation to test landscape methods at the scale of the global and planetary. As he comments, while every discipline is concerned with climate change, "design is the one thing the landscape architect can bring to the table that others cannot."[13] His first project in this arena, the "Atlas for the End of the World," used mapping, supported by statistics, to highlight the conflict between global urban development and biodiversity. The scale then shifts to ground the project in the cultural, ecological, and political specifics of the world's "biodiversity hotspot" cities where the surrounding unique biodiversity is critically threatened by urbanization.

The "World Park" project builds on the Atlas. Global-scale mappings document three walking trails, which transect nations and connect biodiversity hotspots and habitats along the way. Through the cultural practice of walking, these trails aim to encourage humans to participate in the restoration of landscape connectivity, along with reversing the historical role of national parks, which separated culture from a pristine wilderness. To address the challenges of climate change, Richard states, "requires the rationality of the planner, the cunning of the politician, and the imagination of the artist."[14] The World Park project reflects these attributes, working between the two poles of the allegorical and the instrumental. It is a simply communicated yet complex idea which offers a focus to mobilize funds (hopefully obtained from a Musk, Bezos, Gates, or a Winfrey), and it has caught the attention of UNESCO, which is currently exploring its possibilities.

Richard warns that some people might view this approach as an example of a "neo-colonial megalomania," explaining in his writings how mega-eco projects differ from megaprojects.[15] Coming back to his intent to explore the global and planetary scales, I suggest that it is not at the geographic or landscape scale that the World Park project is vulnerable, but at the scale of economic, cultural, and political *disparity*. Like Richard, I want to believe in the power of a big idea to address climatic issues. He clearly sees the potential of the mega-eco project underpinned by landscape architectural thinking as a major way for the discipline to address the loss of biodiversity and global warming. Here is where my earlier reference to "a Bob Geldof presence" kicks in—partly in recognition of Richard's charismatic sensibility[16] but mainly for their shared ambition to mobilize at scale for a greater social and ecological outcome.[17] But for me, there are just too many assumptions of commonality underpinning the World Park project. Most of the examples used to support a mega-eco approach involve one nation, or at most eleven, in the case of the Great Green Wall.[18] Scaling a project to encompass fifty-five nations is where the fun really begins.

This highlights the difficulty of landscape architecture in comparison to architecture. Our work often fails to materialize because forces outside of our control must align. The more ambitious the project, the more alignment required. I am writing this essay from Malaysia, where I have been able to witness how designer Ng Sek San has exploited the cracks of an imperfect political system to achieve the Kebun Kebun Bangsar project—an extraordinary linear community garden within a power line easement in the heart of Kuala Lumpur. Met with considerable resistance, Sek San has persisted and aims for the project to grow into a two-kilometer corridor linking the botanic gardens with the inner city. This is not an argument about "bottom-up" versus "top-down" practice, but rather recognition of the complexity of scale when it comes to negotiating change. Richard and Sek San share a commitment to using projects rather than platitudes to address social, climatic, and economic issues. Maybe only part of the World Park will be realized. Would that be a terrible outcome?

Work, Work, Work

By his own admission, landscape architecture frustrates Richard. A creative and intellectual indifference permeates the discipline—from an uncritical acceptance of *genius loci* (the site) as the source of all ideas, to the moral righteousness currently shaping the response to the climate crisis. In a particularly bruising observation, he comments that "by shifting the problems of culture onto the innocence of nature, works of landscape architecture effectively inoculate themselves from the sort of critique that would apply to any other aesthetic practice."[19] Like the achievements of his great mate Peter England in theater set design, Richard could have left landscape architecture and had success in any number of creative fields. But he elected to stay within. Through projects, exhibitions, writing, and lectures, alongside running landscape architecture programs, research centers, journals, and competitions, Richard has challenged landscape architecture to deepen its engagement as a design discipline.

Frustration is a great motivator. Throughout his career, Richard has been tactical in exploiting opportunities and making them for others. His power of communication and charisma has certainly played a part. As this book documents, he has amassed an extraordinary body of work—some built, many remaining speculative, some acclaimed, others challenged. The idea of the project—which he considers the fundamental way to make sense of and engage with the world—drives this productivity. However, not the project as defined by a site or a brief, but a project as a focus to explore ideas about something—national identity, trauma, loss, the suburb, or the Anthropocene, to name just a few. It is a record of work that challenges the discipline to be braver and smarter, to be experimental and creative, and at times to fail. This is what it means to work between art and instrumentality.

END NOTES

1. The title references an iconic song by The Triffids, who emerged from Perth in the late 1970s. Lead singer David McComb is acknowledged as one of the rare songwriters to capture the sense of isolation and expansiveness of the Australian landscape. It's also a bit of an anthem for expatriate Australians of a certain generation. Have a listen.

2. Don't for a minute think that Richard's reflections herein on his studies at UNSW are exaggerated. Studying a few years later than Richard, I can confirm, among other things, that data punch coding was soul destroying.

3. Hold this thought—this reference becomes more evident towards the end of this essay.

4. Richard Weller, "Inside Room 4.1.3," *Room 4.1.3: Innovations in Landscape Architecture* (Univ. of Pennsylvania Press, 2005), 3.

5. Ibid.

6. See Matthew Rimmer, "The Garden of Australian Dreams: The Moral Rights of Landscape Architects," in Fiona Macmillan & Kathy Bowery (eds), *New Directions in Copyright Law: Vol. 3* (Cheltenham: Edward Elgar, 2006), 134–70.

7. https://aiatsis.gov.au/ngurra

8. In 1998, Richard's work was recognized as such as a finalist in the Seppelt Contemporary Art Award, see https://www.mca.com.au/artists-works/exhibitions/seppelt-contemporary-art-award-1998/.

9. Richard Weller, "Landscape (Sub)Urbanism in Theory and Practice," *Landscape Journal* 27, no. 2 (2008): 262.

10. Interview with Richard Weller (September 26, 2022).

11. Corner completed a master's degree in landscape architecture and an urban design certificate from the University of Pennsylvania in 1986, while McHarg earned a B.L.A. in 1949, an M.L.A. in 1950, and a master's degree in city planning in 1951 from Harvard University.

12. Contemporary academic leadership requires a challenging set of skills and a tolerance for bureaucracy. The ability to balance budgets and attract funding, maintain a career trajectory without being an absent leader, remain an active and engaged teacher, liaise with other disciplines, operate beyond self-interest, manage academic staff, support a new generation of academics, and respond to an increasingly demanding and anxious student body are just some of the demands. And most people are not up to the task. While always chasing big ideas, Richard seems also able to keep the day-to-day demands ticking over. This is a rare skill.

13. Richard Weller, "Afterword," in *The Landscape Project*, eds. Richard J. Weller & Tatum L. Hands, (AR+D Publishing, 2022).

14. See Richard Weller's essay herein.

15. Rob Levinthal & Richard Weller, "The Age of the Mega Eco Project," *Landscape Architecture Magazine* (in press).

16. In 2009 Richard was featured on the cover of the *Sunday Times Magazine*. He was photographed with bare feet wearing a white suit and holding a Rubik's cube superimposed with urban scenes. Without question this was a design rock star moment.

17. Lead singer of the Irish band the Boomtown Rats, Geldof is also recognized for his activism in advocating for equitable and sustainable development in Africa.

18. The problematic top-down approach initially applied in the Great Green Wall project is well documented.

19. Richard Weller, "The Innocent Landscape," *The Architecture Symposium: A Broader Landscape*, National Gallery of New South Wales, Sydney (November 18, 2022).

LANDSCAPE AS ART

What is Nature? You have three minutes...

Nature is everything that happens without any external force • Nature is a group of elements, defined by their progression and reaction to one another • Nature is the encoded, inscribed genetic tendency/ imprint of everything (all matter) that causes its change • Nature is a network of interconnected systems that supports life on earth • Nature is a directional movement towards harmony caused by living beings • Nature is the unplanned growing and decaying biological world that surrounds, contains, and includes us • Nature is everything animate and inanimate on the planet Earth not separate from and including humans and all that is created by them • Nature is everything and thus totally lacking in moral valence one way or the other • Nature is a collaborative system that is not independent. It exists or holds its functions in relation to its surroundings and consists not only of animals and plants, but also humans and other components of the earth • Nature is everything that already existed, not the things made or manufactured or regulated and adjusted by humans • Nature is the antithesis of culture. An assortment of proportions, systems, and aesthetics curated over billions of years. Nature is a word that exists through human definitions but has turned into less of a union of man and nature, and more of a separation • Nature is a perception or idea of what something used to be or an image of space that has not been impacted by humans • The natural world/environment where human settlements and industry do not dominate the landscape. Nature could also be understood as pre–agricultural revolution "untouched" wilderness that no longer exists • Nature is a post-agricultural species' conceptualization of that which is "external" or "other" to that species and its creations. Agriculture enables culture, which in turn leads to the categorization or distinction from "nature." • Nature is all the inherent elements of this planet especially that which hasn't been civilized by human behavior. Nature is pure, wild, born, and clean • Nature is a synthetic combination of all animals and plants, including human. But it's hard to say that human-made environment also is nature. • Nature is a place where we do not live, a place we "return" to or reconvene with when we feel we have strayed from ourselves or become lost. Nature is seen as a truth and a constant, ever waiting • I first thought about the forest, mountain, riverside... Then I thought maybe where there is green there is nature. But green is not enough–nature has to be an original, primitive status in people's hearts and minds • Nature is the environment we live in. And it changes with time. There are laws in nature. We should obey it and learn from it • New ideas of nature transcend its historical duality with culture and includes humans and all the nonhuman life forms and also the interrelationship between them. This is now a question of environmental justice for people of different races, classes, and generations who all have intrinsic value/rights to exist • "Nature" and "nature" are different from each other. "Nature" tends to refer to an environment remaining untouched by humans, while "nature" more generally refers to any landscape. Referencing these definitions it is hard to say there is any "Nature" left on our planet • Nature is what has come into being and includes the outside influences that being has encountered. Nature is constantly changing and is not limited to what has been untouched or what is "pure" • Nature is a complex term that reflects the social, political, and economic conditions of humans • Nature is a cultural construct developed by Western societies to describe that which is not human. While it purports to refer to a concrete set of things, such as plants, animals, and other earth systems, the construct of nature is flexible, transforming over time in relation to different social, political, and ecological conditions • Capital "N" Nature is a cultural construct, antithetically divided and separated from capital "M" Man. Overall, it's just a word, a representation of divisions or unions that we as individuals, as a society, have collectively created or learned. It's something to embrace and to attach ourselves to and to deconstruct • Nature is a word, a big word, that is not fixed but is constantly evolving and co-opted. In this sense it cannot have a strict definition. With that said, I typically think of it as describing environmental systems to which humans are inextricably linked. This is a difficult definition as nature can quickly become a stand-in for everything • Nature is humanity's hope that we are not narcissistic.

A representative sample of responses to the question "What is Nature?" written by students of landscape architecture at the Weitzman School of Design (*left*) [114]. Detail of *Landscape Painting* (Museum of Contemporary Art, Sydney, 1988). Plants grow over a definition of nature printed on a 5 m x 1.3 m canvas kept moist with reticulated water (*right*) [114].

Installation image from the *Seppelt Contemporary Art Award* 1998 exhibition (Museum of Contemporary Art, Sydney, 1988). *Landscape Painting* (left); *The Satellite's Garden*, drawings related to the city of Berlin, backlit and set in a tilted plane of black rutile (front); and designs for the Garden of Australian Dreams at the National Museum of Australia (back) [114, 122, 128].

"The Ghost House" (Central Australia, 1986). Unbuilt concept to construct the frame of a typical Australian suburban home in a remote location in the Australian desert and leave it to decompose [119].

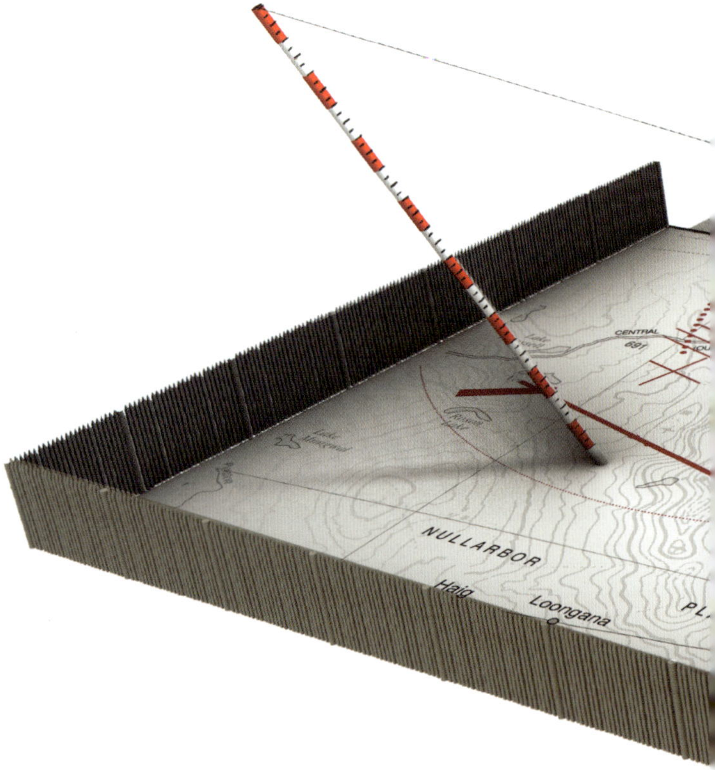
NULLARBOR
Haig
Loongana

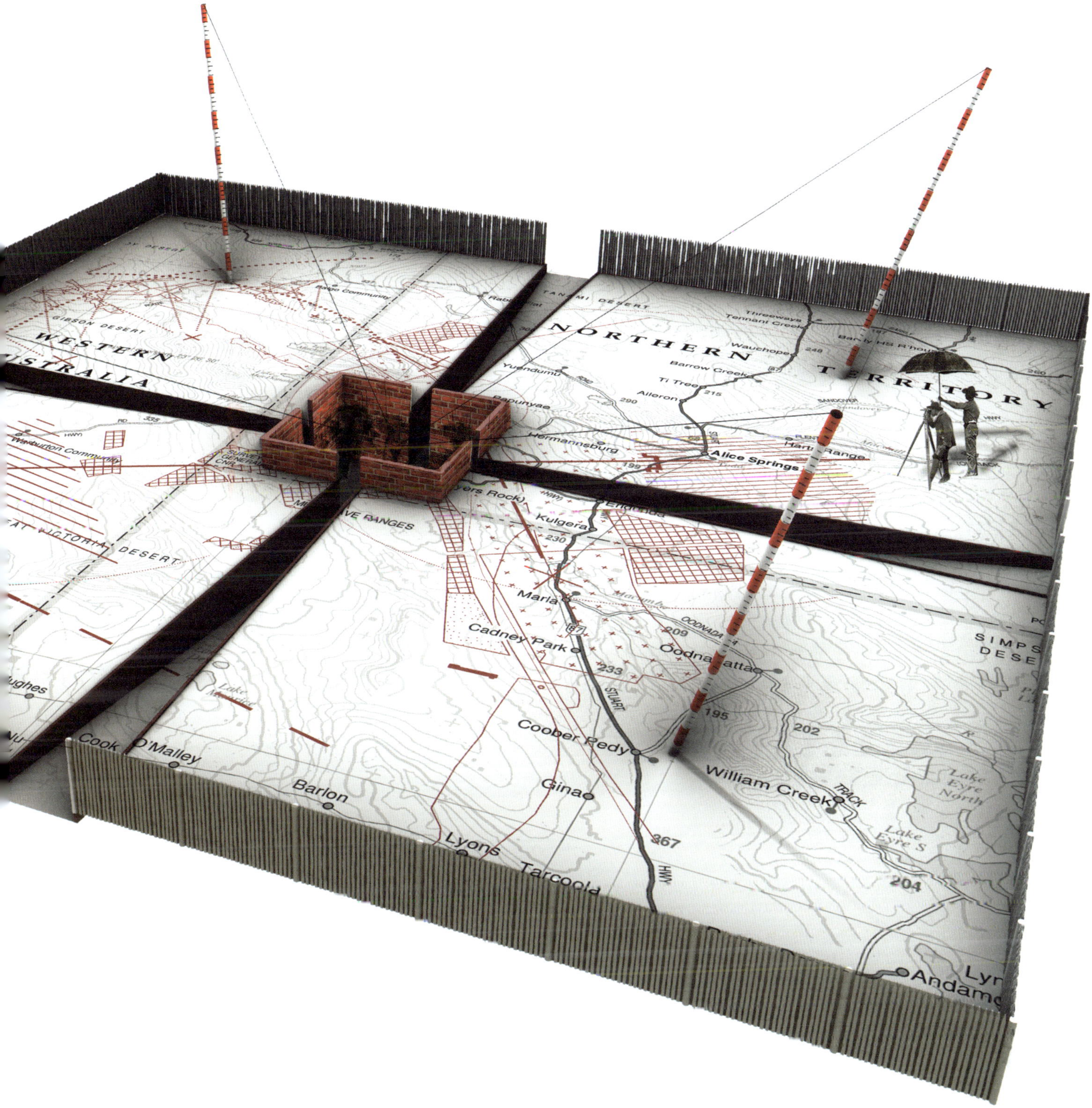

"Australian Garden" (Australia, 1987). Unbuilt design with map surface, a burnt wooden fence, surveyors' poles, and a plumb bob suspended over a sunken room set on cardinal axes [120].

RANGES
DESERT

"Australian Garden" (Australia, 1987). View over the garden's surface (left) and inside the garden's subterranean room with Xanthorrhoea sp and a borehole reaching down to groundwater [120].

GOD LOVES YOU
MIR AUF DIE MAUER AM
1+2. Nov J RUNNINGS

No-man’s land, Potsdamer Platz (Berlin, 1988). © Sueddeutsche Zeitung/Alamy [122].

"The Berlin Room" (Berlin, 1995). Cutaway view of a proposal for a walled water garden in the redeveloped Potsdamer Platz. The garden's concrete wall attracts graffiti and the interior is lined with mirrors reflecting a grove of birch trees planted in the water [123].

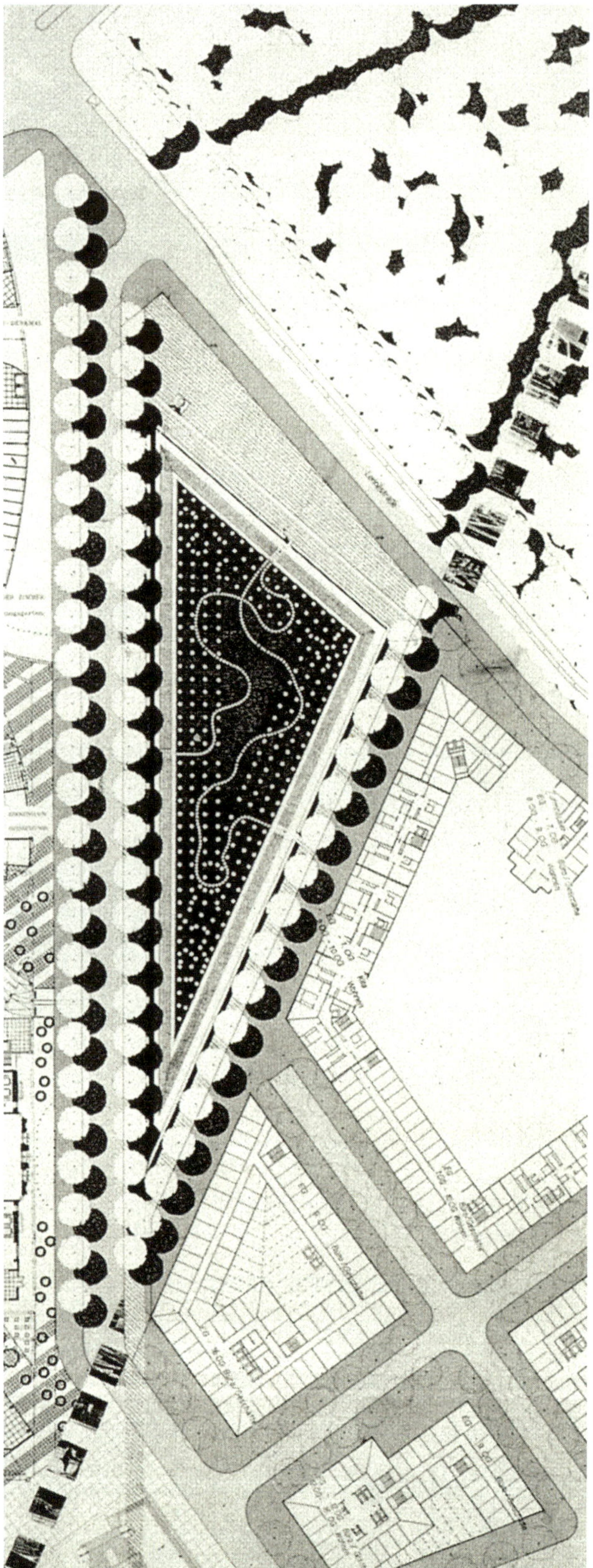

Location and plan of "The Berlin Room" water garden (*left*); including floating images of the history of the Potsdamer Platz (*right*) [123].

"Potsdamer Platz Park" (Berlin, 1991). Overview of a concept design for a new park in Berlin's former no-man's land, conceived as an alternative to the urban redevelopment of the Potsdamer Platz [123].

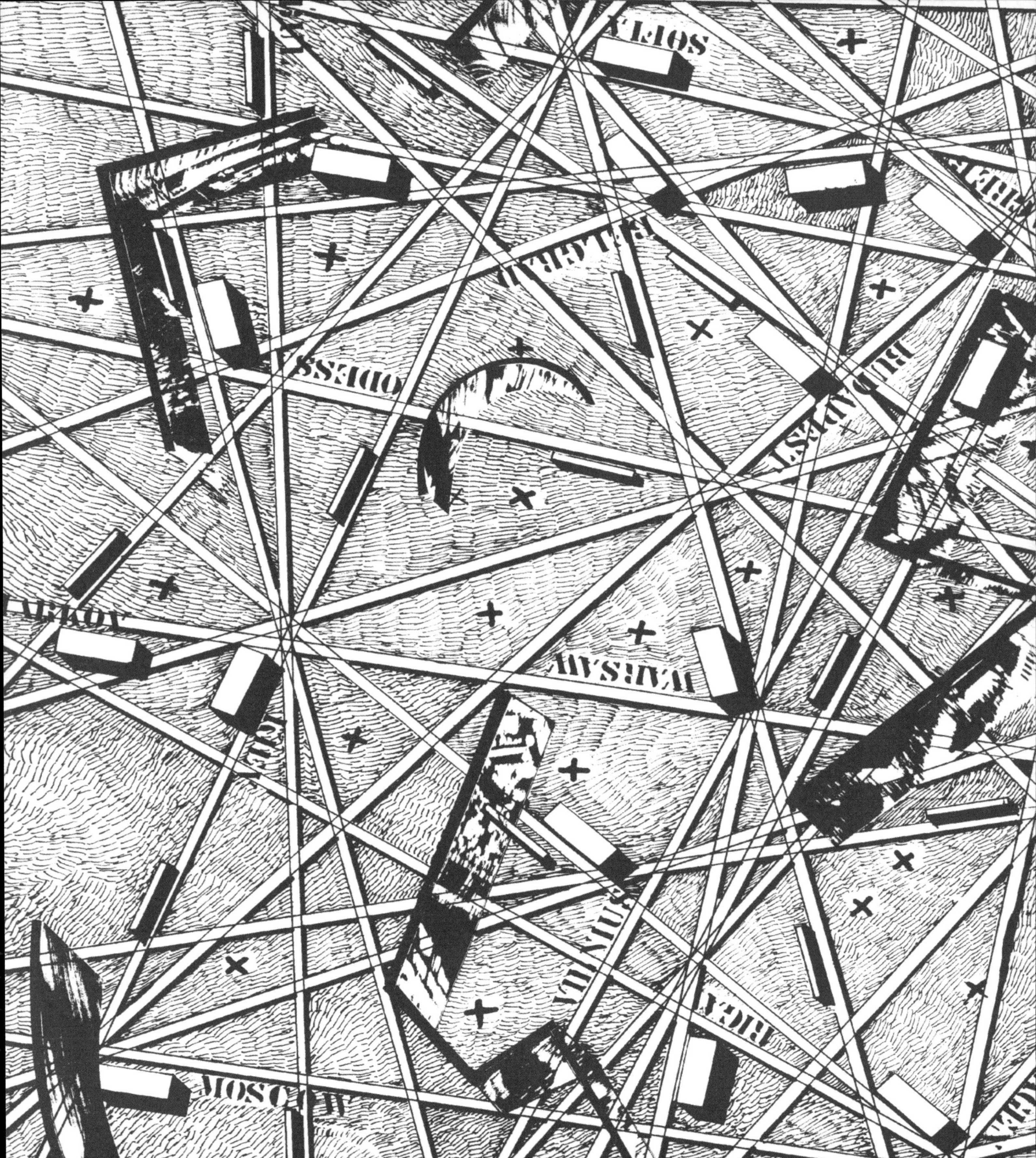
WARSAW
BUDAPEST

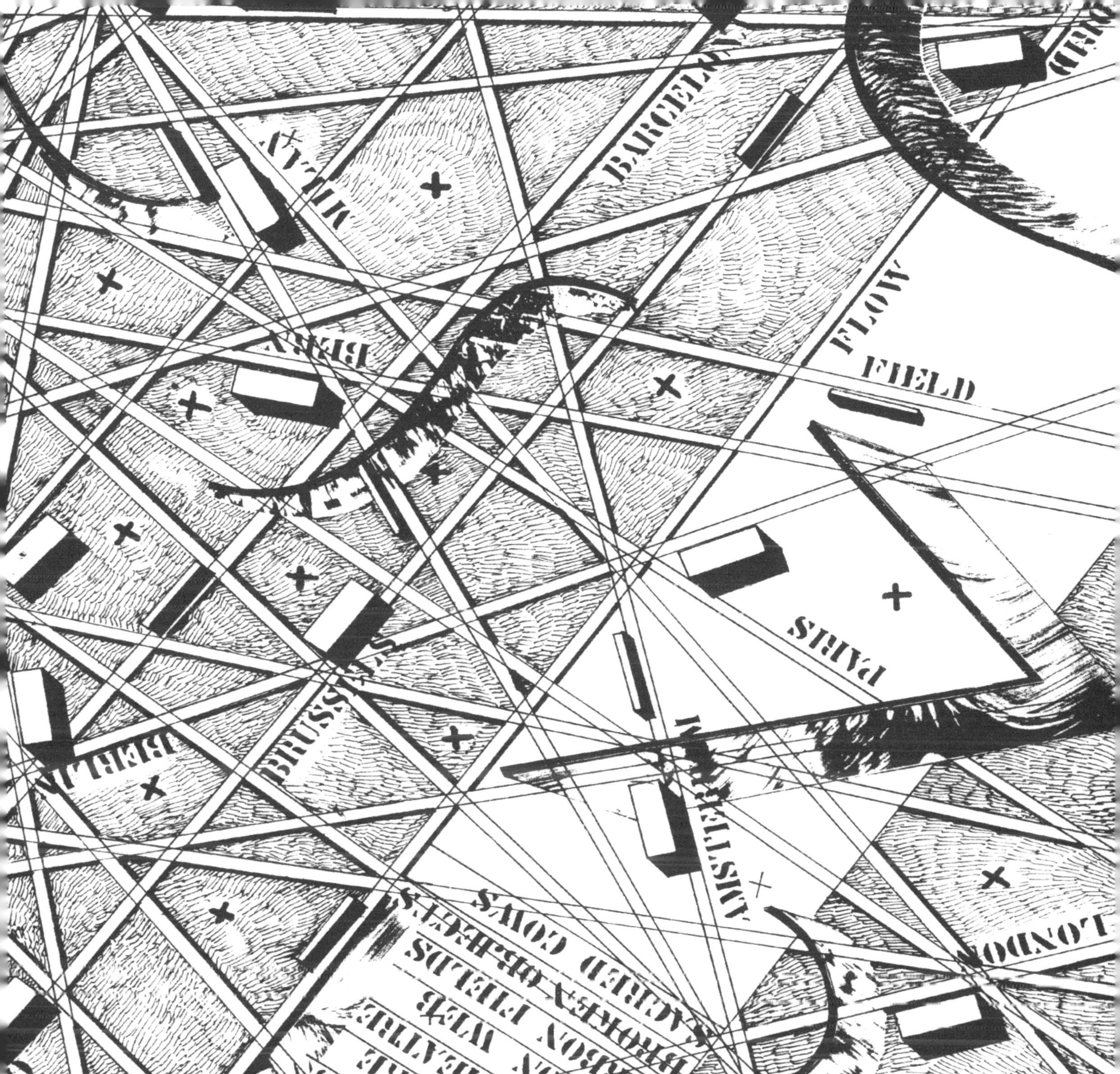

A fragment of the plan of the proposed "Potsdamer Platz Park" showing a network of paths derived from linking the major cities across Europe and including infrastructure for the social and artistic activation of the park [123].

ПОМОГИ МНЕ
HILF MIR. DIESE TÖDLICHE LIEBE ZU

View inside "Potsdamer Platz Park" showing pavilions representing the cities of Europe, moving billboards for art, former military hardware, relics of no-man's land, excavated WWII bunkers, fire pits, a pattern of shadows over the ground plane, and impromptu events [123].

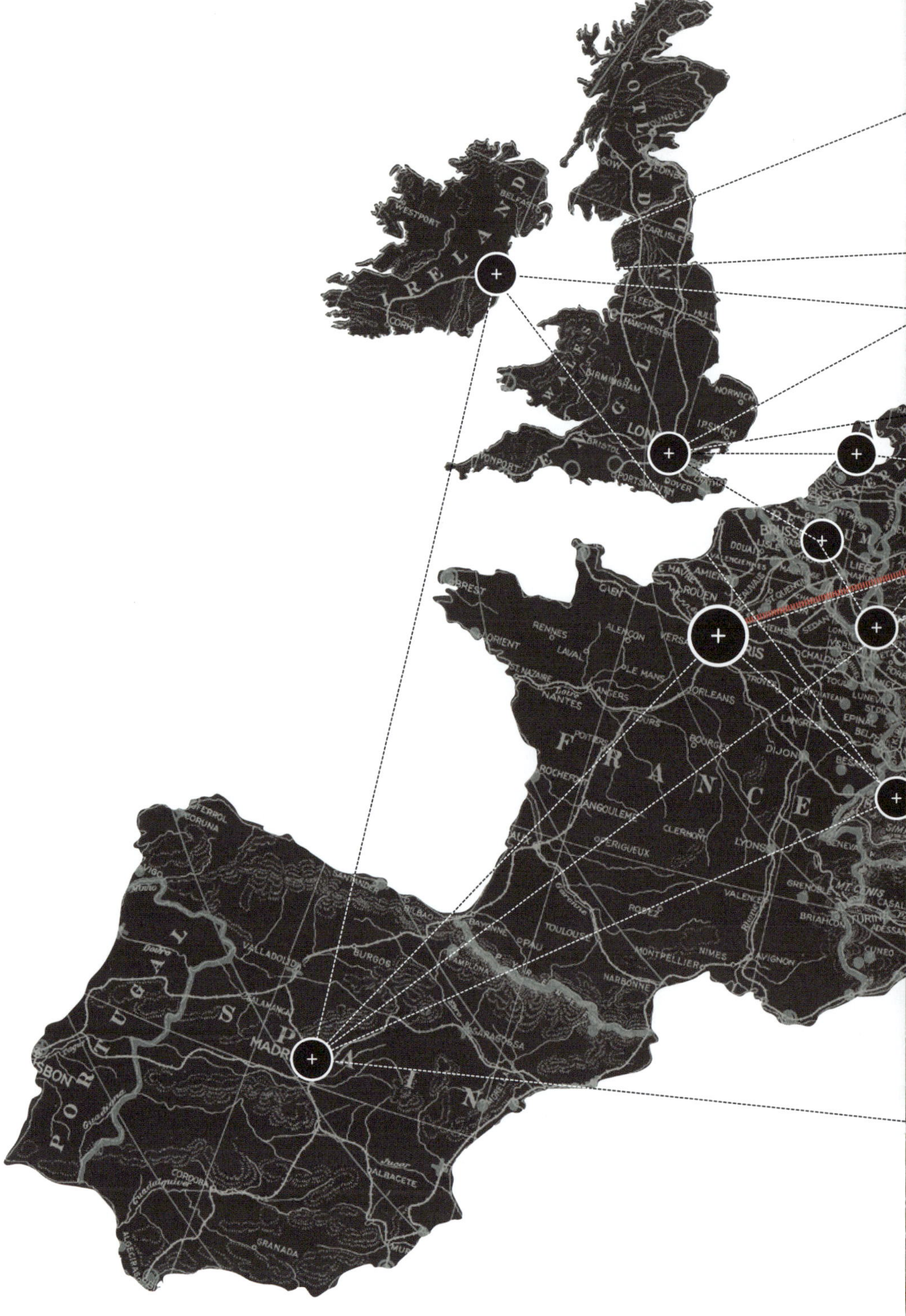
IRELAND
WESTPORT
BELFAST
SCOTLAND
DUNDEE
CARLISLE
LEEDS
MANCHESTER
HULL
BIRMINGHAM
NORWICH
IPSWICH
BRISTOL
PORTSMOUTH
DOVER
DOUAI
AMIENS
ROUEN
CAEN
BREST
RENNES
LAVAL
ALENÇON
LORIENT
LE MANS
NANTES
ANGERS
ORLEANS
TOURS
POITIERS
BOURGES
DIJON
FRANCE
ROCHEFORT
ANGOULEME
PERIGUEUX
CLERMONT
LYONS
GRENOBLE
VALENCE
BRIANÇON
TURIN
MT. CENIS
CUNEO
AVIGNON
NIMES
MONTPELLIER
NARBONNE
TOULOUSE
PAU
BAYONNE
PAMPLONA
BURGOS
VALLADOLID
FERROL
CORUÑA
SPAIN
MADRID
PORTUGAL
LISBON
ALBACETE
CORDOBA
GRANADA
LUNEVILLE
EPINAL
SEDAN
CHALONS
LANGRES

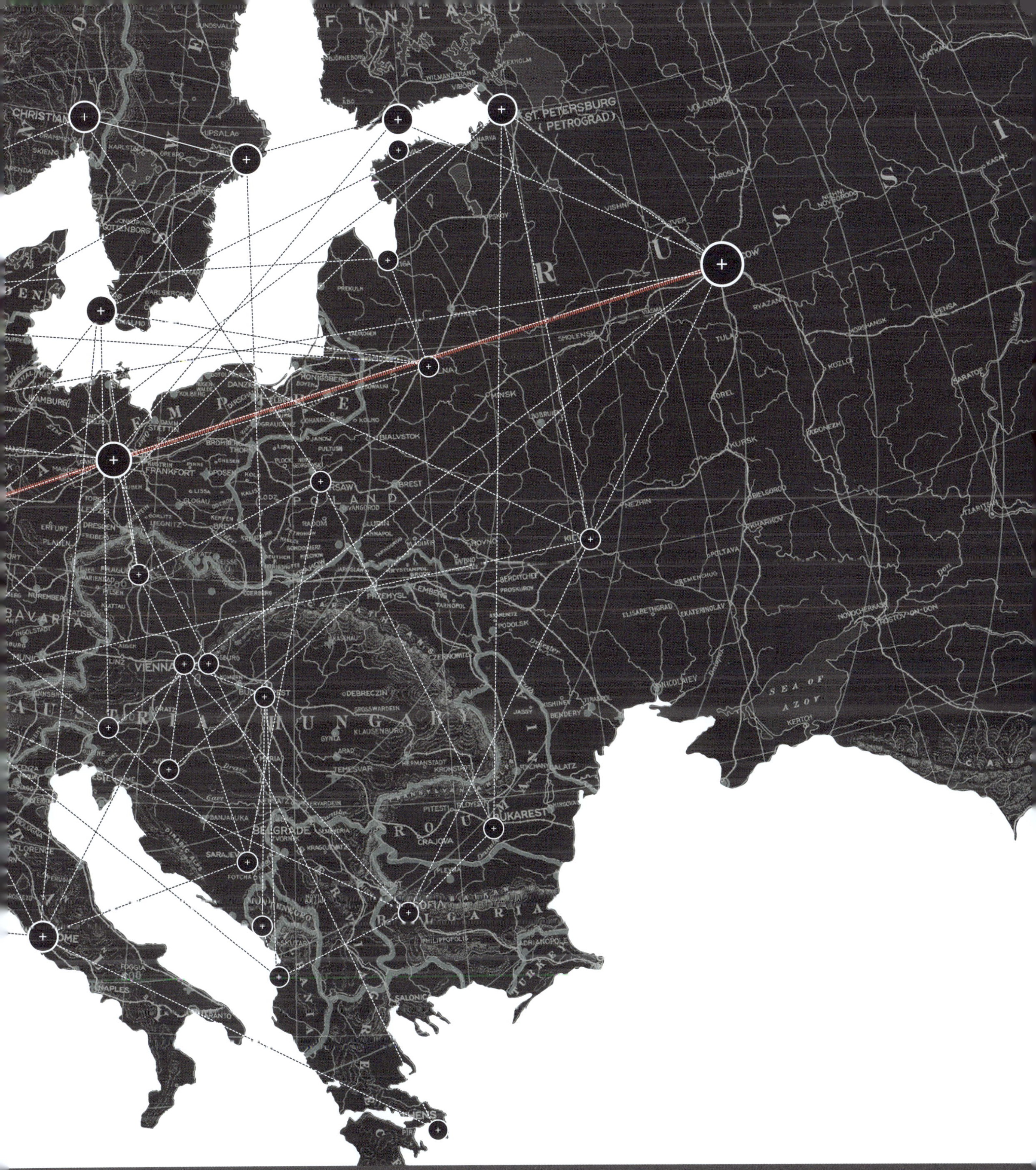

"Paris–Moscow Songline" (Berlin, 1991). An avenue of trees and a cycling and walking trail linking Paris to Moscow through the Potsdamer Platz in Berlin [124].

1

2

"The Herbal and the Bestiary" (Berlin, 1992). A park for experiments in urban ecology in no-man's land, beginning with a field of explosions (*left*) to instigate a process of ecological succession (*right*) [124].

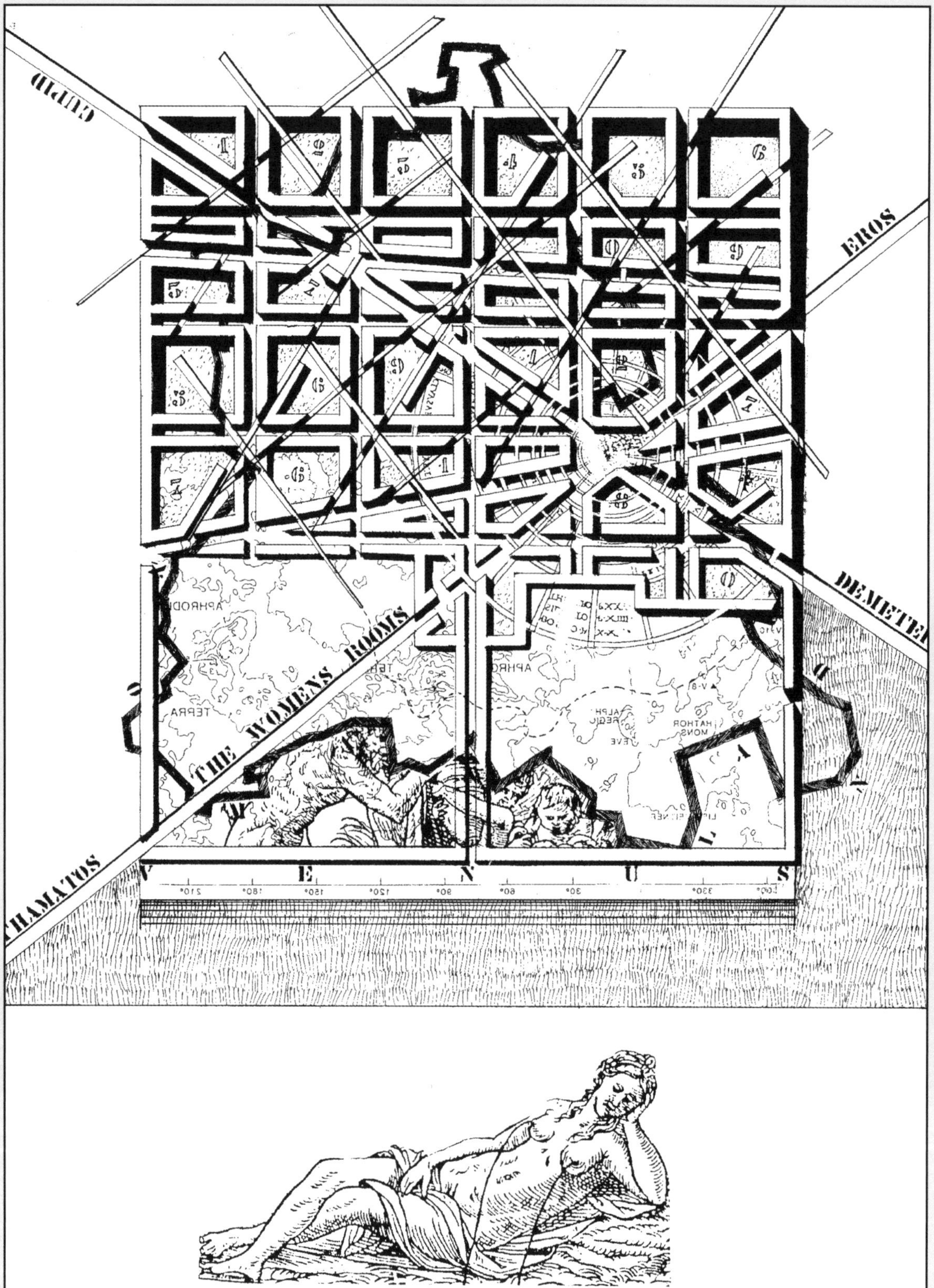

ΠΑΝΤΩΝ ΤΟΚΑΔΙ

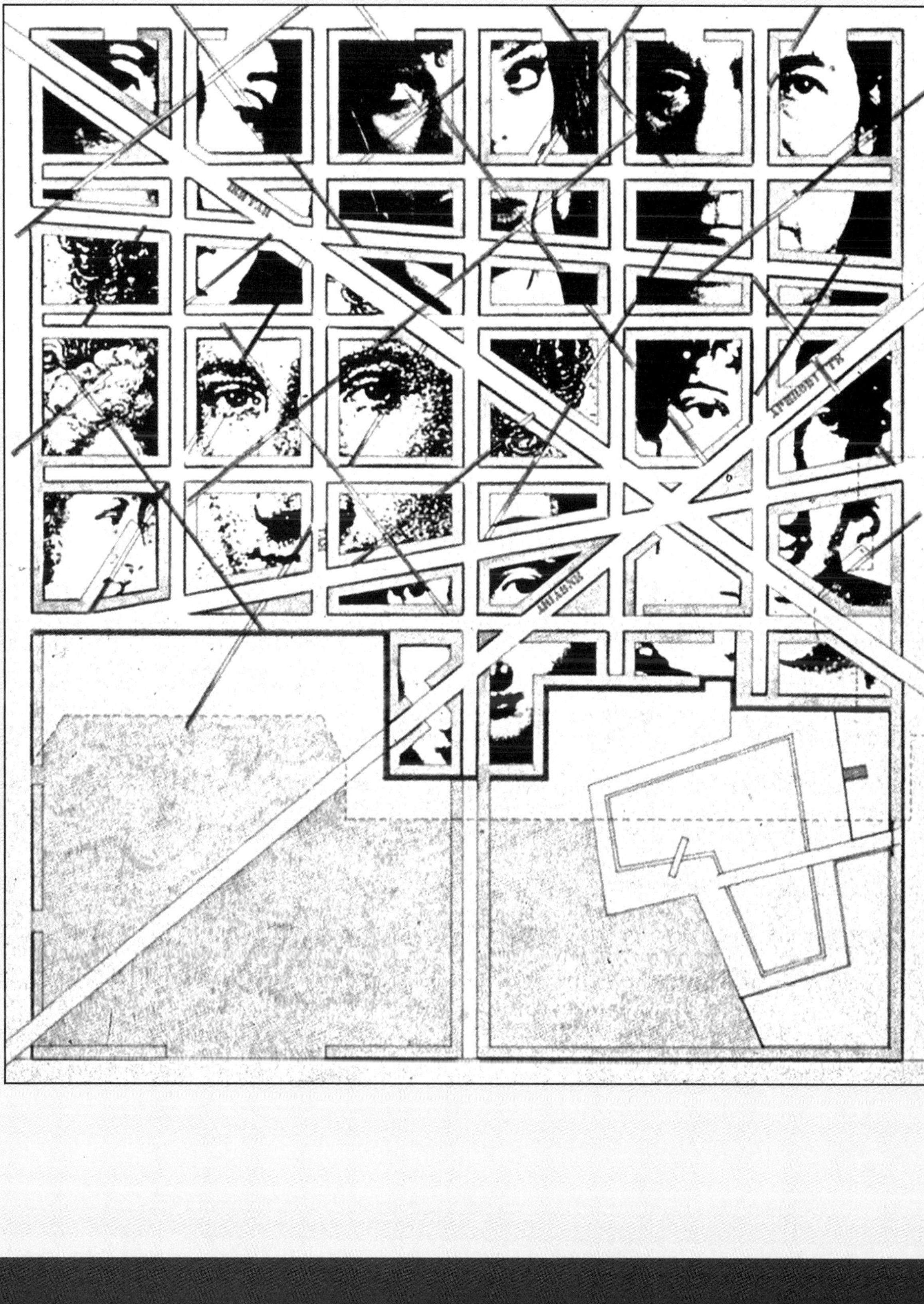

"The Women's Rooms" (Park Monbijou, Berlin, 1993). The concept for a new park on the site of a former aristocratic estate is a labyrinth of hedged rooms, each dedicated to significant women in Berlin's history who are not otherwise acknowledged in the city's urban fabric [124].

Gärten von Monbijou
vorhandener Garten
Büros
Wohnungen
Spielplatz
Rosen
ehemaliges Schloß
Kinderbad
Statue
Landschaftlicher Park
Kinderspiel
Neue Promenade
Sitzmauer
Monbijoubrücke

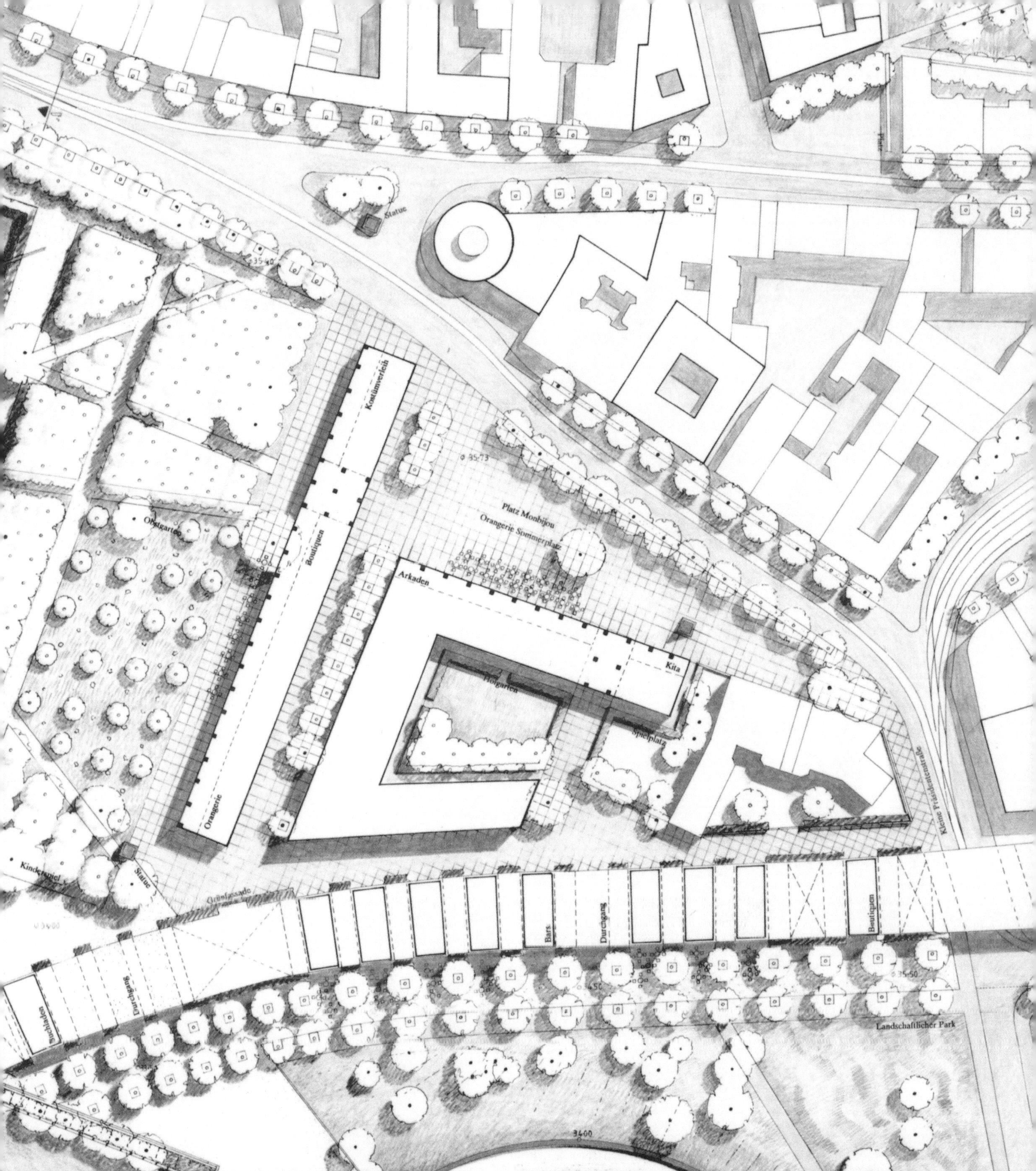

Plan of "The Women's Rooms" as the primary concept for the redesign of Park Monbijou and its surrounds in former East Berlin [124].

View inside the labyrinth of "The Women's Rooms," where rooms are serviced by a costumery to encourage visitors to use the park for masquerade and live-action roleplay [124].

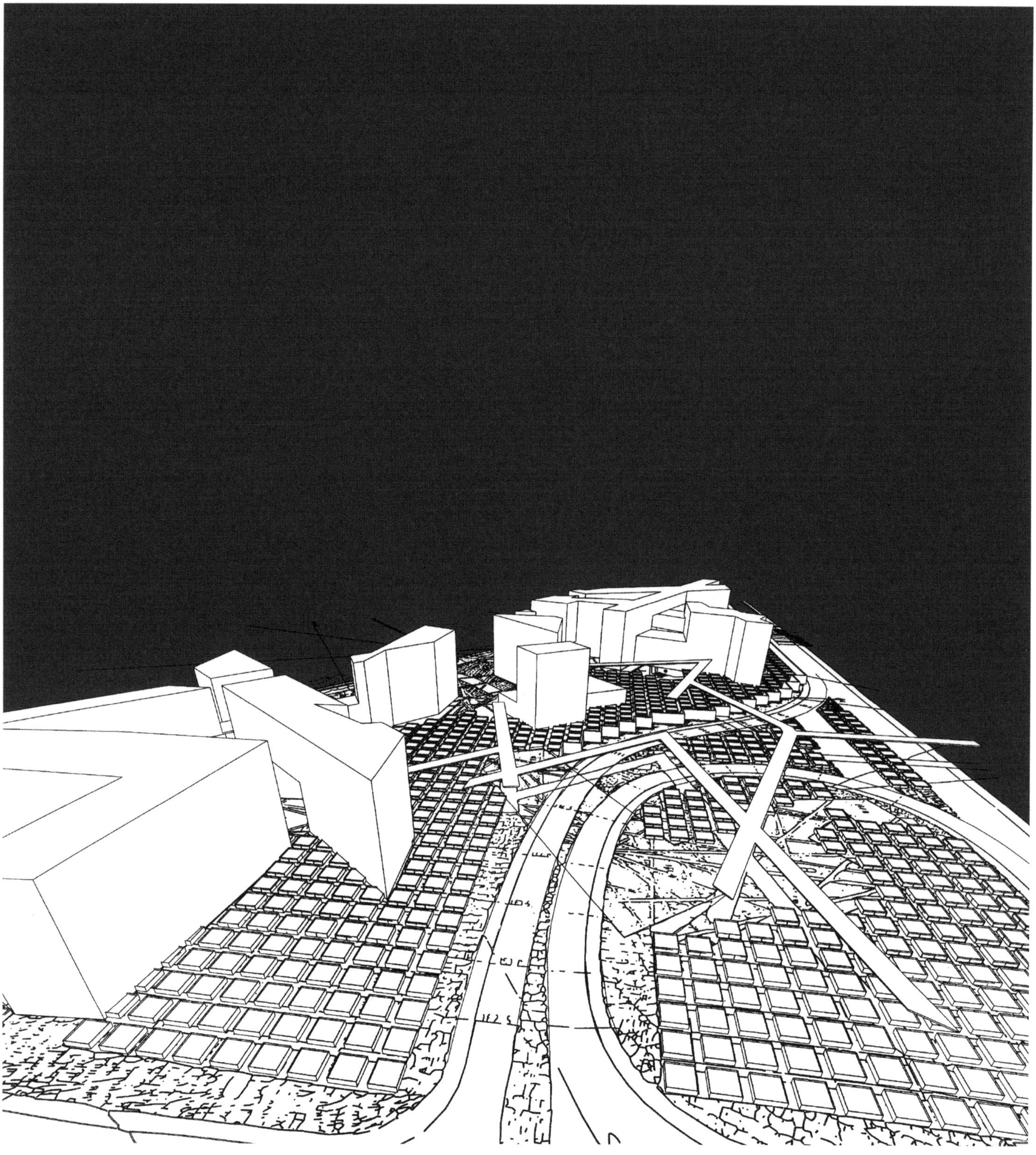

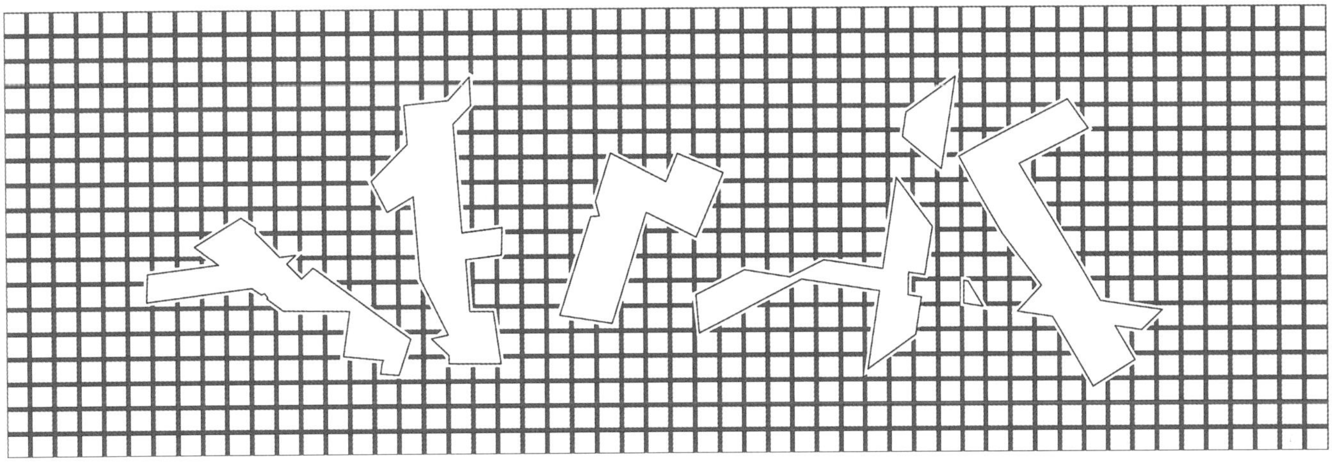

Year 1

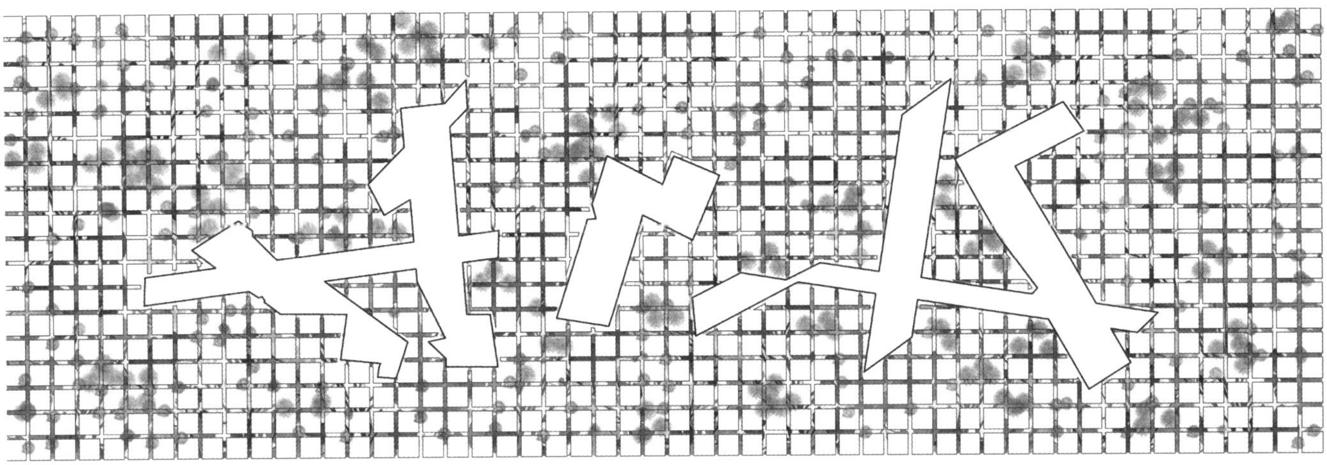

Year 5

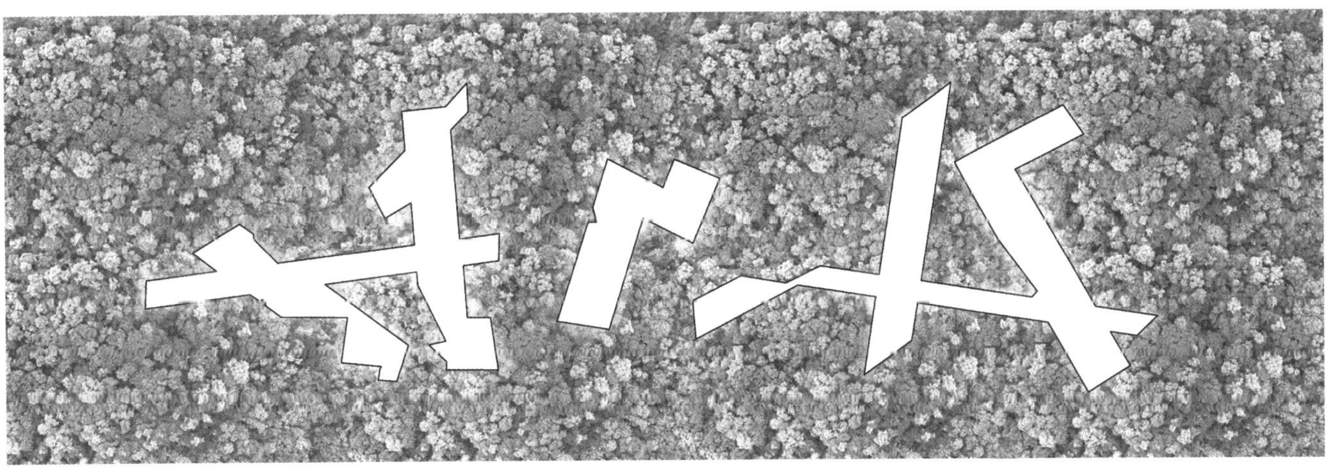

Year 50

"Decomposition" (Wiesbaden, 1993). View of office buildings by Studio Libeskind surrounded by a wooden grid backfilled with soil and seeds and left to grow wild *ad infinitum* (*left*); and diagrams showing the process of succession over a 50-year period (*right*) [125].

Site plan for "Decomposition" showing the landscape design concept for an office park by Studio Libeskind in the year 2040, by which time the original design comprising a grid of soil and seeds surrounding the buildings has matured into an inaccessible, wild forest [125].

TOMBEAU DE JEAN JACQUES ROUSSEAU
Vue de l'Isle des Peupliers, dite l'Elisée, partie des Jardins d'Ermenonville,
dans laquelle J.J. Rousseau, mort à l'age de 66. ans, a été enterré le 4. Juillet 1778.
A.P.D.R.

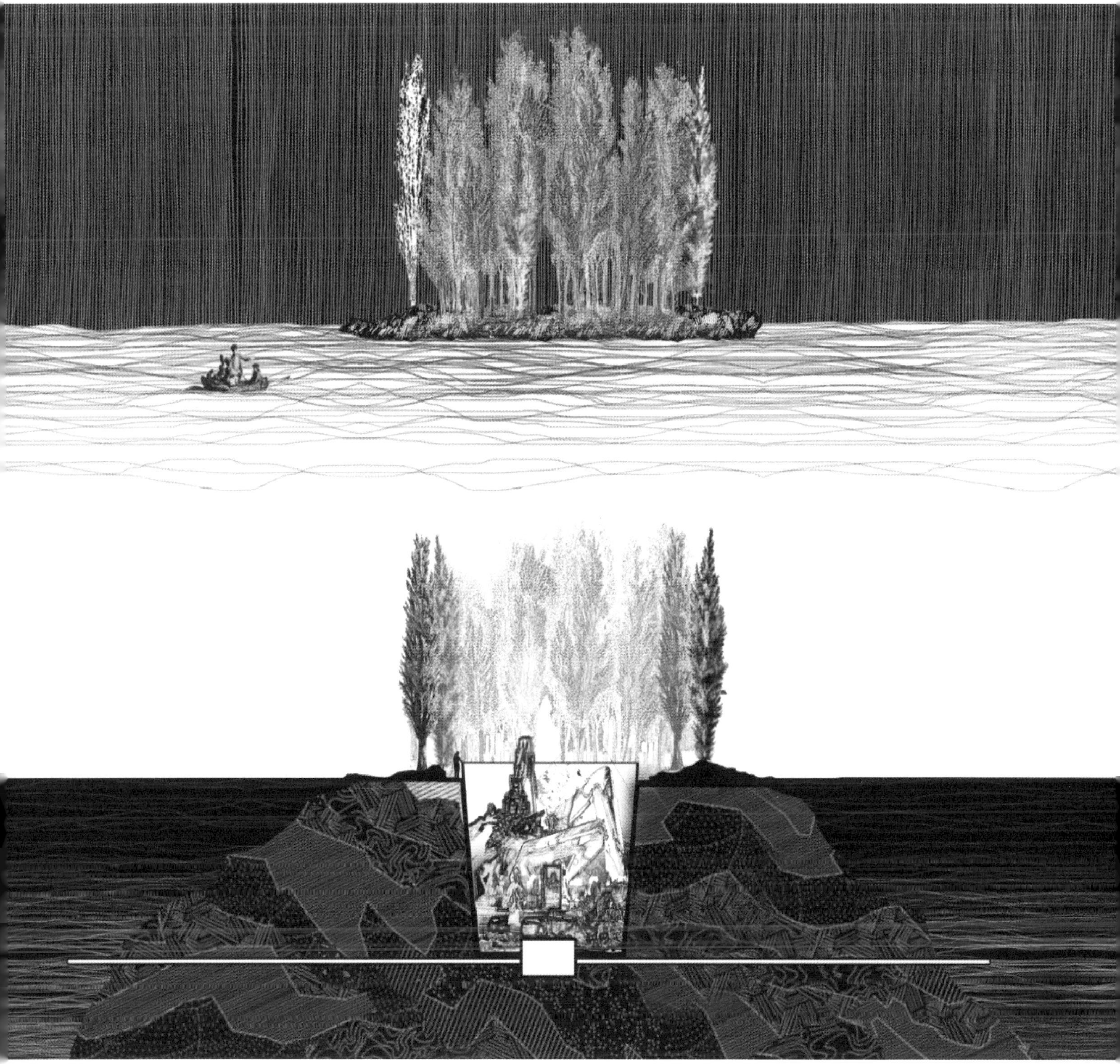

"Île des Machines" (Dessau, 1993). Elevation and section of an island proposed for the exhausted brown coal mines of Dessau which are backfilling with water. The island is a copy of the Île des Peupliers (Isle of Poplars) in Ermenonville, France, where Jean-Jacques Rousseau was originally buried. The island conceals a sunken chamber with relics of the coal excavators [125].

Garden for the Deutsches Institut für Normung (German Institute of Standards) (Berlin, 1993). A large granite tablet proportioned to the dimensions of an A4 page (a standardized product) with a thin film of running water under which are samples from the history of script [126]. Images courtesy of Müller, Knippschild, Wehberg.

33°50'50''

"Animale Ignoble" (Sydney, 1995). Concept for the industrial landscape of Sydney's Cockatoo Island to be rewilded with Moreton Bay figs (*Ficus macrophylla*) so as to form a new roost for Sydney's population of flying foxes (*Pteropus poliocephalus*) [126].

Ficus macrophylla
Cockatoo island 1995

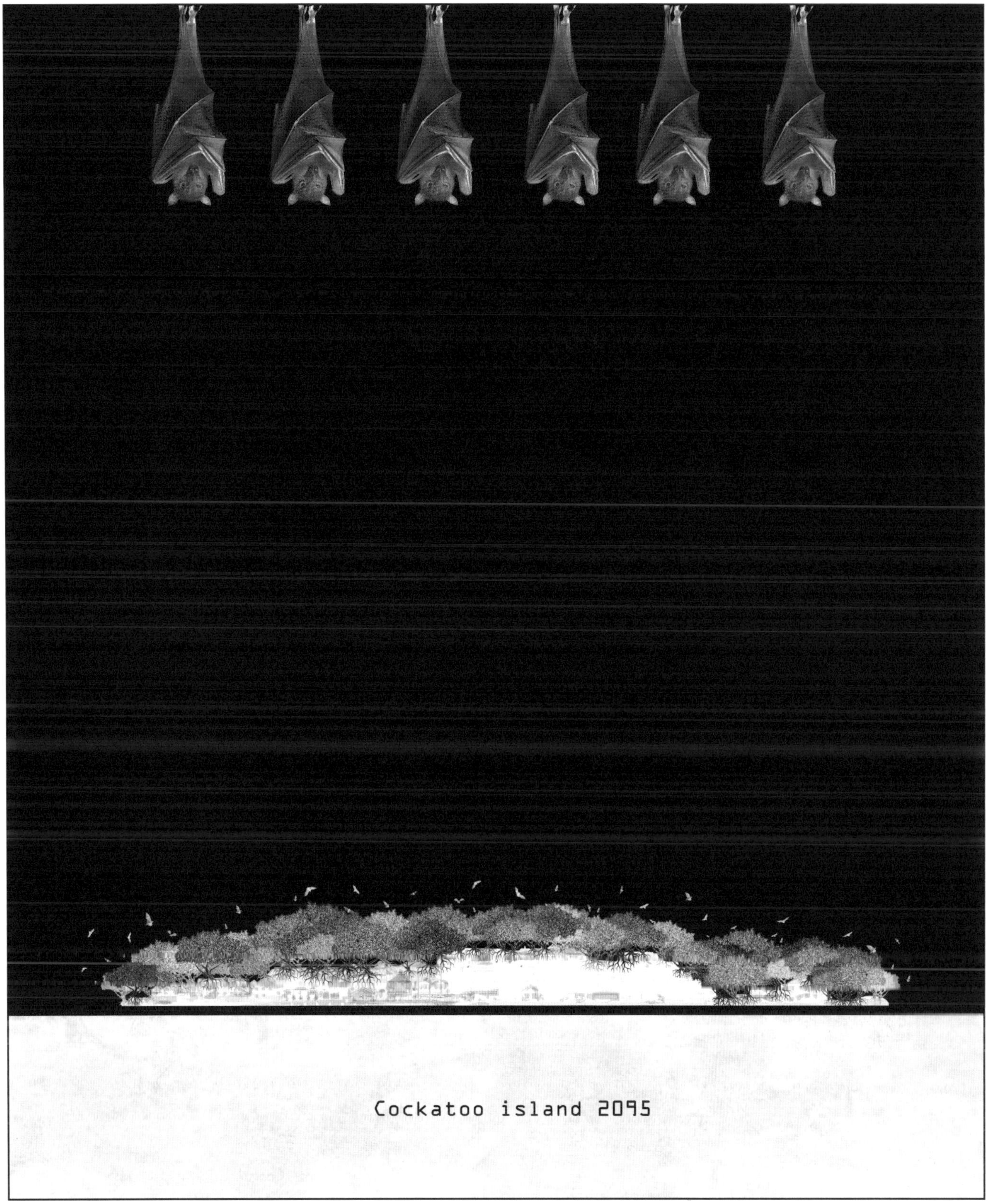

"Animale Ignoble" (Sydney, 1995). After 100 years the former industrial landscape of Cockatoo Island is a mature forest of ficus macrophylla and home to Sydney's flying fox population [126].

National Museum of Australia (Canberra, 2001). Set on an axis directed toward the national landmark of Uluru, in the center of Australia, the museum links the Indigenous spiritual heartland of Australia with its white political capital [127]. Image: John Gollings (2001).

Construction of the Uluru Axis at the National Museum of Australia [128]. Image: Vladimir Sitta (2000).

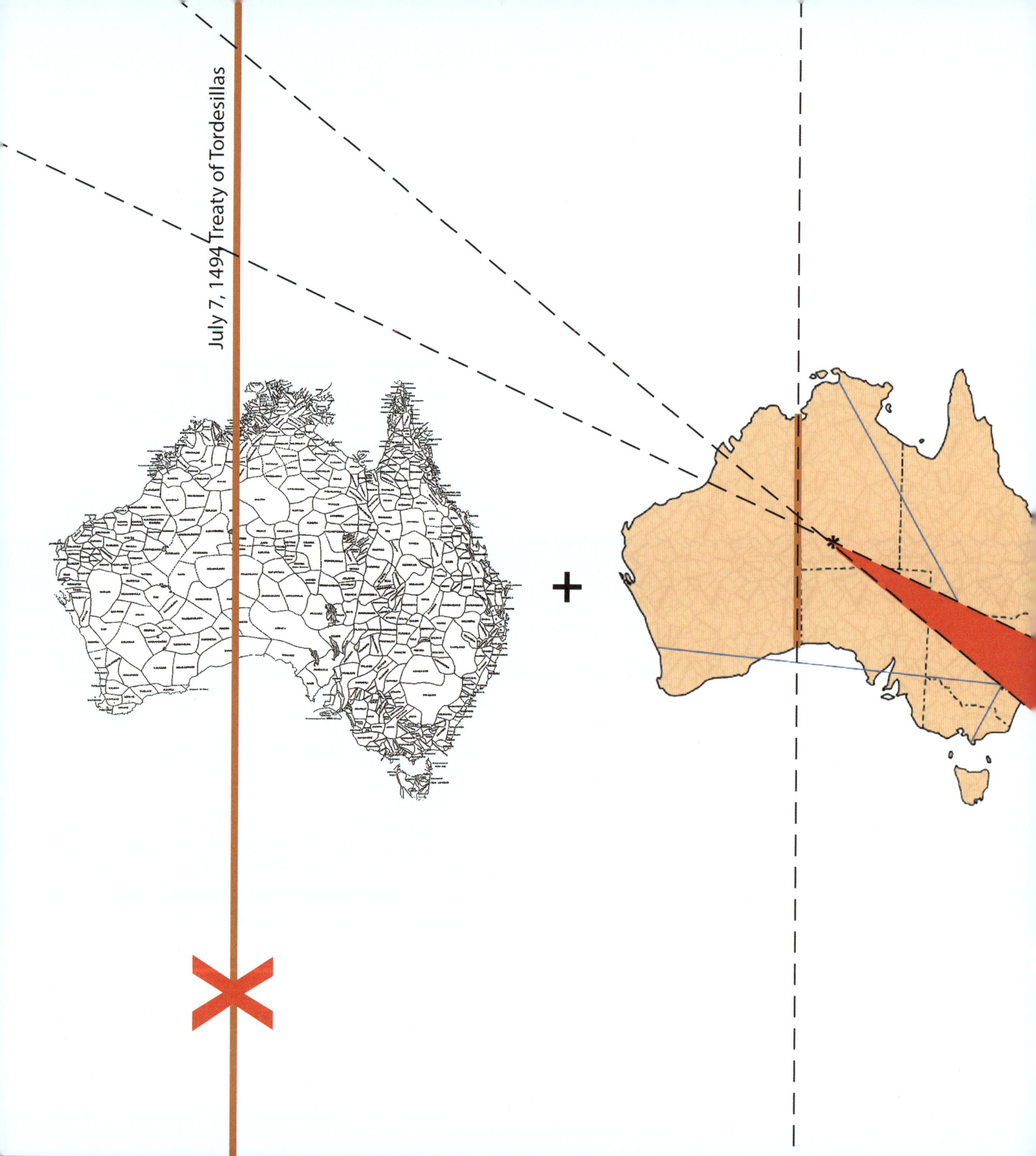
July 7, 1494 Treaty of Tordesillas

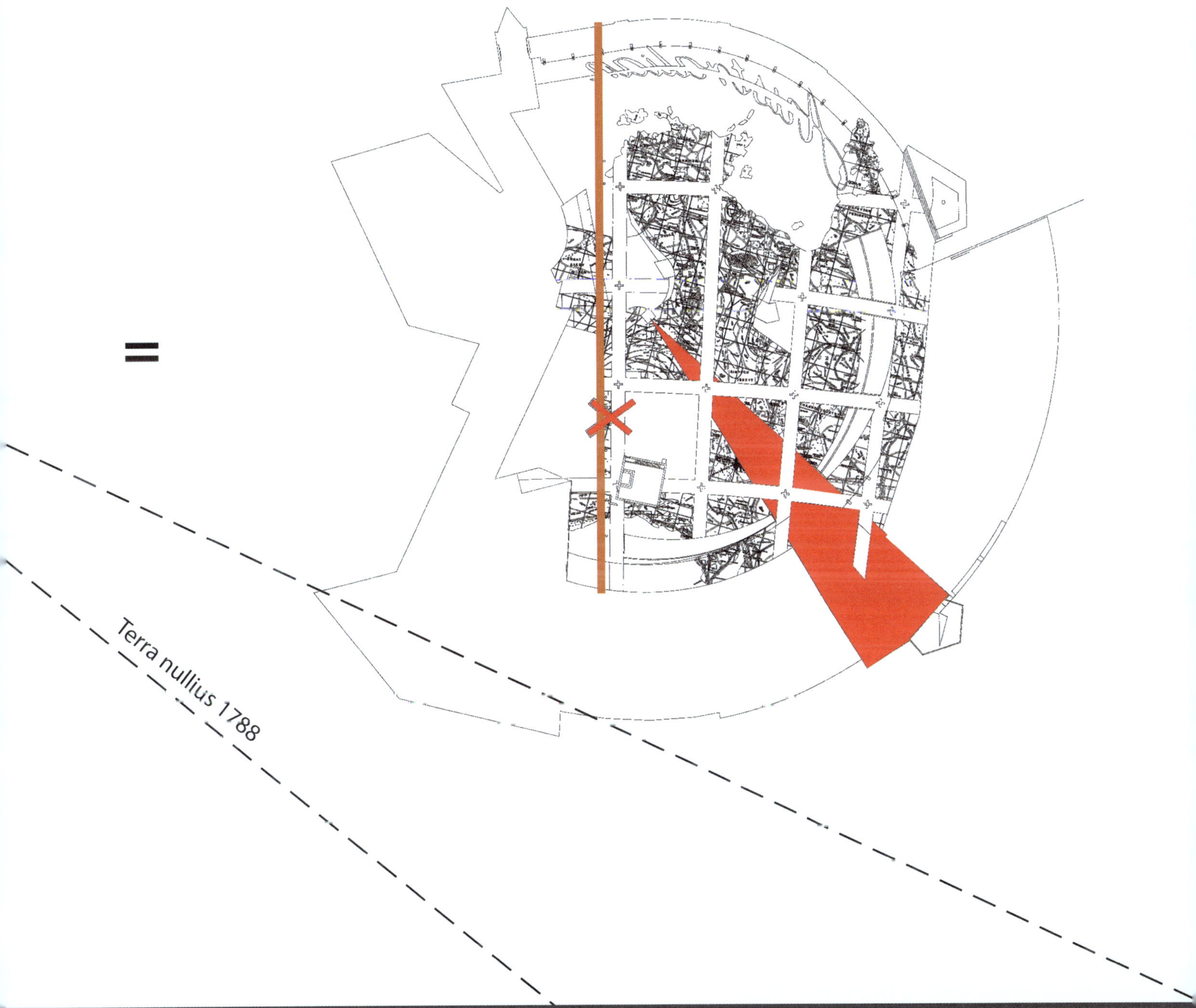

Concept design for the Garden of Australian Dreams at the National Museum of Australia (1996). Diagrams showing Aboriginal cartography (*left*) and European cartography (*middle*) of Australia, which are combined to make the garden's primary surface pattern (*right*) [128].

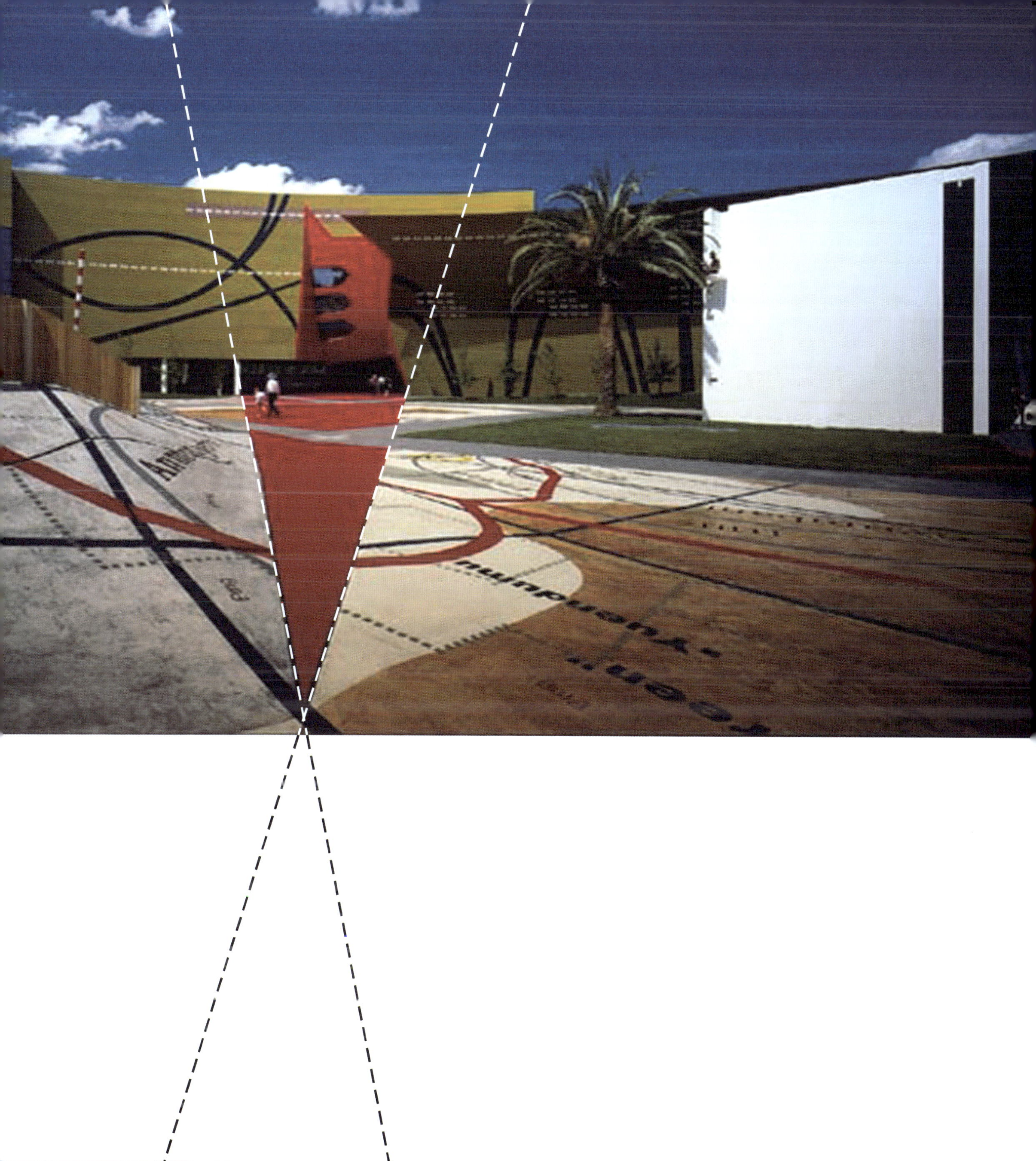

Detail from the Garden of Australian Dreams at the National Museum of Australia. A red cross bisects a yellow line representing the border between east and west Australia. The end of a red wedge marks Uluru on a map of Australia. At this point in the garden stands a camera obscura [128]. Image: John Gollings (2001).

Arabana
Glendambo
balay
rumah

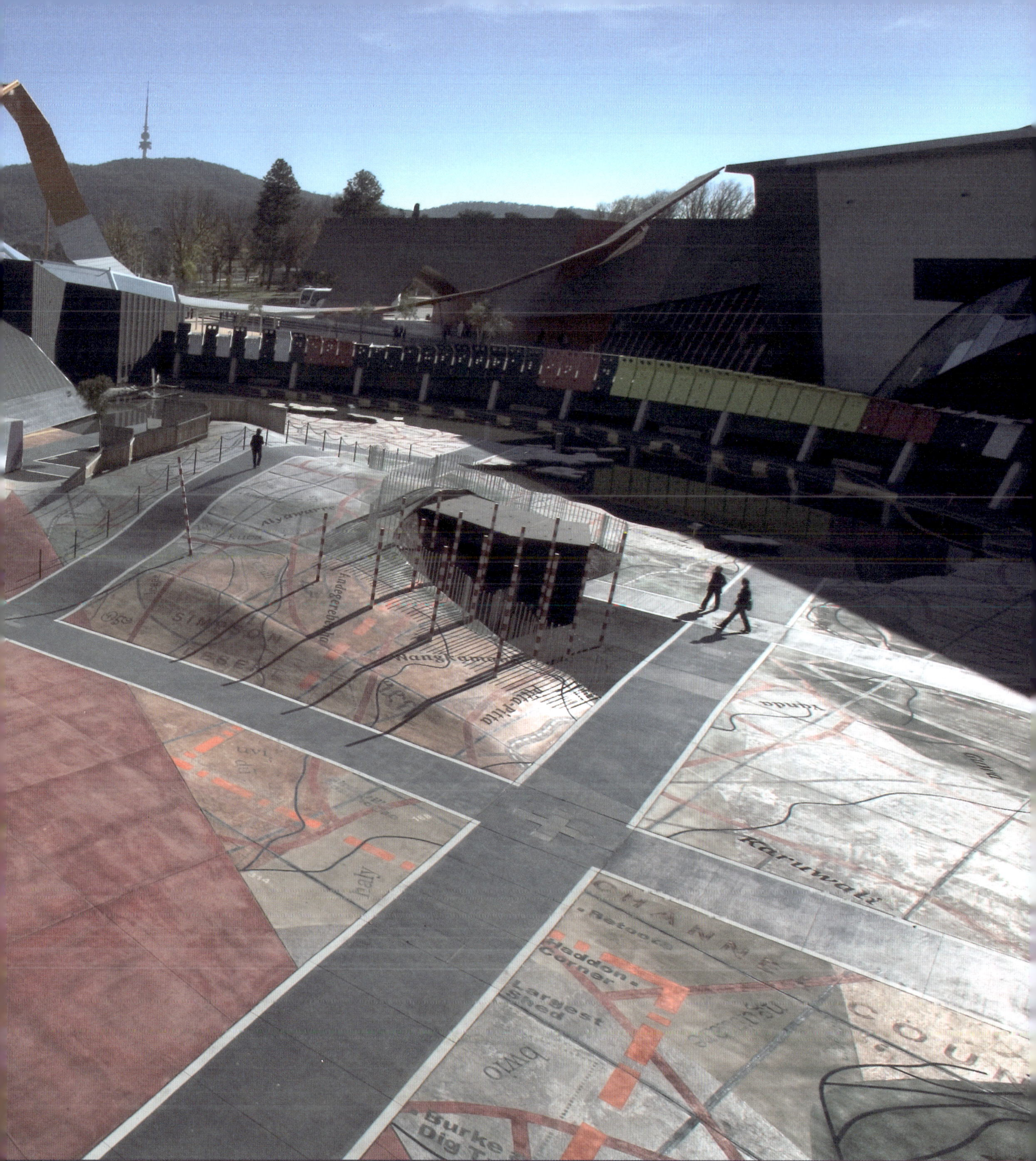

The Garden of Australian Dreams at the National Museum of Australia [128]. Image courtesy of National Museum of Australia (2001).

CHANNE
Betoota
Haddon Corner
Largest Shed
haly

View of the Garden of Australian Dreams from the gallery of the National Museum of Australia [128]. Image courtesy of National Museum of Australia (2001).

á shaa

View of the Garden of Australian Dreams from the entrance to the National Museum of Australia. In the foreground is Australia's northern coastline and *"Australian"* copied from the national currency and written in reverse [128]. Image courtesy of National Museum of Australia (2001).

Former Australian Prime Minister Gough Whitlam in the Garden of Australian Dreams standing amidst a cluster of blue poles referencing Jackson Pollock's painting, which was purchased by the Australian Government under Whitlam and came to symbolize Australia's cultural renaissance [129]. Images: Vladimir Sitta (2001).

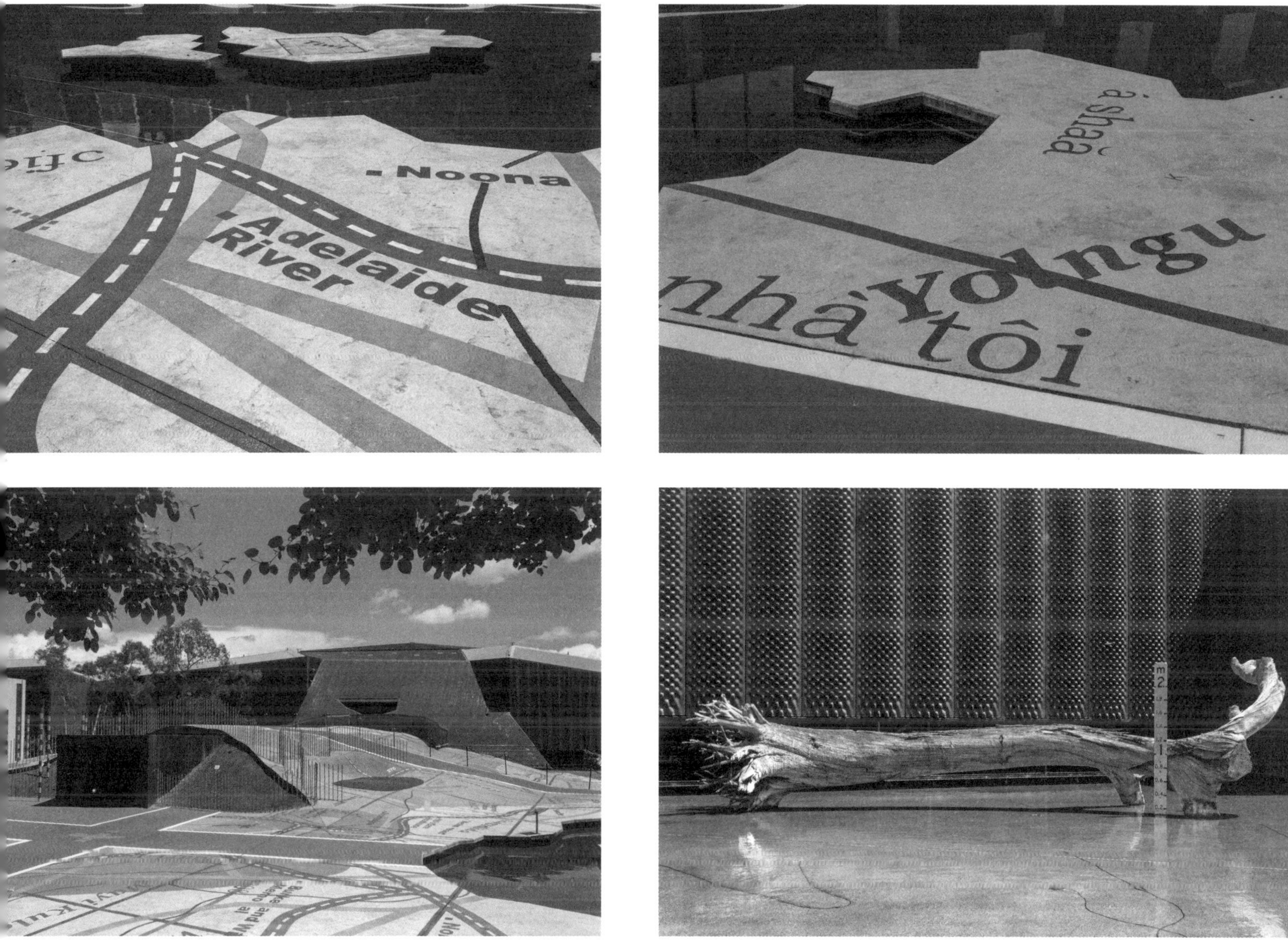

Detail images of the Garden of Australian Dreams at the National Museum of Australia [128]. Images: Hugh Swann (2022).

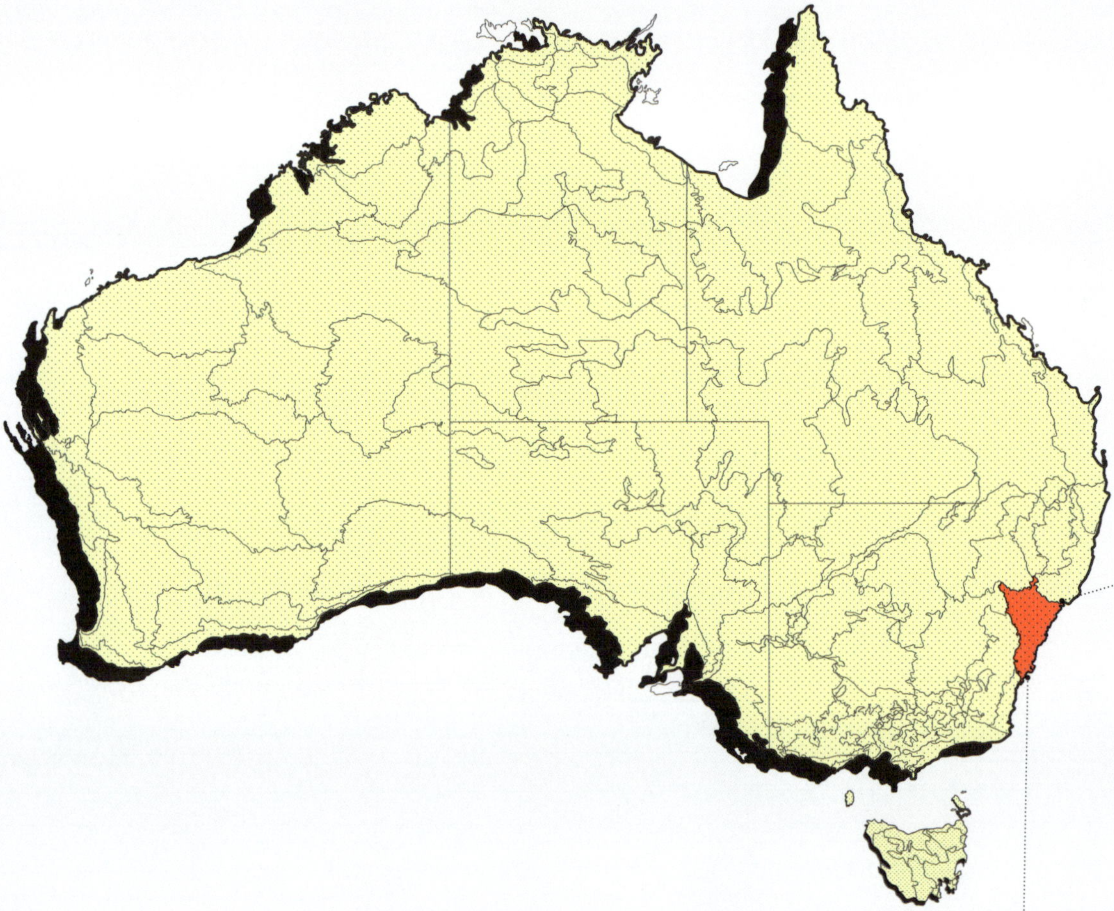

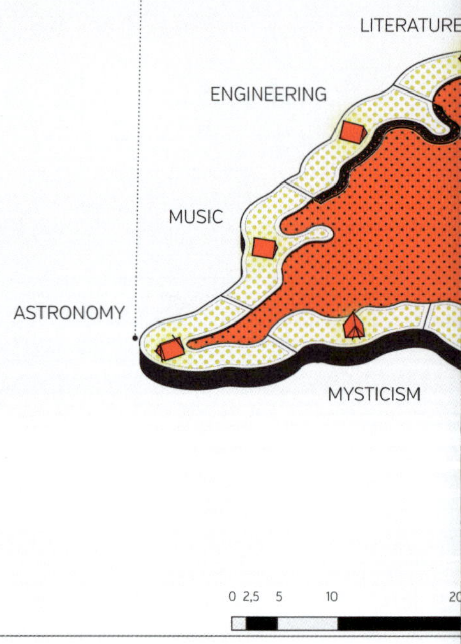
LITERATURE
ENGINEERING
MUSIC
ASTRONOMY
MYSTICISM
0 2,5 5 10

DARKINJUNG

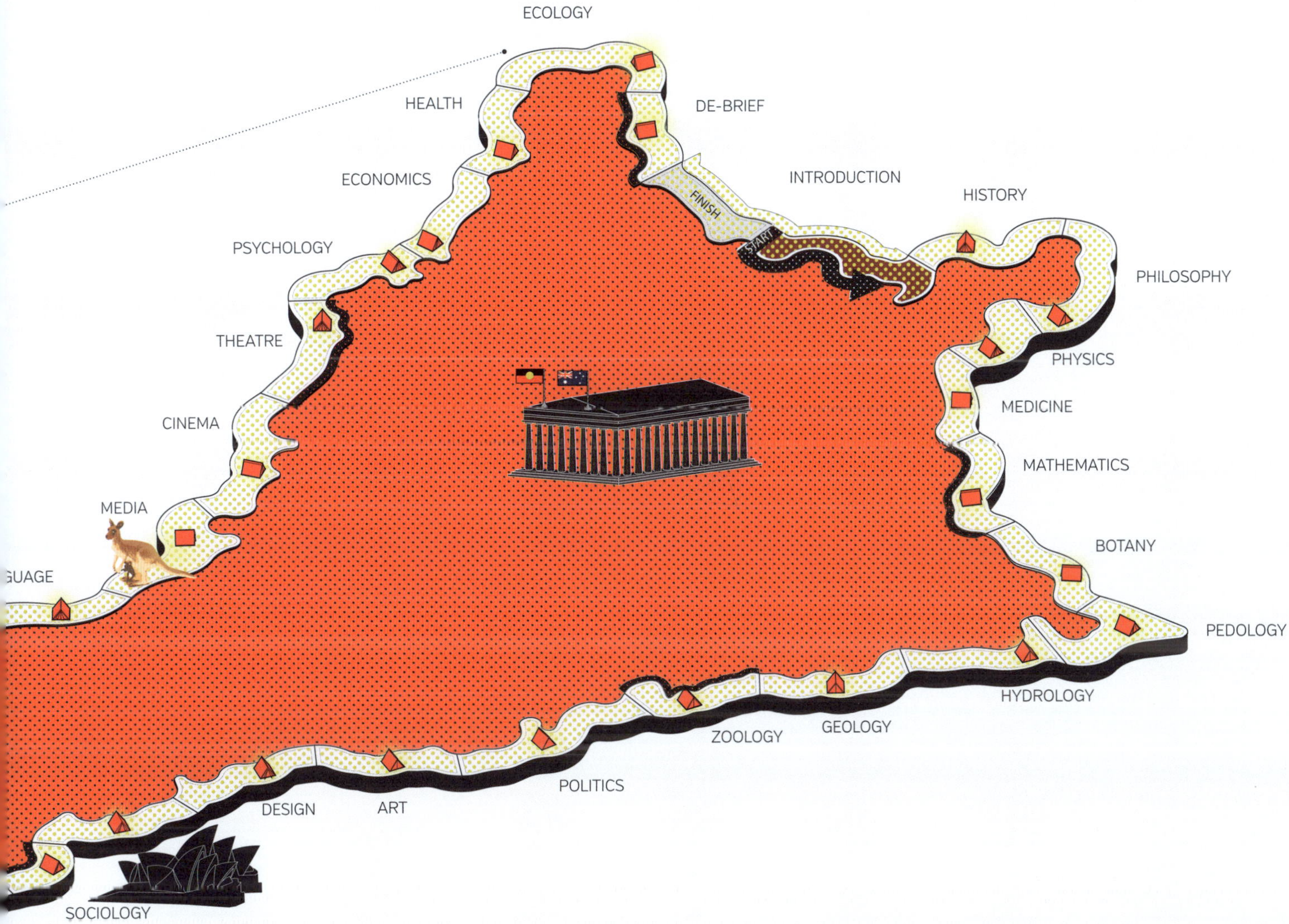

PERIPATOS

5 KM 50 KM

"Future Generations University" (New South Wales, 1996). A proposal for a university campus where teaching spaces are distributed along the 1,000 km boundary of the Darkinjung Aboriginal lands in eastern Australia [131].

PAUL AMBROSE
b. CHARLESTON. W. VA-1969

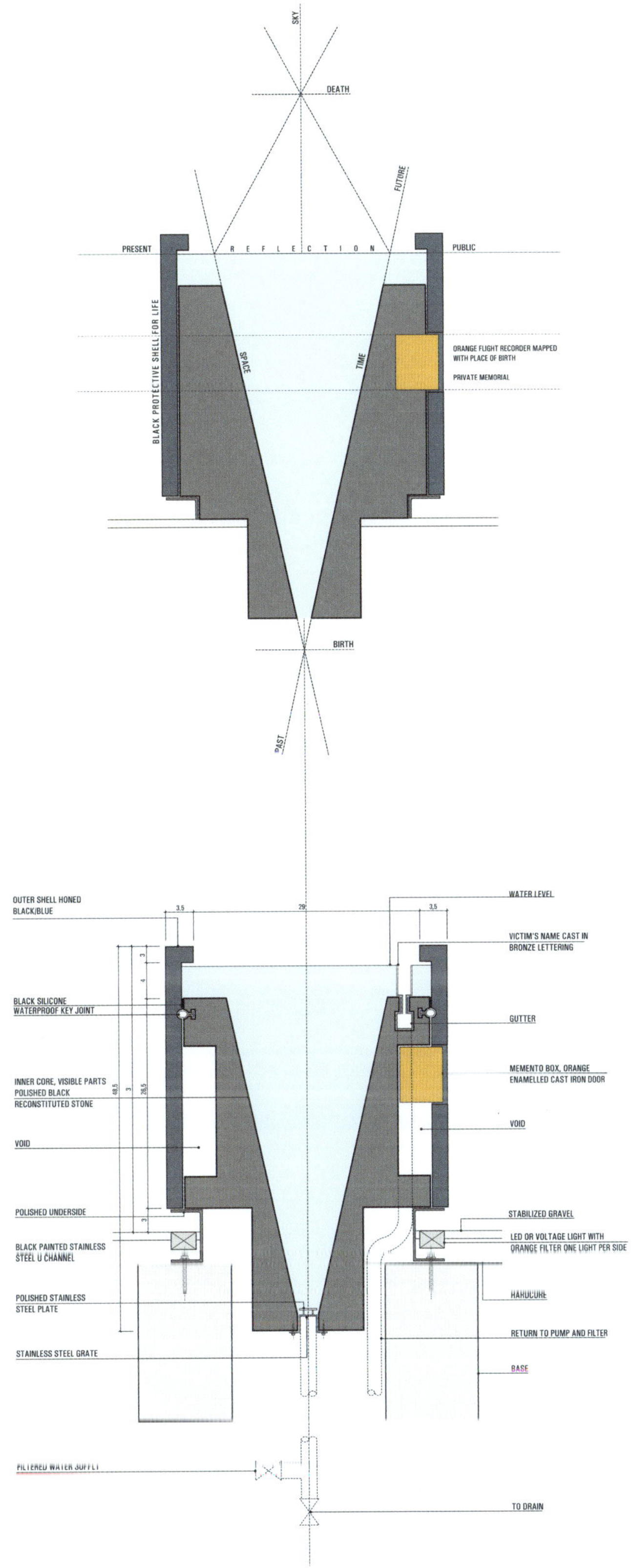

Unbuilt design for the Pentagon Memorial (Washington, DC, 2002). A memorial comprising 184 "black boxes," one for each of the victims of the September 11, 2001, terrorist attack on the Pentagon. Each box contains the victim's name and place and date of birth inscribed at the surface of dark water reflecting the sky [131].

Detail of the unbuilt design for the Pentagon Memorial showing an orange container for private keepsakes, which can be inserted by relatives into a black box dedicated to each victim [131].

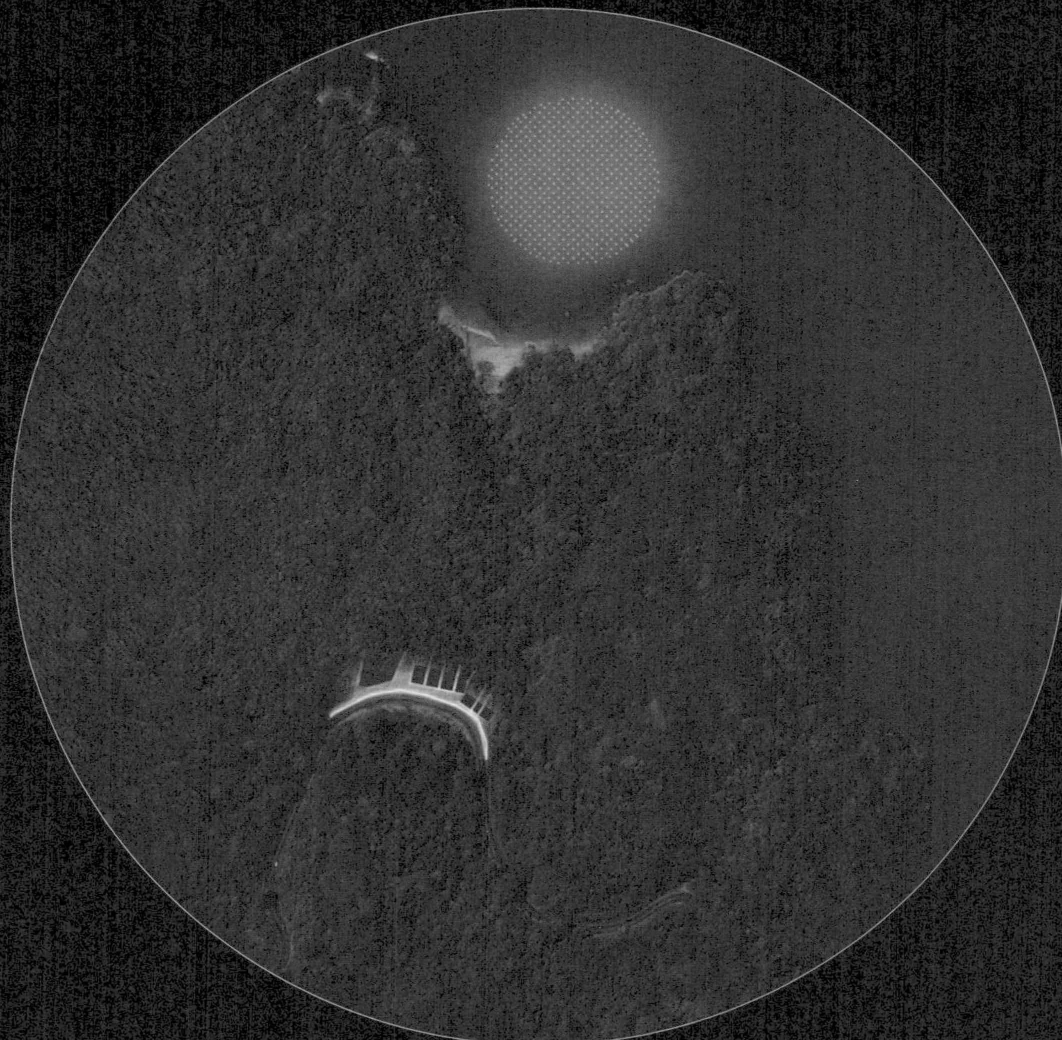

Unbuilt design for the Memorial to Victims of the Tsunami (Thailand, 2005). Site Plan showing a field of solar-powered lights in the ocean and museum (*left*). Diagram (*right*) of the memorial's grid of lights fixed to the sea floor and fluctuating with the perturbations of wind and water [132].

View of unbuilt design for the Memorial to Victims of the Tsunami from Khao Lak headland to the memorial's floating grid of solar-powered lights [132].

View of unbuilt design for the Memorial to Victims of the Tsunami from Khao Lak beach to the memorial's floating grid of solar-powered lights [132].

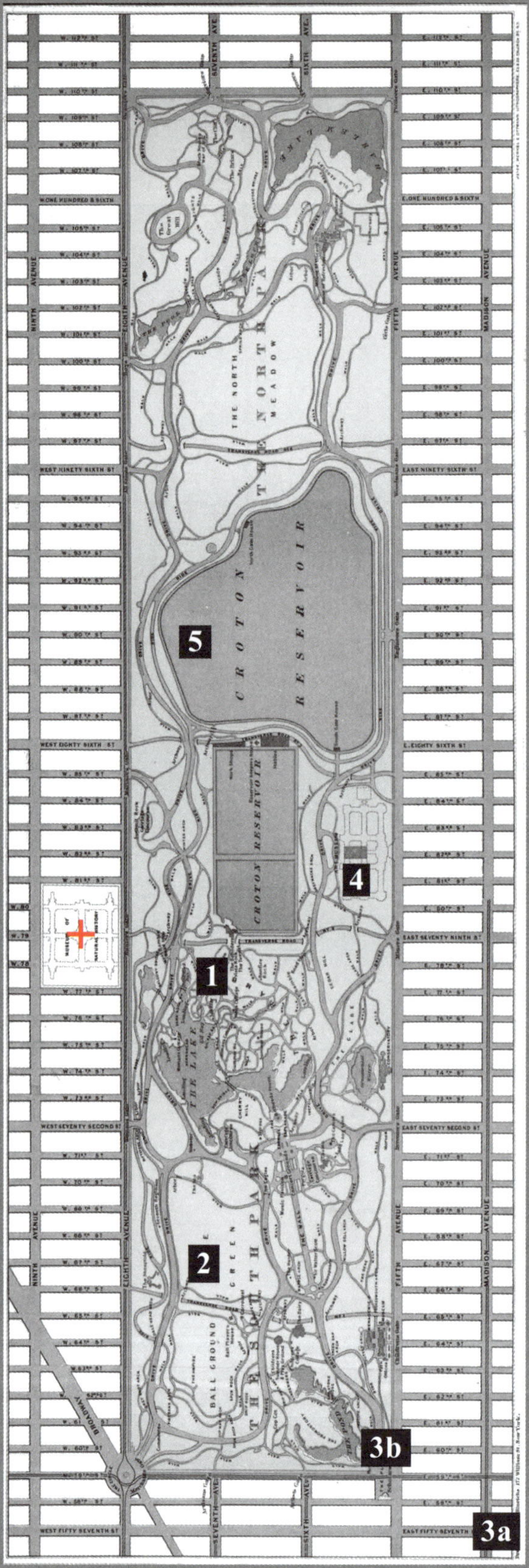

1. The Savage State

2. The Pastoral State

3. The Consummation of Empire

4. Destruction

5. Desolation

"The Course of Empire Circuit" (New York City, 2022). A proposed walk in Central Park leading to vistas which embody Thomas Cole's five allegorical paintings—*The Savage State*, *The Pastoral State*, *Empire*, *Destruction*, and *Desolation*—collectively known as *The Course of Empire* [133].

"The Course of Empire Circuit" features a copy of the iconic boulder that anchors each of the five paintings in Thomas Cole's *The Course of Empire* series. Designed to look like an asteroid, in this case it is cantilevered off the roof of 432 Park Avenue to signify "Empire," the fourth painting in Cole's series [133].

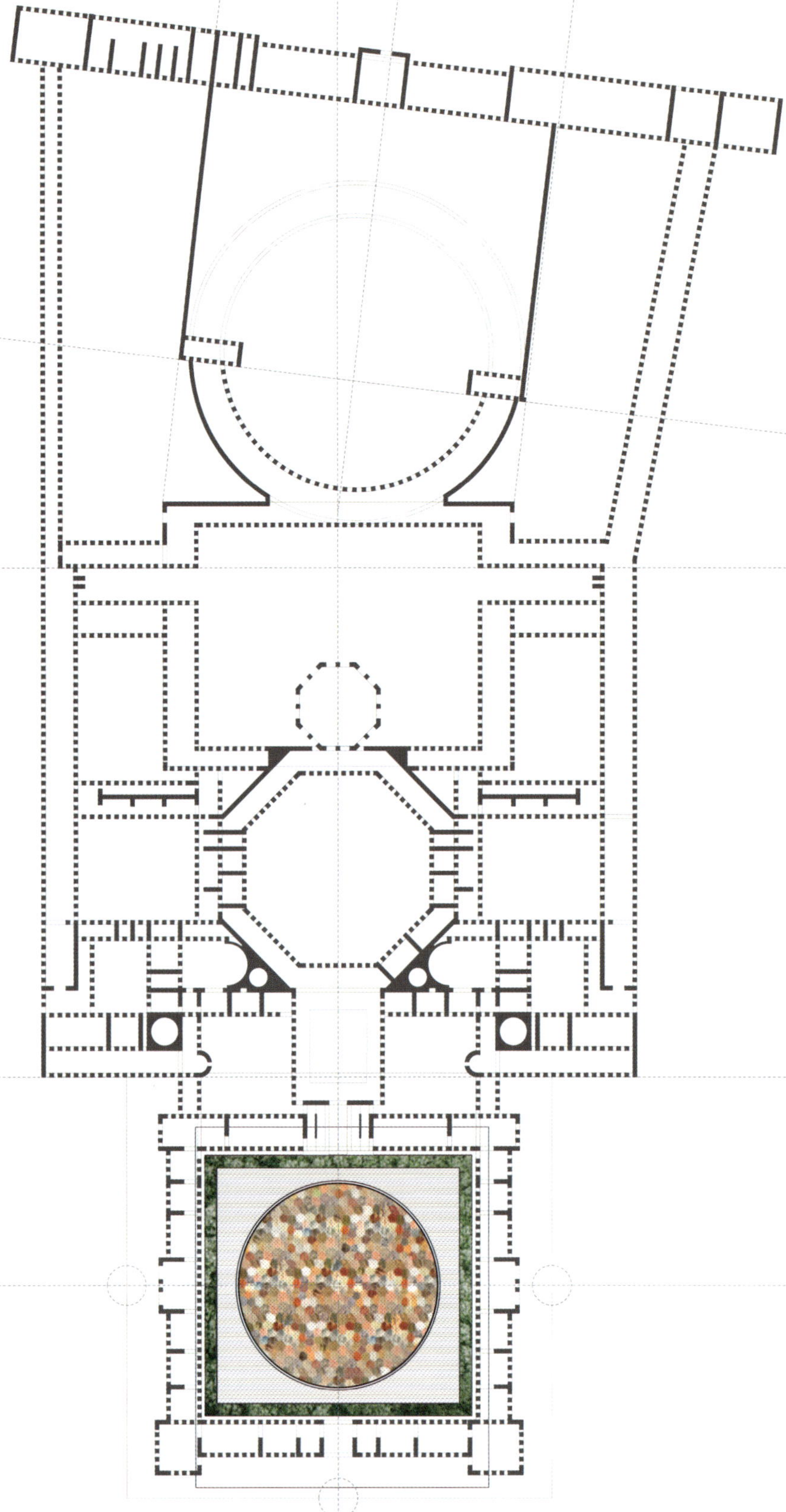

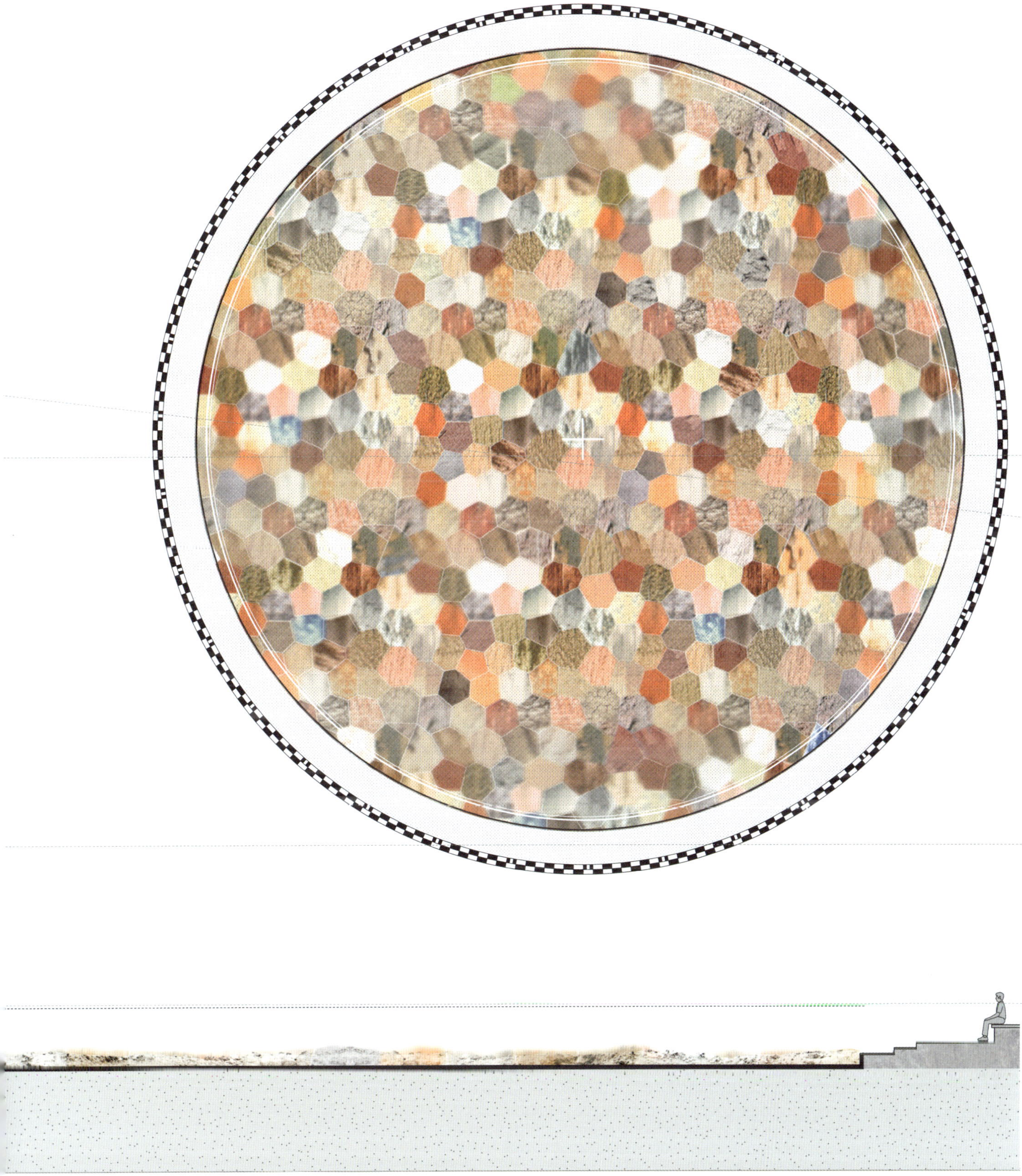

"Garden of the Anthropos" (Paris, 2022). Plan of a hypothetical monument to the Anthropocene located in the Louvre Museum's Cour Carrée comprising samples from the earth's diversity of soils [134].

View of the hypothetical “Garden of the Anthropos” monument to the Anthropocene [134].

“Weather Balloon” (Paris, 2022). Proposal to float a hot-air balloon over the Jardin des Tuileries in Paris based on the cartoon of a thought bubble with a carbon molecule serving as the gondola [134].

ESSAY BY RICHARD WELLER

FROM ART TO INSTRUMENTALITY AND BACK AGAIN

It must have been one morning in late February in 1983 when I awoke to my mother shouting that she had just called the university and they'd said if I showed up before 5:00 p.m. that day I would be accepted back into the landscape architecture program. Unconvinced that landscape architecture was either an art or a science (let alone both, as the professors had claimed), I'd dropped out two years earlier and spent the time since living wild on beaches and in rainforests along the east coast of Australia. But now, back in Sydney with nothing better to do, I did as my mother urged and made it to the campus before the deadline. And I have loved it, and, it must be said, also hated it ever since.

To start, I love the very word *landscape*: its gravitas, its ubiquity, and also its quotidian banality. I mean, on the one hand, landscape carries the weight of the world, indeed it *is* the weight of the world, and on the other, it's just something you stand on while waiting for the bus. And like most landscape architects, I have a deep love for the land—it filled every aspect of my childhood and is therefore something I remember as innocent. I know now of course that landscape is anything but innocent and I am especially critical of the way my profession trades on images as if it were. That said, I do now believe in landscape architecture's romanticism that both art and science come together in forming an ecological worldview, and that the profession's highest calling is stewardship of the land at a planetary scale. By the same token, I realize this is hubris and practically impossible. I also loathe the way this grandiose sensibility translates into saccharine images of "nature" and reduces design to self-righteous displays of sustainability. And while I believe in the profession's commitment to democratic public space, I am suspicious of design that venerates "the community" as the font of all wisdom. In this vein I also agree, in principle, with landscape architecture's respect for and incorporation of Indigenous landscape knowledge, though not when it is tokenistic or romances the noble savage.

I love the way landscape architecture reads places as layers of time and is sensitive to the more-than-human aspects of place, but not the way this can be reduced to prescriptions that limit design experimentation. And I resent the way this striving for holism that underpins landscape architecture is trivialized by clients and other consultants. Finally, I love landscape architecture's deep garden history—the allegory and theatricality of the garden—but dislike the way this so easily translates as trite decoration.

The point is that, without easy resolution, I have spent my career wrestling with these contradictions. I think they lie at the core of what it means to be a landscape architect and are what makes the discipline so interesting, so pertinent, and yes, so frustrating. These contradictions and the issues they involve can be conflated in the single definition that landscape architecture is an *art of instrumentality*, or, to shift the emphasis slightly, an *instrumental art*.

Art

In both theory and in practice, on every project, the landscape architect has to strike a certain balance between artistic subjectivity and the instrumental needs and constraints of any piece of land. Frederick Law Olmsted's design of Central Park, for example, is routinely lauded as a triumph in this regard. It reconciled prosaic matters such as water management and traffic flow within a spectacular rendition of a range of romantic landscape aesthetics, all underpinned by a reformist social agenda. Robert Smithson, arguably the most important landscape artist of the late twentieth century, interpreted Central Park as a great work of art. For him the park was art, not because of its painterly scenes, but because its picturesque qualities emerged from the way raw nature is engaged in its construction, setting in motion what Smithson saw as a constantly evolving synthesis of humanity and geology. Others will find myriad other meanings or feelings in the work, and whether Central Park is a great work of art depends, of course, on one's definition of art.

In fact, landscape architecture is a craft before it is an art, and there is much that art can do that landscape cannot. By the same token, there is much that landscape can do that fine art cannot. Much of that is instrumental; landscape must function economically, socially, and ecologically, but for this to be more than something a robot could produce, it has to be undertaken artfully, by which I mean that it must not only be refined in terms of the craft of construction, but conceived as a philosophical intervention between culture and nature and something situated critically within the history of aesthetics.

Smithson worried that as art moved out of the art gallery and into public space, its rigor as art would likely dissipate. And he was right: public space is never a blank canvas. And even if it was, those charged with designing it—namely, landscape architects—do not typically set out to make it into art, nor are they trained to do so. That is, even though they situate and justify their work in between nature and culture, landscape architects rarely set out to make explicitly philosophical or critical claims about contemporary culture, and they rarely lay out their designs as forms of agitation and innovation in relation to the history of aesthetics or contemporary visual culture. In the rare instances in which they might try to do so, they quickly come up against landscape's inherent limitations as a sculptural and semantic medium, not to mention the censorial wrath of clients and bureaucrats for whom landscape is nothing if not "nice."

As much of this collection of work shows, I make works of landscape architecture that are *not* nice. Instead, I have tried to foreground landscape as a medium and a mechanism of cultural critique, and I have intentionally attempted to situate design projects within, and against, landscape's aesthetic traditions. So yes, it is fair to say that I have tried to make *my* landscape architecture as a form of contemporary art. And I have been keenly aware that this pretentious experiment risks making neither good art nor good landscape; be that as it may, the compulsion to try is, for me, greater than the fear of failure.

The way to evaluate the work in this book is probably not so much about adjudicating whether it satisfies some definition of art or not, as it is about placing each project within its own genre (garden, memorial, urban design, research project, etc.) and asking whether the artistic inclinations embedded in the work help make it any good, and in turn whether this is of any relevance to the evolution of the discipline as an art of instrumentality.

The difference between my work and much mainstream landscape architecture is that it emerges more from an engagement with contemporary culture than from a veneration of *genius loci* (the spirit of place). In the Church of Landscape Architecture this is heretical because at least since Alexander Pope's epistle to the Earle of Burlington in 1731, in which he implored designers to "let *Nature* never be forgot" and to "consult the *Genius* of the *Place* in all," landscape architects have primarily drawn their inspiration from and tried to tailor their craft to the preexisting landscape conditions of the places in which they work.

In my time, *genius loci* was influentially resurrected and complicated by the Norwegian architectural philosopher Christian Norberg-Schulz, and rationalized as "a sense of place" by geographers. This was then appropriated by landscape architecture to serve as its postmodern desideratum, and in the wake of twentieth-century modernism, sensitivity to the genius of place is very well advised. Of course, site matters and only those intoxicated with utopian ideology could ignore it, but in landscape architecture, site-specific sensitivity quickly calcified into either a formulaic reading of a site's biophysical layers through the lenses of the natural sciences, or alternatively, symbolic incantations over spirits long since gone.

Designing a place means engaging with both the cultural and biological processes at work in a given locale in equal measure. It also means triangulating this with a self-reflexive awareness of one's own limited and idiosyncratic worldview. There are two ways around this becoming either incapacitating on the one hand, or superficial on the other. The first is for the designer to cultivate their own site-specific romanticism by attempting to empty their mind of Cartesian anxiety through a combination of immersive intuition and educated observation. At worst, this can lead to little more than clichés of an all-too-easy harmony between subject and object, while at best there are landscape architects such as Craig Burton in Australia, Martí Franch in Spain, Günther Vogt in Switzerland, and Teresa Moller in Chile, who devote their lives to auguring places deeply and carefully and can produce beautiful and sensitive designs.

The second, less common approach is what I call a critical romanticism of place. This approach makes the "problem of place"—not just the place itself—the subject of design. This is a subtle but important shift. Instead of seeking and claiming to tap into the aesthetic and ecological essence of a place, it means worrying that there are infinite "places" in any one place and considering that they are all, to varying extents, fictions. It is also to ask in whose interest this sense of place is being decided and expressed. It means worrying about how, on the one hand, *genius loci* can provide identity and strength for those oppressed and betrayed by modernity, but on the other, it can also be the way the colonizer digs in so as to secure their political hegemony and their ecological self-preservation. It means staying with the tension between a longing for "home" that is implicit in seeking a sense of place and an equal and opposite desire for liberation from parochialism. It means staying with the frightening instability of landscape as a synecdoche of nature and our tremulous situation within it.

This insistence on questioning the authenticity and righteousness of seeking a sense of place needs, however, to be tempered by two important and interconnected facts. First, in the long run there can be no enduring modernity in the unforgiving and fragile Australian landscape—or anywhere for that matter—unless it adapts to and is embedded within the specific ecological conditions of the landscape. Second, by way of atoning for their crimes, the colonizer must go through the process of deconstructing the legal and aesthetic lies they have imposed on Indigenous people and the land. So understood, landscape becomes the medium through which a reconciliation between modernity and tradition and the colonizer and the colonized can take place. Easy to say.

Landscape architecture, then, necessarily draws its conclusions from an amalgamation of other disciplines, such as ecology, geography, history, anthropology, and sociology, but, above all, its greatest source of inspiration and authority is that good old thing called nature. And because in popular culture, nature and landscape are synonymous, and because this nature is now cast in terms of crises and victimhood, it follows that landscape architecture is generally perceived, and in turn, received, as righteous. There is no question—and climate change makes this more acute every day—that by carefully designing places instead of just exploiting them, landscape architects are on the right side of history, but while righteousness might be good for a designer's sense of self, it is not necessarily good for aesthetics. Design that looks benign, as works of landscape architecture usually do, masks other economic and cultural forces which are not. In this way, what may have begun by resisting the evil genius of capitalist modernity, ends up serving it. Realizing this, and then trying to do something about it, presents the designer with an irreconcilable conundrum: either move the landscape project toward the criticality of art, or abandon it altogether for politics. Despite its impossibility, an *art of instrumentality* tries to hold onto both and turn them through the optimistic agency of design.

The problem is that because on the surface of things landscape architecture is so virtuous, it can get away with representing complex things like relations between culture and nature, and relations between the colonizer and the colonized, as more or less just a walk in the park. By shifting the problems of culture onto the innocence of nature, works of landscape architecture effectively quarantine themselves in a prelingual zone where they are protected from the sort of critique that would apply to any other aesthetic practice engaging with such complex and controversial subjects. Going back to the eighteenth century, this is landscape's great trick: it plays the innocent bystander, the backdrop to history, when in fact it has always been the whole theater. More to the point, in the Anthropocene—in the planetary form of the earth system, or what scientists are now referring to as "the critical zone"—landscape is becoming the script. Landscape architects know this, but caught up in the chicanery of commercial development, their efforts to create a sense of place that might yet ground modernity in place translates all too easily into glib contextualism: the environmental equivalent of elevator music.

The paucity of intentional meaning in much landscape architecture could hardly be more disproportionate to the magnitude of the profession's overarching mantra to *design with nature*. In his celebrated work *Keywords*, Raymond Williams describes nature as one of the most complex words in the English language. It is no surprise, then, that it is unclear which nature exactly landscape architects are referring to as they go about designing with "it." The nineteenth-century philosopher John Stuart Mill provides us with four enduring options in this regard: 1) nature as everything; 2) nature as not culture; 3) nature as things as they ought to be; and 4) nature as the potential of things. Landscape architects, like the general public, tend to mean definition 2, which then, according to their expertise, becomes a sign of definition 3. But by reinforcing a dualism of nature and culture as definition 2 does, the two natures they elide—nature as not culture, yet as things ought to be—are contradictory. One is left then with definitions 1 and 4—that is, nature is everything and its potential. Ontologically true as these two natures might well be, they are as good as useless as an epistemological basis for a profession. I mean, other than "anything goes," one is hard-pressed to draw any ethical or aesthetic mandate from *nature as everything*. There is however a fifth definition of nature, one which for whatever reason Mill didn't feel it necessary to include, namely, that before it is anything else, nature is a cultural construct. This is not to say nature is all in one's head, but it is to recognize that one's head has a lot to do with it.

Along these lines, for many years I've been teaching a seminar called "The Culture of Nature," centered on the problem of nature in Western (and some Eastern) thought. The course is a history of the sciences and the arts emphasizing the way ideas translate into the design of places and things. It has eleven lectures: Words, Flora, Fauna, Paradise, Utopia, Orientation, Machines, Landscape, Environmentalism, Anthropocene, and Cyborg, which, aside from technical training, is about all you need to think like a landscape architect.

Each year, the first thing I ask each student to do is to write down their answer to the question "What is Nature?" [p. 22] They have three minutes to respond. After class, I type the answers into a single document and circulate it to the class so that everyone can reflect on what is, for all intents and purposes, a multibrained snapshot of what we collectively think the world, aka nature, is. The answers generally fall into one of Mill's four categories, but over the years more and more students are quick to realize that before it is one of these four, it is indeed a cultural construct. With the advent of the Anthropocene, what this shows is that nature has become a profoundly unstable referent. This instability is, I think, the primary characteristic of our historical moment and one which most works of landscape architecture either choose to ignore or assiduously repress.

Over the years, very few students have taken the riddle to its logical conclusion and given the correct answer that nature is really just a word. My own confusion about this word-of-all-words became the primary subject of an installation in the Museum of Contemporary Art in Sydney titled *Landscape Painting*, which I created for the Seppelt Contemporary Art Award 1998 [p. 23–25], an annual event where a small, select group of designers and artists are invited to present summations of their practices. In this installation, a dictionary definition of nature is printed on a large canvas surface onto which pockets of soil with living plants are stitched. To the sound of an electric pump embedded in the artwork, a film of water runs constantly over the canvas so that the plants, along with algae and fungi, can grow. Over the period of the three-month exhibition, the text dissolves into the ecology of the surface of what is effectively a painting that paints itself.

Landscape architecture's maxim par excellence is to design with nature, an expression coined by Ian McHarg. By calling his 1969 magnum opus *Design with Nature* instead of Design with Landscape, McHarg gets himself and the discipline into all sorts of philosophical trouble. Influenced by the likes of big thinkers such as Patrick Geddes, Lewis Mumford, and Buckminster Fuller, McHarg's use of nature elevated what was for all intents and purposes just a simple land use planning method to an all-encompassing teleology of evolution. In venerating nature as such, McHarg sidestepped the problem of art (human subjectivity) by claiming that his method of land use planning would result in the "higher art" of humanity ultimately finding its place in the natural order of things. Although his intention was a "higher" level of (spatial) symbiosis between "man" and "nature," the title and the method of his work recapitulate nature as an object within the Western canon which the landscape architect, backed by science, stands outside of and can rationally interpret so as to then prescribe how culture should be corrected. McHarg's method was brilliantly simple and replicable, and in terms of making big basic decisions about land use—such as, don't build in flood zones—he was right. But it also reduced design to instrumentality, computation, and bureaucracy. With no room for chaos or design nuance and artistic subjectivity, this is not how culture, or for that matter nature, necessarily even work.

Ideologically, the landscape architecture department at the University of New South Wales where I studied was split between two camps: analogue representation and site design in accordance with interpretations of *genius loci* on the one hand, and large-scale McHargian landscape planning based on digital landscape suitability analysis on the other. By "digital" I mean punch cards pushed into "the computer"—a behemoth with its own room in the geography building that occasionally printed out incomprehensible pixels. The difference between the camps lay not with intent—for both *genius loci* and McHargian suitability analysis ultimately strive to ground modernity in local ecology and local culture—the difference was in scale and method.

The difference is that while both are grounded in an analysis of the landscape as described by the natural sciences, the former pays more attention to the detail of the cultural landscape and—to a certain degree—engages the designer's aesthetic subjectivity. This is the semantically rich and theatrical world of the garden. Inversely, by repressing artistic subjectivity in favor of empirical analysis and procedural method, McHargian planning foregrounds the scientific nature of the ecological landscape. It soon became apparent that this binary between design (the garden) and planning (the ecological landscape) in my school extended to the profession as a whole, and, as this book documents, it has taken me an entire career to go to both ends of the spectrum to try and sort out my own version of a rapprochement between the two.

In my design school in the early 1980s, there was no serious studio culture to help us grapple with the complexity of issues related to place, method, and representation. While there was a sense of reformist optimism in the department—landscape would now redeem modernism—the topics and sites we worked on were trivial and only ever reviewed in terms of functionality, spatial composition, and *genius loci* lite. Along with McHarg's *Design with Nature*, our key text regarding the field's formal legacy was *The Landscape of Man* by Geoffrey and Susan Jellicoe. There were no theory classes to speak of and there was no engagement with the emerging international discourses of postmodernity and the aesthetics of postmodernism as they had started to take hold in both art and architecture. This institutional torpor, along with the profession's intellectual and creative vacuity at the time, was extremely frustrating, but it was also, ironically, good for one thing—it motivated self-education. And in my case, that motivation has powered an entire career. It has also provided me with a healthy degree of self-doubt, which helps resist any form of certainty and hold the design process in a liminal, open-ended space for as long as possible. In my case, it also inspired an iconoclastic approach to design.

The most important iconoclastic images passed under the desk in the design school in the 1980s were Charles Moore's Piazza d'Italia in New Orleans (1978) and Bernard Tschumi's Parc de la Villette in Paris (1983). Although in downtown New Orleans it might well be a ridiculous and failed public space, in carefully cropped photographs, Piazza d'Italia appeared as a dazzling work of theater. This was exciting at the time because the cities of the so-called developed world were anything but theatrical. They were not pleasurable, imaginative, carnivalesque places that celebrated urban living; they were nine-to-five machines—cold, empty husks left in the wake of international modernism. In a flash, Moore's chintzy montage gave us permission to broach the city as a stage and use history as a cut-and-paste catalogue. And while on the one hand this opened the sluice gates for the flotsam and jetsam of postmodernism, on the other, per Charles Jencks and Robert Venturi, it could also be taken seriously and used as a vocabulary.

As for Tschumi's winning design for the Parc de la Villette; there were over 470 entries in the competition, and all but three were parks as we know them. Brazenly and bravely, the three entries by the architects Bernard Tschumi, Rem Koolhaas, and Zaha Hadid jettisoned the bucolic idyll of a park and replaced it with extensions and intensifications of the culture of the city. Hadid's version of contemporary landscape was a graphic abstraction lifted off the surface of the earth. OMA's was a flexible, indeterminate kit of parts, and Tschumi's winning scheme comprised surfaces, lines, and grid points superimposed upon one another with intentional discordance. Replete with references to contemporary French philosophy, Tschumi described his park as the biggest building in the world. Koolhaas similarly excised landscape's aesthetic baggage (and its environmental burdens) by simply referring to his design as "scape." The refusal by these architects to conform to the traditional dualism of culture (city) and nature (park) was an important development, but binaries are not resolved, or absolved, simply by the excision of one half. As built, Parc de la Villette today is a field of thirty-five empty architectural follies, and forty years later, Parisians are still at something of a loss as to what to do with them. Similarly, had it been built, OMA's graphic striations, which still enjoys iconic status in the realm of paper architecture, could just as easily have become a field of random junk dating as quickly as it was evidently drawn. In any event, the important thing in the case of La Villette was that the death knell of the picturesque had now been rung. That landscape architects have been trying to resurrect it with their sappy photoshop renderings of nice people in nice places ever since is testament to the indelibility of this British aesthetic invention and the inordinate conservatism of the profession and its patrons.

Along with Piazza d'Italia and Parc de la Villette, other landscapes designed by artists, such as Jean Dubuffet's Jardin d'émail (1974), Daniel Buren's Palais Royale (1985), Isamu Noguchi's various works, and a little later, Arakawa and Madeline Gins's Site of Reversible Destiny in Yoro, Japan (1995), could be assembled to build an alternative landscape lexicon that wasn't pastoral, picturesque, or eco-paradisiacal. These projects demonstrated the potential of not being constrained by *genius loci* and whatever aesthetic advances have been made in landscape architecture over the last fifty years are indebted to them.

To be fair, landscape is a very difficult medium to aesthetically advance in any radical manner. Certainly for the public, a park is a park is a park. It is not some sort of social and ecological experiment, let alone an architectural exegesis on poststructuralism, as Tschumi would have it. It is a place to feed ducks, walk the dog, and generally marvel at flowers and photosynthesis. And so, what Hadid, OMA, and Tschumi overlooked in their designs (as have those of us who were deeply influenced by them) is that topography and plants are the reliable building blocks of landscape design, and that biophilia, especially for people in high-density urban environments, is real. For example, with good vegetal and topographic structure, parks such as Jardin du Luxembourg and Central Park—arguably the two best urban parks in the world—are not only theatrical and functional, they are also immensely pleasurable.

Of course, today both can also be read as conservative and reactionary spaces. But this is to overly confuse politics with parks. I am not suggesting their forms be replicated, nor am I suggesting that landscape architecture only play paradise lost to architecture's utopia. I am suggesting that the cliché of landscape has deep illusory traditions that warrant imaginative and critical reinterpretation, not just outright rejection, or mindless repetition. And it is not just *avant-garde* architects who ignore this history, it is also landscape architects who have become so pious and doctrinaire with regard to environmental and social issues as to be incapable of exercising what James Corner refers to as "the landscape imagination." Many of the profession's award-winning practices have learned that "nice," picturesque landscapes are a winning formula, but every time they use this old trick to win a job the discipline is set back. Complicating matters is that when a landscape architect does try to do something other than "nice" they can play into the hands of clients who see landscape as a cheap form of branding. The challenge, then, for the designer is to turn this into something more than just advertising.

When the Parc de la Villette competition was announced in 1984, the profession in Australia was comprised of either puritans preaching a strict Australian sense of place (European geometry and European plants were *verboten*), or commercial practices glamming it up for their neoliberal pimps. To avoid both, instead of working in a landscape architecture practice, I turned to the art scene in Sydney where unemployment was *de rigueur*. To supplement my limited education, I interloped on theory classes in the local art school, where the French intelligentsia now had a stranglehold. Talk of Barthes, Baudrillard, Derrida, and Deleuze was loose and fast, though I'm not sure anyone really knew what they were talking about. Or if they did, then they had not yet worked out how to translate it into making art that was anything more than a scrappy addendum to verbose critical theory essays. Nonetheless, I took it all very seriously and set up a studio to focus on painting big canvases. There were signs that I could actually do this, but being a serious painter and making a few pictures with paint are two very different things, and so, after a few grimy years, this romance ran its course.

During that time (1983–89), I remained tethered to the design world by regularly entering design competitions. The first of these, done in partnership with a like-minded mate, was for Sydney's Taylor Square, a gritty traffic intersection at the epicenter of the city's thriving gay community. Our submission of a big glow-in-the-dark copy of Michelangelo's David was evidently lost on the jury. In another, for a chunk of the Hudson River waterfront in Manhattan, we plowed a cruise liner into the city's western flank, called it the "Love Boat," and ripped open the hull so the city's artists could have their way with it. Alas, to our disillusionment, these "designs" and many more like them all went into a void. As it happened, my mate, Peter England, saw no future in landscape architecture's Calvinism and went on to build a successful career in theater set design. I went back to questions of Australian identity vested in land and the problem of *genius loci* that lies at the core of the discipline.

The first "project" in this vein, born of Australia's jingoistic buildup to its bicentenary in 1988, is titled "The Ghost House" [p. 26-27]. It is a copy of my suburban childhood home—or any suburban home for that matter—relocated into the central Australian desert and left to decompose. The Ghost House is sited on the British lie that Australia was a "terra nullius," a land devoid of Indigenous peoples. Because of this, under the house of my childhood—under every Australian house—there are ghosts suspended in the unimaginable pain of (almost) total loss.

In the early 1980s, I read Patrick White and pored over the works of Australian painters such as Arthur Boyd, Sidney Nolan, Jeffrey Smart, and Tim Storrier, all of whom plumbed the troubled depths of what might be meant by an Anglo-Saxon Australian sense of place. Instead of finding solace in place, White's characters are driven mad by the Australian landscape, and instead of grand vistas, the painters depicted diminutive antiheroes lost in both time and space. This sensibility translates into the "Australian Garden" [p. 28–31], which has elements that would stay with me throughout my life: the burnt fence, the mapped surface, the geometry of the *hortus conclusus*, surveyor's poles, a room. I was not concerned about whether a design such as this would be built or how it would be used. It is obviously useless. This "garden" is a set piece in which everything is selected and situated to play a symbolic role, an approach that would fully materialize in my approach to designing the National Museum of Australia a decade later.

Around this time (1986), I met the landscape architect, master craftsman, and eastern European refugee Vladimir Sitta. He said he could get me some work—my first real job—with a new group that was forming in Sydney called Creative Design and Technology (CDT). Sitta and I shared a mutual disdain for the profession's lack of creativity and its mounting postmodern hypocrisy, but little did we know that we were both about to jump from the frying pan into the fire. CDT was run by an enigmatic American with a background in advertising in Tokyo and a newly minted architecture degree from the AA in London. He was now in Sydney to sell a vision of redeveloping the city's extensive postindustrial waterfronts based on the Baltimore Harbor model. As I would later find out, he was also in Sydney because it was relatively close to Jakarta, the headquarters of a New Age cult known as Subud, of which CDT was ostensibly an entrepreneurial extension. After only a few weeks in his employ, he said he could not work with me unless I undertook a grand tour, with him as my guide. No, not the Parthenon and the Pantheon; he insisted we visit Edmonton Mall (the world's largest shopping center at the time), EPCOT in Orlando, Tokyo Disneyland, and Baltimore Harbor, among other assorted horrors. Similarly, Vladimir, who had a penchant for avant-garde theater, was sent to New York for reeducation and paid to do nothing other than visit Broadway musicals. Needless to say, this was all quite bizarre, but what our enigmatic American was endeavoring to do was convince us that popular culture in general and theme parks in particular could be used as profitable catalysts for more idealistic forms of development. And the more we disagreed, the more he tried to convince us.

The way it worked was CDT would convince investors (mainly Japanese banks) to bankroll "the office"—a loose collection of script writers, animators, architects, and other creatives—so we could work on visioning projects of our own invention that might one day be of value to investors. Among others, we did this for Sydney's Darling Harbor, Singapore's Marina Bay, and New York City's Coney Island. The coup de grâce, however, was a concept for creating an "eco-resort" of massive tree houses serviced only by dirigibles, deep in the rainforest of Kalimantan in Borneo. As the story went, the vague location of this project was determined by Subud's spiritual leader, who had apparently placed his thumb on a map and instructed those gathered at his feet to "build the new city here." Accordingly, we flew into the unmapped center of Borneo in a military helicopter to try to locate this sacred site, and with nothing more than some random snapshots of the ubiquitous forest we returned to the Sydney studio to draw tree houses and dirigibles so the concept could be pitched to investors and Indonesian politicians. The argument was that the investment stream of the eco-resort would save the rainforest from imminent mining and logging, that is, until it morphed into a new City of God, as Subud's disciples always intended. Three decades later, there is no eco-resort and no new city and Kalimantan has been plundered for timber, palm oil, and minerals.

Exhausted by the ethical conundrums of such projects and the cultish aura that surrounded them, after a few years I decided to pack my portfolio and get out. The exact rationale escapes me now, but I flew to Cairo on a one-way ticket. It was probably something along the lines of retracing Western history, as this would explain my eventual route from Aswan to Jerusalem to Berlin. My reason for passing through Israel was also because my father—along with the entire German (Christian) farming community of Sarona, now a heritage precinct in central Tel Aviv—had been arrested by the British at the age of four and sent to Australia for seven years of internment in a remote rural (prison) camp. After some time spent (illegally) in the West Bank learning of the Palestinian struggle firsthand, I headed for Berlin, where the Wall had just fallen. I was broke, and the only thing I knew about the city was that the beautiful German design journal *Daidalos* was produced there. I looked them up, asked about work, and was directed to James Stirling's office, who in turn directed me to Müller Knippschild Wehberg (MKW, now Lützow 7), "the best" landscape architects in town. They were surprised that someone from Australia would just knock on the door unannounced, and even more surprised when I said I didn't want to work for them. Instead, I proposed to do a competition with them on the condition that if we did happen to win a prize, we'd split the cash fifty-fifty. Deal!

A competition had just opened for the Moabiter Werder, a five-hectare site on the river Spree, and after six weeks of hand-drawing we submitted an overworked scheme. As luck would have it, we came in second (to Dieter Kienast), and with my cut of the winnings I could now settle down and focus on what really interested me—the 160-kilometer strip of no-man's land [p. 32–33] encircling the former West Berlin. My position was that this land should not only stay open and public, but also that it should not be sanitized and gentrified by design. This was not an original insight into the city—the beauty of Berlin's *terrain vague* was well known and much loved by many, not least of all Wim Wenders, whose black-and-white film *Himmel Uber Berlin (Wings of Desire)* played nonstop in a small local cinema. The academic exercise I set myself, however, was not to frame Berlin's post-Cold War character, but to try to *design* parts of it in a way that would aid and abet the remarkable propensity Berliners had for self-organized use of ruins and wasteland. In other words, I was asking if a form of landscape architectural antidesign could be catalyzed by design.

After the Berlin Wall came down in 1989, the Potsdamer Platz and surrounding area was a field of rubble with nothing but a small mound marking the site where Hitler had killed himself in the bunker below. In its sublime dereliction, the Potsdamer Platz was beautiful in its emptiness. Alas, development hates a void, and so in 1991 a master plan by Richard Rogers was unveiled by the government, with Daimler Benz appointed as its landlord.

Rogers's scheme was bullied into place as the winner of a competition it was not even originally entered in. A prominent loser in this competition was Daniel Libeskind, who submitted the most extraordinary and most unlikely maelstrom of urbanism I've ever seen. Because of my association with MKW, who were his go-to landscape architects, I was able to contribute a landscape component to this competition entry. The idea was that under Libeskind's new city would be a new ground created by earth imported from all nations. Libeskind liked this idea but scooped it up into a massive (angel's) "wing" hovering over the whole site in which, according to him, Germany's Bundestag (parliament) would convene.

Rogers's master plan followed the nineteenth-century template that could still be seen etched into the ground of no-man's land. This business-as-usual approach to the question of the Potsdamer Platz was profoundly disappointing. For some, rebuilding the city as it was before the war would be an act of intentional amnesia, whereas apologists argued that the city's form needn't change just because shameful historical events had taken place there.

Either way, if it was the halcyon days of the 1920s that its planners sought to selectively channel from its fraught history, they soon learned that the resurrection of the form and the resurrection of the spirit of a place are two very different things. Thanks to Rogers and the starchitects who subsequently lined up to get their snouts in the trough, the Potsdamer Platz is today a soulless, generic enclave.

There was one triangular parcel in the master plan left empty, and in 1995, a competition called for ideas. Titled "The Berlin Room" [p. 34–37], the proposal, again in partnership with MKW, was to build a large concrete wall around the entire site to secure a sanctum of memory within. This is achieved by lining the entire interior of the concrete wall with mirrors to reflect a bosquet of birch trees set in dark water. On the water float small, engraved images (daguerreotypes) selected from the twentieth-century life and death of the Potsdamer Platz.

Aside from admiring Libeskind's competition entry for a new city, I believed—and continue to believe—that instead of urban development, the Potsdamer Platz and its surrounds should have been seen as an extension of the Tiergarten (Berlin's Central Park) and reserved as an open public space. This new public space would be one that retained the Potsdamer Platz's raw poetry of dereliction but one that also provided infrastructure for artistic and social activation. The question, then, was what kind of infrastructure?

The "Potsdamer Platz Park" [p. 38–43] is an attempt to answer this in eight parts. 1) Excavate some of the earth to reveal and let light into parts of the bunkers of the former Reich chancellery; 2) import earth from all nations and ceremoniously deposit it on-site to form a new symbolic ground; 3) create a ground pattern of gravels, paving, and grasses based on the shadows of the palimpsest of the site's history; 4) insert large fire pits regularly across the site to attract impromptu gatherings of people; 5) distribute old war machinery and remnants from no-man's land across the site; 6) overlay across the whole site a network of paths derived from a map linking all of Europe's capital cities to one another with straight lines; 7) add large moving screens (art billboards) to run on tracks adjacent to the pathways; and, finally, 8) at each node in the network (where each of the European capitals would be on a map of Europe), insert a copy of Le Corbusier's Dom-Ino House as a frame to be altered by designers/artists representing each respective city. These buildings function thereafter as public art embassies where each nation is responsible for curating their own events in the building in the park. In short, the Park at Potsdamer Platz is a combination of Parc de la Villette, an expo, a biennale, and Burning Man.

The geometric template of the Potsdamer Platz Park was derived from the broader geography of a newly unified Europe. Coupled with this symbolic implosion of territory is an additional proposal linked to the Park for an avenue of trees and a cycling and walking path heading east from Potsdamer Platz to Moscow and west to Paris. As well as marking a significant historical trans-European axis, the "Paris–Moscow Songline" [p. 44–45] encourages people to leave the city and immerse themselves in the different time and space of rural landscapes, to become nomads again. With its introverted park and extroverted path, the design of the Potsdamer Platz Park begins an elastic approach to sites and their boundaries that can be found in different ways in many of the projects in this collection.

The second project conceived in answer to the question of designing antidesign in the former no-man's land of Berlin is "The Herbal and the Bestiary" [p. 46–47]. The Herbal is an experimental landscape and the Bestiary is a building where the project's custodians meet and host events related to the theme of contemporary ideas and representations of nature. The Herbal begins as a grid of poles marking the location of explosives across a large part of the former no-man's land. The explosives are detonated to form an instant topography that loosens the compacted ground and retains water, thus establishing the basic conditions for weedy processes of ecological succession to ensue. This process is managed by an on-site gardener and used by ecologists as a place to conduct a range of experiments related to urban ecology. Wooden enclosures, which the public can peek into but not access, close off these experiments and also incubate endemic plants, which can then be transplanted throughout the 160-kilometer strip of no-man's land to help create an urban greenbelt.

The risk of overly scripting and underdesigning sites that both these previous conceptual projects for no-man's land run, comes to the fore in a competition entry titled "The Women's Rooms" [p. 48–53] for Park Monbijou ("my little jewel") in former East Berlin. From the mid-seventeenth century, Park Monbijou had been a small palace and ornate garden continuously renovated by aristocratic women. Damaged during the war and razed in 1959, the site was a typically nondescript scrap of socialist public space until 1992, when the competition called for its redesign as a contemporary public space. The concept was to dedicate the new park to a group of significant women (from 1649 to the present) who, except for Rosa Luxemburg, are otherwise not commemorated in the urban fabric of Berlin. To that end, a maze of hedges subdivides the site into rooms, each containing the bust of a notable woman. The rooms are also furnished as social spaces, and an adjacent building rents costumes so that the park becomes the set for fancy dress, masquerade, and live-action roleplay. The Women's Rooms came second to a then unknown Dutch firm called "West 8" who clinched first prize with the sort of pragmatism that makes it easy for juries to eliminate more experimental ideas. Today, Park Monbijou is a modest green space, just like any other.

In 1992, Studio Libeskind, MKW, and I won a competition for an office complex in Wiesbaden that forcefully advanced landscape as an experimental idea. For the buildings (titled "The 10th Muse"), Libeskind produced a cluster of chaotic forms that warranted an unconventional landscape response. The proposal, titled "Decomposition" [p. 54–57], was to cover the entire exterior of the site in a wooden grid which interpolated the site's existing topography by one meter. Constructed of plywood hoardings, the grid is backfilled with soil and seeds and left to decay and grow with zero maintenance. Office workers could use roof gardens, but not the gridded ground plane of the site. Eventually, say after fifty years or so, the site would become a forest and envelop the architecture, while retaining a trace of its original Cartesian geometry. In short, the ground for Libeskind's figure was a landscape of entropy.

During my time in Berlin I worked occasionally as a studio critic at the old Bauhaus in Dessau. But it wasn't the famous school that impressed me, it was the exhausted open-cut brown coal mines [p. 58] at the edge of town. To scramble down into this mine-scape is to enter another world, one terraformed by monstrous excavators, their skeletons left wherever they clawed out their last load. The only signs of biological life in these old mines are insects entombed in flecks of amber littered throughout the soil. Groundwater is slowly seeping in to reclaim the excavations.

The idea of creating an island of this landscape seemed apt not only because it anticipates the incoming groundwater, but also because its romanticism is enhanced by the ambience of industrial ruination. But what kind of island? The concept of the Île des Machines [p. 58–59] is an island planted with a grove of poplars so that when the mine fills up with water it would appear as a picturesque feature in the lake. This form of island is also a copy of the famous Île des Peupliers in the French garden of Ermenonville, where Jean-Jacques Rousseau was originally buried in 1778. It is also a copy of a copy, for just over the horizon from the Dessau mines there is a second Île des Peupliers commemorating the famous philosopher in the eighteenth-century gardens of Wo'rlitz. A few small rowboats at the lake's edge would encourage people to take leisurely trips out to the new island, whereupon they would find that the poplars conceal a large, deep, concrete chamber in which a collection of the old excavators is assembled. The chamber also includes a new working machine—a small pump house helping to aerate the lake's fetid, incoming waters.

During this period in Berlin I was also producing concept designs for some of MKW's commercial practice. One of these that I consider of some significance is the Deutsches Institut für Normung (German Institute of Standards) [p. 60–61], built in 1993. The design is based on the idea that a piece of A4 paper—itself a standardized product—has fallen out of the building and landed in the courtyard. Instead of the landscape being a nonlingual image of "nature" out the window, in this case a history of written script is inscribed on the garden's surface and projected back at the viewer. The text makes no sense, signifying instead language itself. In this way, the nature/culture dyad that is axiomatic to so much landscape architecture is turned into a semantic feedback loop asserting that the garden and whatever claims it may make to representing nature are linguistic constructions.

Back in Australia from the mid-1990s onward to help Craig Burton, a colleague and former professor of mine, build an idealistic new program in landscape architecture at the University of Western Australia, I chose to work on select projects that had what I considered to be some form of academic merit. The first, for Sydney's Cockatoo Island titled "Animale Ignoble" [p. 62–65] in 1996, marks a continuation of interest in designing antidesign and deploying entropy, though in this case, coupled with a turn toward the nonhuman. A former shipyard and military depot, Cockatoo Island is an industrial relic awaiting new use in the midst of the world's most beautiful (and probably most expensive) harbor. The well-intentioned government wanted to reprogram the island as public space; developers of course saw a bonanza of housing for the rich. The problem with the former is how to maintain the island as a viable public asset, and the problem with the latter is that any overt privatization of Sydney Harbour's public land is political suicide.

The alternative proposed here is not to give it to people at all, but to seed the entire island with Moreton Bay fig trees *(Ficus macrophylla)* and give it all to Sydney's population of grey-headed flying foxes *(Pteropus poliocephalus)*. Every evening at sunset these enigmatic creatures (known locally as fruit bats) swoop over Sydney to feast on the Moreton Bay figs in the city's eastern suburbs. While their nighttime antics are an accepted part of Sydney's nocturnal ambience, their daytime roosts in the suburbs can conflict with human activities, and so by designating the island as theirs, this conflict could be mitigated. It would also give the island a unique, powerful, and new *genius loci*.

The original idea was to prohibit humans from entering the island for a hundred years, enough time for the fig trees to turn the site into a veritable Angkor Wat of industrial ruination. After this time, a restaurant and bar could be opened on the island to facilitate some nocturnal life for humans, though even this concession seems unnecessary to me now. In any case, Cockatoo Island is now a public event space, yet another postindustrial art space in Sydney's never-ending bid to prove to the world (and Melbourne) that it's more than just a lovely harbor.

Whereas the question in Berlin had been one of designing antidesign, the question in Australia, as the nation approached the celebration of the centenary of its federation in 2001, was one of design's complicity in constructions of national identity. Melbourne-based architects Ashton Raggatt McDougall (ARM), who had a reputation for making this question a subject of their architecture, invited me to join them in a competition entry for the National Museum of Australia [p. 66–83] in 1996, which ultimately won and was built. With this win, Vladimir and I launched Room 4.1.3, a landscape architecture practice devoted to experimentation that we vowed would never sell out. We held onto that idealism for a decade before I shifted to academic research and Vladimir returned to being a sole practitioner doing small sculptural gardens for rich clients who would agree to let him do whatever he wanted. Today he is back in Prague, teaching, doing the odd project and endlessly drawing small surreal spaces in his sketchbook.

To understand the National Museum of Australia's design you need to understand ARM's *modus operandi*. In the 1980s Steve Ashton, Howard Raggatt and Ian McDougall were some of the first Australian designers to explicitly turn the cultural cringe (a feeling of inferiority on the global stage) from something to be ashamed of into something that could be exorcised, even flaunted, in a productive manner. ARM recognized that countering the problem of the global through recourse to the landscape of the local (critical regionalism) or alternatively, simply mimicking international styles, were both dead ends. Their modus operandi instead is to foreground selected influences and turn the act of appropriation irreverently through a critical culture of the local. While jokes and the one-liners are certainly not beneath them, ARM have developed a method whereby the original referent, usually a sign already laden with meaning is sampled and then pushed through a range of digital and semantic operations so that it becomes something new – a process they refer to as "mongrel rapture." For example, the National Museum of Australia and the affiliated Australian Institute of Aboriginal and Torres Strait Island Studies (AIATSIS) in Canberra are both cobbled together by sampling parts of Libeskind's Berlin Museum, Le Corbusier's Villa Savoye, Giurgola's Parliament House, and Utzon's Opera House. With exclusive reference to representations of landscape (maps, paintings, laws, texts) and not the landscape itself, Room 4.1.3's design for the landscape architecture of the museum deploys a similar technique of citation.

The big initial landscape move for the National Museum was to take Walter Burley Griffin's original mandala for Canberra and add a new line to it. Whereas Griffin's various axes fan out from the parliamentary center to the nation's other state capitals, this new line—the Uluru Axis [p. 66–69]—links Canberra to Uluru. In this way, the nation's white political capital is directly linked to the monolith in the center of the country that signifies Aboriginal Australia in both popular and political culture. This axis between white and black Australia, inscribed across the site, is then knotted by the buildings and spaces of the museum into a more complicated configuration, a literal manifestation of what in the humanities is referred to as "entanglement."

The museum knots itself around a central open space we called the Garden of Australian Dreams [p. 70–83]. As a rule, this "garden" only includes elements which refer to representations of the Australian landscape, not the landscape itself. In other words, as discussed previously with regard to *genius loci*, this project makes the problem of place, not the place itself, its subject. The ground plane of this garden is a concrete graphic surface created from a compilation of maps of Aboriginal Australia and the cartography of modern Australia. Important elements of this include the Pope's line [p. 70–71], the first European inscription to unwittingly bisect the

Australian continent. This line of longitude was first drawn around the globe by Pope Alexander VI according to the 1494 Treaty of Tordesillas, which subdivided Spanish and Portuguese trading interests. By being simply copied onto maps over time, the line now serves as the border between western and eastern Australia.

In the garden, the Pope's line is crossed with a large red X [p.70–72]. Although it is typically a sign of negation, Aboriginal Australians, under duress, often signed legal documents with an X instead of writing their names. The X is then countersigned with the signature of Australia's first Prime Minister, Sir Edmund Barton (1849–1920). Additionally, a large red wedge [p. 73–75] points to the location of Uluru on the mapped surface of the nation, reiterating the orientation of the Uluru Axis inscribed across the museum's entire site outside the garden. A camera obscura, which the public can enter to witness a live image of the garden upside down, stands at the apex of this red wedge.

Upon the garden's cartography is an array of symbolic items including a white room, a tilted line of trees, a garden gnome modelled on early European imaginings of antipodeans, a tunnel, a dead tree, surveyors' poles, a flood gauge, a fence and lawn with a small pool, blue poles, and the word "home" written in the many languages of Australia's multicultural communities. Locations where Aboriginal Australians were massacred are also marked on the map. Additionally, written (in reflection) around the garden's entire eastern flank and half under water, is the word Australia [p. 78–79] in a font lifted directly from the national currency. Symbolism aside, this project was also a very early, and somewhat clunky attempt to build a continuous, morphing, computer-generated surface.

The design's use of symbolism was controversial for a range of reasons. The first was that by superimposing Aboriginal cartography on the nation's colonial cartography, vexed questions of land rights between white and black Australia are foregrounded. The second believe it or not— was that the museum's executive committee took particular issue with a group of blue poles [p. 80-81] in one corner of the garden. The committee wrote us to cease and desist from including them in the design. They didn't say why, but it was understood that because these poles refer to the painting *Blue Poles* by Jackson Pollock, originally purchased for the National Gallery by former Labor Prime Minister Gough Whitlam [p. 80] in 1973, they were considered offensive to the Liberal-National Party in government at the time. Whitlam draws the ire of conservatives because he is a left-wing icon of Australia's late twentieth-century cultural renaissance. By specifying a blue paint that didn't use the word "blue," we worked around this petty form of censorship, and the poles are there to this day. Unexpectedly, Whitlam also showed up on the opening day of the museum and posed for photographs in the garden with the offending poles.

More serious was that just before Queen Elizabeth II and Prime Minister John Howard were due to open the museum on March 11, 2001, the museum's executive committee realized that the entire building, designed by ARM, appeared to be covered in braille. As if anyone could read it (let alone feel it), some of the braille was frantically altered by the addition of silver discs to the building's facade. But the shit really hit the proverbial fan when journalists got hold of the fact that a big chunk of the museum was derived from a copy of Daniel Libeskind's Berlin (Holocaust) Museum. Transposed from Berlin to Canberra, this reference offended just about everyone, including Libeskind; and yet the question remains, was there a form of genocide in Australia? Is there a form of ongoing genocide in Australia? One can also ask, as ARM often do, why architects cannot make a new building with overt reference to—not plagiarism of—another?

Convinced of a leftist conspiracy, the government launched a formal inquiry into the aesthetics of both the architecture and the landscape architecture of the museum. Bureaucrats and scholars pored over every detail of the design in a quest to uncover signs of political bias and subversion. This gave certain politicians and critics the imprimatur they needed to then call for the museum's demolition forthwith. Thankfully, governments come and go, and the museum is still there as originally designed. Its design helps tell the story of a confident, multicultural nation, one able to laugh and cry over its history; one trying, yet still failing, to face its demons.

A boldly designed postcolonial national museum can register powerfully in the symbolic order of things, but symbolism only goes so far. It is only one part of the deeper question of design's role in relation to the complicated, ongoing process of reconciliation between colonizer and colonized. The question for me then is how to stake a claim in the symbolic order of things *and* design something that also "works": in other words, how to design something that makes positive change as opposed to just representing positive change? In the discipline of landscape architecture, this is to draw a line between landscape as scenery *(landskip)* and landscape as instrument *(landschaft)*. A project where this ambition for the landscape project starts to take shape is for the "Future Generations University" [p. 84–85], which I and a large interdisciplinary team were commissioned to envision in 1996, the same year the National Museum was designed. The Future Generations University was to be dedicated to the study of environmental sustainability and developed on a large rural site an hour's drive north of Sydney. The client asked for the traditional form of a university to be reimagined, so rather than just designing a campus, our proposal was to reimagine the university curriculum and relate it to the indigenous geography and culture of the region.

The big idea was to expand the site of the university from its actual landholding to the boundary of the Darkinjung nation, the regional Indigenous community on whose land this institution would sit. The proposal was for the new university to fund the development of a walking and cycling trail punctuated with hostels and campsites every thirty kilometers for the 1,000-kilometer length of the Darkinjung boundary. Students at the new university would then take a full semester to walk and cycle this 1,000-kilometer boundary trail engaging along the way in an educational program set by scholars-in-residence in the various hostels. In this way, the educational experience is symbolically and actually grounded in Indigenous culture and merges traditional forms of pedagogy with physical landscape experience.

The use of symbolism in design reaches its apotheosis in designing memorials, and for this reason they have always been of great interest to me. The Pentagon Memorial [p. 86–89] competition to commemorate the 184 victims of the 9/11 terrorist attacks on a site directly adjacent to where American Airlines Flight 77 came down is a case in point. What to do? How to combine the intensely private nature of death with a public display of patriotism? How can a memorial now be anything but a footnote to Maya Lin's brilliant Vietnam Veterans Memorial in Washington DC? Surely we can't just build more black granite walls.

The answer in this case was to create not one memorial to the event, but 184 memorials, one for each of the victims. Each memorial is a personalized black box that appears to hover slightly above the ground, containing a deep pool of water that reflects the sky. At the surface of the water is the victim's name and place and date of birth. The black box is a literal reference to the black box flight recorder to which authorities turn for explanations of aviation disasters. Black boxes are however not black, they are in fact bright orange so as to aid in their recovery. As a reference to this, families can insert mementoes into a small orange chamber, which is then inserted into the side of the larger black box. In this way, the design combines the very private and very public nature of this event in one.

Like the Pentagon Memorial, the Memorial for Victims of the Tsunami [p. 90–95] that devastated Southeast Asia in 2004 was also a finalist from a very large number of entrants. The site chosen by the Thai government for this memorial (and a museum) was a pristine, coastal national park. To avoid impact on the landscape, we stretched the museum long and thin and pushed it hard up against a nearby road, and then sited the memorial out in the ocean. The memorial is made of solar-powered navigation lights used for shipping. The lights come on automatically when the sun sets, and with the addition of a beveled glass rim, they sparkle during the day. The lights are set on a grid, forming a one-hundred-meter circle, and are tethered to the ocean floor with enough slack to account for tidal fluctuation. As such, the memorial strikes a tension between geometric order and liquid disorder.

Ultimately, the jury selected a scheme that was both museum and memorial in one, a big pagoda sited smack-bang in the pristine rainforest. Only architects with little appreciation of site impact would think this a good idea. As we had expected, the museum never materialized, and because the winner made the museum and the memorial one and the same, the families of the victims got neither. A decade later, the government created the Ban Nam Khem Tsunami Memorial Park, which includes a wall of victims' names and a boat ruined by the tsunami.

Designing commemorative places for events such as 9/11 and the Boxing Day Tsunami provides tangible specificity for the designer to work with. A more difficult challenge is to create symbols of the age. The next three projects, one in New York and two in Paris, take on this challenge. All three are symbolic responses to the dawn of the Anthropocene through the medium of public space.

The heroes of the early Anthropocene are people like James Lovelock, Lynn Margulis, and Al Gore. But surely we can't just prop more humans up on pedestals: the Anthropocene is not a great human achievement, it is an indictment. It requires reflection on the fundamental values and mechanisms of modernity that have now brought the world to the brink of ecological collapse. The emblem of this is the city itself. So how to make a monument to the subject of the city in general?

The New York project answers this by bringing together two epic landscapes: the first is the allegorical landscape depicted in Thomas Cole's (kitsch) masterpiece *The Course of Empire* [p. 96], now hanging in the New-York Historical Society directly overlooking Central Park on 76th Street. The second is Central Park itself. Set out across five canvases painted between 1833 and 1836, Cole renders the same vista through five different phases: the savage state, the pastoral or Arcadian state, the consummation of empire, then its destruction, and, finally, desolation. A single boulder perched on a precipice in the background of all five paintings tells the viewer they are witnessing the same place at five different times. With this conceit, Cole maps the classical notion of cyclical time and the golden age onto America's manifest destiny to issue the warning that venal empires tend inexorably toward their end—an axiom that applies today, even if his simplistic teleology from savagery to Western civilization does not.

To now map Cole's narrative of the rise and fall of civilization onto the Anthropocene, the proposal is to create a new circuit [p. 96–99] within Central Park's existing picturesque scenery that leads the visitor to five views. Each view—signified by the insertion of a copy of Cole's signature boulder—relates to Cole's five phases of classical history. For example, to effect Cole's first scene—the so-called savage state—the boulder is placed above the arch in the park's wildest zone, the Ramble. The setting for the pastoral state is Sheep Meadow, and the consummation (of empire) is dramatically achieved by adding the boulder to the roof of 432 Park Avenue. (Alternatively, the Grand Army Plaza could be reshaped as a ziggurat of terraces with the boulder balanced on its pinnacle.) For the fourth scene, Destruction, the boulder is cantilevered off the edge of the Metropolitan Museum's rooftop sculpture garden, and finally, the mood of Desolation is invoked by placing the boulder in the waters of the Jacqueline Kennedy Onassis Reservoir. As indicated in the visuals, the fake rock that would for practical purposes be fabricated for each scene is also reminiscent of an asteroid so as to shift the course of empire to the scale of a cosmological extinction event, albeit one now engineered by humans.

Crossing to Paris, in the wake of the 2015 climate accord, it seems both opportune and appropriate to zero in on the center-point around which the city's tumultuous modern history has spun—the Cour Carrée in the Louvre. This magnificent yet inhospitable courtyard, at the core of an institution venerating humanity's highest artistic achievements, is the perfect setting to frame the question of what a "Garden of the Anthropos" [p. 100–103] might be.

In Greek mythology, Prometheus—the god of foresight—makes humans (the Anthropos) at Zeus's behest, from clay. The proposal for this garden is to gather as many soil samples from around the world as possible (there are close to 1,000 different types in the World Soil Museum in Wageningen) and lay them out to fill a sixty-meter-wide circle in the center of the Cour Carrée. The soils are mixed with lacquer for durability and can be roughly shaped so as to create a range of microtopographies that blur the samples at their edges. On the one hand, the diversity of form, texture, and color of the soil samples are testament to the richness and beauty of the earth; on the other, the encrusted soils appear as a vast desert in the heart of the city, a barren world and the prospect of a dead planet.

The edge of the circle holding the soil samples is formed by a sit-wall comprised of black and white concrete blocks. The black and white blocks are reminiscent of the surveying equipment used in archeological digs. Imprinted into the top of each block are what the paleontologist Jan Zalaciewicz calls technofossils—everyday things made by humans such as plastic bags, toothbrushes, and iPhones. To give the collection coherence and particular relevance to the Anthropocene, each technofossil is an object derived from fossil fuels. Framing the circle of soils is a square grass embankment with espaliered trees and seating in the Parisian style so that visitors can stay a while and reflect on this world in microcosm.

The final project in this trilogy signifying the Anthropocene is titled "Weather Balloon" [p. 104–105] and is sited in the Jardin des Tuileries, a short walk from the Cour Carrée. The proposal is to float a custom-made hot-air balloon, shaped as a cartoon of a thought bubble, above the gardens. The reason for this is that it was from this point in 1783 that the physicist and professor Jacques Charles first launched a hydrogen balloon and completed an unprecedented flight of thirty-six kilometers. Watched in awe by dignitaries and the masses, Charles's yellow-and-red striped balloon, replete with a regal gondola, heralded the beginning of an age of technological optimism and confidence in human ingenuity. Colored black and red after the carbon molecule, and suspended above a pool of oil, this thought bubble marks the beginning of a new age—a climate-changed age—where such optimism and confidence are now significantly harder to summon.

Instrumentality

Insofar as landscape architecture is predicated upon a belief that humans can form a deeper union with the landscape, it is fundamentally romantic. Rather than repress this wellspring of much that is good in the human spirit, today's romantic has to ask how romanticism translates into the badlands of the Anthropocene. Today's romantic must confront the denatured, damaged, and depleted ecology of the twenty-first century without Vaseline on the lens. To engage with, rather than just aestheticize, the slow-motion disaster of today's landscape, the romantic must attempt to infiltrate the systems of agriculture, industry, and urbanization in an effort to redirect them from self-destruction. To even attempt this, the landscape architect needs the imagination of an artist, the rationality of a planner, the cunning of a politician, and the evidence-based knowledge of a scientist.

A discipline also needs a theory of change and methods to suit, and apart from rote-learned McHargian planning or its slightly more sophisticated doppelganger "geodesign," landscape architecture has had little more than the vagaries of *genius loci* in its quiver. Consequently, at the turn of the twenty-first century, despite making claims to planetary stewardship, the profession found itself with little structural influence beyond the scale of public spaces in rich cities. Out of frustration with this, the discourse of landscape urbanism—the argument that the landscape, not just the building block, be taken seriously as the basis for urbanism—gained momentum. The polemic of landscape urbanism, of which I was a part, expanded landscape architecture's purview to include urbanization in its totality, not only its voids and edges. Landscape urbanism's importance was, and is, that it turned landscape architecture away from paradise and redirected it toward utopia. This is to situate contemporary landscape architecture not only in the history of gardens, but in the history of urbanism, and to reread that history as one in which landscape has played a crucial, yet underestimated role. The Garden City, Broadacre City, and the Modern City are not just urban designs, they are *landscape* visions, and the question landscape urbanists asked was what might be meant by the Ecological City. Since postmodern architects (apart from the neoconservative new urbanists) have largely abandoned the subject of urban design, and planners have become so preoccupied with sociology and policy, landscape urbanists saw an opportunity to become, as Charles Waldheim so memorably put it, "the urbanists of the age."

For this academic posturing to translate into practice not only would landscape architects have to somehow assume positions of leadership on urban design projects, they would also have to demonstrate how, by bringing the landscape to the fore, they would produce a better form of urbanism. The answer to this challenge lies in first returning to the scale of McHargian landscape planning and then nesting the urban design project within it. Instead of just producing big land use plans—development here, and not there, as McHarg's generation had done—landscape urbanists sought to also shape urban form as a synthesis of buildings and open spaces not only tuned to the specific ecology and culture of a place, but nested within larger cultural and ecological systems. In practical terms this meant expanding the landscape architectural remit to encompass a working understanding of the logistics of urban development, including zoning, density, building typology, transportation, and real estate values. This also meant landscape architects encroached on other professions' territories.

Fearing that landscape urbanism could only mean more green space in cities, which in turn spells the dissolution of traditional urban grids, the Congress for the New Urbanism (CNU) soon rallied its troops and in 2013 published a nasty demolition job titled *Landscape Urbanism and Its Discontents*, edited by Andrés Duany and Emily Talen. They needn't have worried: as is the case with any fashionable, academic shift in design culture, landscape urbanism's aestheticization—its liquidized grids and stylized diagrams of ecological flows—quickly incubated its own obsolescence. Unable to bring the mainstream landscape architecture profession with it, and largely unsubstantiated by built work, the "urbanists of the age" soon melted back into the academic ether from whence they had come. That said, urbanism is now a core component of landscape architecture curricula in many graduate programs, and the prospect of the city yet evolving into a more sophisticated ecological system, as landscape urbanists say it must, remains a beacon for research and invention. One thing is for sure—a truly ecological urbanism is no simple, green thing. It means reformulating not only the city's built form, but also bringing its supply chains within the purview of design, and in this sense the work of landscape urbanism, both in theory and practice, has not so much come and gone, as it has only just begun. If cities are to survive the Anthropocene, they have no choice but to evolve into more sophisticated ecological machines.

Perhaps in part attributable to the discourse of landscape urbanism, today, landscape architects do find themselves at the table on major urban design projects and, depending on their influence among other consultants, can play a substantial role in the formulation of such projects. Fortuitously, around the same time that I joined in the landscape urbanism conversation (2005), insisting that it be grounded in and tempered by practice, a development authority in Perth asked me and my University of Western Australia colleague Tinka Sack to master-plan a suburban development for 40,000 people. The client said they wanted to build a suburb "as if the landscape really mattered."

OK!

Landscape "matters" to orthodox suburban development [p. 158–159] in three ways: the first comes in the form of environmental regulations pertaining to ecological assets such as wetlands, riparian corridors, and remnant habitat. While it can be sold to home buyers as a backdrop of sweet nature, this type of landscape is generally perceived by developers as a problem because it locks up potential real estate and messes with the geometric efficiency of the development plat. The second comes in the form of public open space, prescribed by law as 10% of the developable area set aside for recreation and stormwater retention. This landscape is essential to the suburban idyll, and as such, developers are prepared to invest in it, so long as it doesn't complicate the rollout of the development. The third way in which landscape matters concerns topography. Home buyers and home builders generally prefer level blocks, so developers will manipulate (not to say obliterate) topography to that end. They will also do whatever they can to minimize the expense of earth moving (cut and fill) operations, which leads to a clumsy combination of curvilinear streets and terraced blocks. Curvilinear streets and cul-de-sacs are also preferred by developers because they help with the ludicrous yet necessary sales pitch that each house is in a "unique" position.

But if landscape was *really* to matter in suburbia, the preservation of topography, vegetation, and water would more strongly determine its design. Housing would be designed to suit topographic nuances and oriented towards the sun to maximize passive energy. All drainage lines would be restored as living streams and all stormwater harvested and cleansed through "treatment trains" of interconnected public spaces. Instead of disconnected open spaces, public space would be linked together by linear green spaces [p. 159] so as to encourage exercise and create biological and hydrological connectivity through the development. These linear spaces would in turn be connected to areas of well-buffered remnant habitat aggregated together to connect the neighborhood to the district, and the district to the region. Finally, if landscape really mattered, its design as a holistic structural system would come first in the development process. All this is to say that if landscape really mattered to suburbia it would be designed with all living beings in mind and not just "putting parsley on the pig."

These axioms became the guiding landscape principles for the new suburb of Wungong [p. 160–169], a 1,500-hectare (3,700 acres) site on the outskirts of Perth. The master plan attempts to create a robust landscape matrix whereby all remnant habitat and drainage lines are buffered and restored, and the entire site is striated by thirty-meter-wide avenues, each with four rows of indigenous trees set 200 meters apart. Avenues of trees (indicated with blue lines on the master plan) are a good thing in the suburban context for several reasons: they are relatively simple and cheap to construct, and over time become visually impressive; they can also be used to collect, filter, and convey stormwater from the surrounding developments; they serve as conduits for airflow and the movement of biodiversity through the site, and their linearity encourages people to exercise, especially when they lead to neighborhood pocket park destinations (as indicated by small yellow squares on the plan). Finally, the sequencing of the avenues across the site also serves to predetermine the urban form of the subsequent infill development (indicated in gray on the plan), and encourages developers to use orthogonal, solar-oriented grids instead of curvilinear geometry to achieve best fit. Everyone agreed this was a good, robust master plan—that is, everyone except the developers.

This is a big housing development with a dozen or so different developers, each working their own parcel of land as a part of the whole. Whereas we saw the avenues as making a whole that would be greater than just the sum of its parts, individual developers saw them as an imposition, compromising their ability to style their own enclaves to achieve points of difference in the market. This began a decade of tussle between the rigor of the master plan and the flexibility the individual developers said they required. While as a work of landscape urbanism the design earned accolades, its final form is a compromise, and we are not yet able to measure if the built product is an improvement on the status quo.

Importantly, the design of the landscape matrix for the site of the Wungong development fits, like a puzzle piece, into a larger metropolitan Landscape Structure Plan [p. 161]. Based on the advice of local ecologists, this plan put forward a matrix of green infrastructure (patches and corridors) to be retrofitted into the existing city and secured in advance of the development front in greenfield zones. The value of a whole-of-city landscape structure plan such as this is that individual development projects such as Wungong can be keyed into it to ensure ecological systems are embedded and networked from a local to a regional scale. Such a plan also gives developers certainty as to what can and cannot be developed, and establishes the amount of investment required to build a whole-of-city green infrastructure network.

This landscape structure plan for the Perth metropolitan area also laid the spatial basis for a three-year research project, and ultimately a book, titled *Boomtown 2050: Scenarios for a Rapidly Growing City* [p. 162–169], funded by the Australian Research Council (ARC). The aim of the research was to produce alternatives to the status quo of low-density suburban sprawl using the city of Perth as a case study. Sprawl is not only big business, a freestanding suburban home is still considered the epitome of the Australian way of life. To date, suburbia has served the nation well, but as Australian cities move ever closer to becoming megacities (with populations of ten million or more), the dream of a quarter-acre block is harder to find, harder to afford, and harder to sustain. What was the edge of the city in my childhood is now middle-ring suburbia, where the original quarter-acre blocks have been "battle-axed" to squeeze a second home into backyards, and apartments now cluster around transit hubs and shopping centers. So far have Australian cities now sprawled that it can take hours to get from their peripheries to their centers, and while Australian capital city planning reports all advocate for transit-oriented infill development (TODs), they also continue to underwrite further sprawl that is widely recognized as socially, environmentally, and economically untenable. By the same token, infill development in TODs on a scale commensurate with long-term population projections is also likely to produce negative urban outcomes. Planners and designers have so far been unable to demonstrate how adding large numbers of people to Australia's cities will be achieved in a way that is both good for the incoming residents and for those who already live there. As such, planning reports for Australian cities rarely show spatially accurate images of the long-term future according to their own policy settings.

The Boomtown 2050 research project attempts to draw attention to this problem and offer alternative scenarios. It begins with accurately modelling business-as-usual development in the city of Perth extrapolated through 2050 population projections. This then serves as a benchmark against which a range of alternatives can be created and to which they can be compared. By visualizing multiple alternative scenarios using the same population metrics, the public is provided with a set of spatially accurate options for the growth of the city that can be easily understood and reasonably discussed.

Importantly, in this study we developed alternative forms of both low-density sprawl *and* high-density infill without coming down explicitly in favor of either. In other words, the key to engaging the media, the public, and the professions involved in urban growth was for us as authors to remain neutral. This is not to say that the scenarios themselves are neutral; on the contrary, each of the various scenarios take certain criteria—say, for example, the fact that people want to live within walking distance of the beach—and by turning them through 2050 population projections we render their pros and cons obvious. To maintain neutrality, the way in which the scenarios are imaged had to be spatially accurate and easily understood while avoiding any excessively utopian or dystopian tropes. The scenarios of the Boomtown 2050 project do not pretend to be plans, they are visual tools to prompt a more informed public debate about the future of the city.

The greenfield development scenarios that the Boomtown 2050 project puts forward as alternatives to conventional sprawl are POD City, Food City, Car Free City, Seachange City, and Treechange City. POD (Performance Oriented Development) City [p. 162–163], takes Ebenezer Howard's Garden City original of small towns of 30–50,000 people living at four times the density of typical suburbia surrounded by generous greenbelts, and brings it into the twenty-first century. That is, to absorb Perth's projected 2050 population growth, forty-eight new PODs, would be required. The PODs would constitute a government-led new town program, where the design of these new towns would compete for market share and bring contemporary social and ecological values and technologies to bear on the Garden City original.

The urban form of Food City [p. 164–165], is a braid of housing, industry, and agriculture in linear formation. In this way, Food City equates density with local food production and local industry to minimize the length of supply chains and commute times to jobs. It also establishes the potential for recycling water, nutrients, and energy in the urban landscape. The next scenario, Car Free City [p. 165], adds a grid of light rail transit to Food City. The transit system services a grid of housing (at four times the density of typical suburbia) with open spaces dimensioned to provide both sufficient recreational space and productive farmland to sustain the population living in the immediate vicinity. Two additional scenarios, Seachange City [p. 166] and Treechange City [p. 167], offer alternatives to suburban sprawl at a regional scale. Seachange City anticipates an aging population wanting to live in low-density development within a walkable distance of the beach. By extrapolation, this scenario intentionally demonstrates the implausibility of large numbers of people living in such a configuration, thus preparing the community for a more open-minded attitude to higher density development in relation to high-amenity contexts such as the coastline. Treechange City responds to a certain sector of the market who wish to move out of the city and live on large rural lots. This housing and lifestyle option is then combined with carbon sequestration forestry and solar energy production.

The infill development scenarios that the Boomtown 2050 project put forward as alternatives to conventional transit-oriented development are Sky City, River City, and Surf City [p. 168–169]. To encourage Australians to take up high-density living as a lifestyle option, Sky City maximizes high-density infill development in areas of high natural and cultural amenity. River City focuses on maximizing affordable density directly along transit corridors within walking distance and visual catchment of Perth's two major rivers. Similarly, Surf City proposes high-rise buildings and a new transit corridor along the city's 130 kilometers of coastal ridgeline so that residents could live within walkable distance of the beach but not impede the views of extant housing.

If there is an answer to the city's future, then the Boomtown 2050 project argues that it lies, in part, in all these scenarios and more. The scenarios show that the future needn't be reduced to only low-density sprawl on the one hand or TODs on the other. In this way, the research served to bring a certain level of "design thinking" to a city whose twenty-first-century fate is otherwise being decided by a status quo of planning bureaucrats, land developers, and nimbies. The issues facing the city of Perth are germane to all of Australia's major cities. A nation of twenty-six million people in 2022, Australia is forecast to possibly reach over sixty million by 2100. The question of how this growth can be absorbed is critical. This problem was the subject of a two-year research project conducted in partnership with my colleague Julian Bolleter through the Australian Urban Design Research Center, culminating in a book titled *Made in Australia: The Future of Australian Cities* [p. 172–177].

The point of departure for this study is the mythology that big cities are better than small cities. Certainly, megacities (ten million or more people) like London and New York are economic and cultural powerhouses, and while they are exciting for tourists and luxurious playgrounds for the rich, they rate poorly in global livability assessments. For the bulk of their citizens, life in such megacities is not a ladder of opportunity, and many instead find themselves trapped in a permanent underclass with poor living conditions. Made in Australia argues that if Australia's existing cities can only offer further sprawl and TOD infill, then as their populations approach megacity status, the high livability that these cities have hitherto enjoyed will drop precipitously.

The first form of urbanization this study explored is that increased density in Australian cities could be related directly to the amenity of public open (green) space, or what we call GOD—Green Oriented Development [p. 170–171 Because the density of housing within a walkable catchment of the many large open green spaces in Australian cities is very low, there is an opportunity for zoning to incentivize significantly higher density development around such an amenity. In this way, higher density living becomes more of a lifestyle proposition than merely living close to public transport and shops as prioritized by transit-oriented development.

The second form of urbanization this study explored is that through a national program of decentralized development, Australia's existing major cities can intentionally avoid becoming megacities. In a word, this means Australia should actively try to create megaregions rather than megacities. Identified as ribbons of continuous light as seen in satellite imagery, there are now over forty megaregions in the world. These regions are polycentric conurbations comprising one or more large cities networked into regional constellations of proximal smaller cities. As such, megaregions tend to be well connected in terms of transportation and communication systems, and because their territory transcends the sprawl balloon of any single city, they offer their citizens a broader range of housing, employment, and lifestyle options. On a national and global scale, megaregions—the most famous being the northeast corridor from Boston to Washington, DC, in the United States—are political, economic, and cultural hubs serving as incubators of innovation and wealth creation.

What is often overlooked in the literature of megaregions, however, is that their positive cultural and economic attributes are not just because of development—ultimately a successful megaregion is dependent upon being embedded in a healthy environment. While scholarship and policy related to megaregions has focused on their bright lights, it is the dark matter of the landscape that ultimately underpins a megaregion with the ecosystem services (clean air, water, food, biodiversity, and open space) its citizens require. In other words, megaregions are a new form of *landscape* urbanism and have much to recommend them as population growth ensues.

Unlike the world's megaregions, which have developed organically over time, Australia has the opportunity to now consciously plan its megaregional growth. Instead of letting extant cities sprawl so far that they break apart at the edges and spill over into regional landscapes in an ecologically and socially unsustainable manner, megaregional development can be orchestrated through a combination of government incentive and landscape analysis to ensure that economic viability and environmental precaution are built into the development process. The only way to incentivize this in the case of Australia's population centers is by the creation of high-speed rail corridors and high-speed telecommunications linking its existing big cities with strings of new smaller regional cities [p. 176–177]. To that end, the *Made in Australia* study proposed the creation of an East Coast Megaregion and a West Coast Megaregion [p. 174–175] as the two armatures of Australia's twenty-first-century urban growth. Connected with national immigration policy, this growth can enhance Australia's modern multicultural success story, boost its economic productivity, and do so without squandering its limited and fragile biological resources.

Working on these Australian research projects related to suburban sprawl and megaregional decentralization revealed how little we really know about peri-urban landscapes. This is understandable because, following the money, the profession of landscape architecture has focused primarily on public space related to urban design in city centers. And yet, as the eminent landscape ecologist Richard T.T. Forman has often said, the really interesting and important zone to consider is the city's periphery: it is there that nature and culture intertwine in critically important and mutually dependent ways.

A turn away from city centers toward the peri-urban, at least in theory, was announced by an important exhibition at the MAXXI gallery in Rome in 2015. Titled Roma 20-25: Lifecycles of the Metropolis [p. 178–181], the exhibition explicitly took its cue from, and saw itself as, an extension of the famous *Interrota* exhibition of 1979. The original *Interrota* was held by the Italian Incontri Internazionale d'Arte, and assembled twelve renowned (male) architects to each take a panel from Giambattista Nolli's 1736 plan of Rome and "interrupt" it with their own architectural intervention. This was largely about architectural aesthetics and issues of contextualism in the wake of modernism, whereas the *Roma 20-25* event turned its attention to the larger landscape scale of peri-urban Rome.

Teams from different universities around the world were assigned portions of this territory and asked to speculate on its future. The program at the University of Pennsylvania (Penn), which I was now chairing, was assigned a large area northeast of Rome characterized by peri-urban sprawl, ancient agricultural landscapes, and weedy ravines. The proposal we developed was to use this land for the location of a new recycling and composting industry with a whole-of-city plan to redirect Rome's food waste. Some of the soil produced by this industry could then be used to fertilize the ravines as catalysts for environmental restoration of the land, as well as engendering related urban development and other new land uses [pp. 180–181]. This, we argued, could be actively supported by the celebrated environmentalist Pope Francis, as well as Italy's major fashion houses, who would produce the bags and bins and advertising campaigns (Prada Loves Shit, Green Gucci, Dirty Dolce, etc.) to mobilize Romans into an active composting program.

Of course, the scrappy peri-urban landscape of any city is an interesting liminal zone, but if one wants to engage with the clash of nature and culture that Forman refers to in a way that has more pertinent relevance to today's planetary environmental crisis, then one has to leave the old world and focus attention on the new. To that end, with a small research team at Penn in 2014 I decided to begin an analysis of urban growth and land use in the world's biodiversity hotspots [p. 190–191], thirty-six regions where irreplaceable biodiversity is threatened with extinction. The first phase of this was published by both National Geographic and Scientific American in late 2016 as the *Atlas for the End of the World – Atlas for the Beginning of the Anthropocene.*

The first modern atlas, the *Theatrum Orbis Terrarum* (The Theater of the World) [p. 182–183], was published in 1570 by the Flemish book collector and engraver Abraham Ortelius. Despite missing entire continents, the *Theatrum* was lauded for its accuracy and quickly became a bestseller. Whereas the *Theatrum* outlined a world of healthy ecosystems ripe for colonization and exploitation, some 500 years later, the *Atlas for the End of the World* [p. 182 –201] rakes over the remains. The Atlas is, of course, not about the end of our world, it is about the end of Ortelius's world; it is about the end of the world as a God-given, unlimited resource and concomitant myths of progress.

The *Atlas for the End of the World* begins with something called "The Problem of the Two Worlds" [p. 184–185]. In the image, you see two worlds highlighting different sets of information from the same vantage point. On the left, an urbanized planet—the result of a 10,000-year process of agricultural, architectural, and infrastructural expansion. This, in the Western canon, is what we arrogantly call Culture. In the second world to the right, you see only the archipelago of the world's current (2022) Protected Areas, an ad hoc collection of over 250,000 fragments of remnant habitat fenced off from the extractive landscapes that surround them. In the Western canon this is what we erroneously call Nature.

Now, you could say the process of urbanization is an evolutionary success story—*Homo sapiens sapiens* (the wise ones) have colonized an entire planet and, on the face of it, appear to be thriving—and yet, as the shock of climate change sinks in, it is becoming clear that our success also contains the seeds of our demise. And not just *our* demise, for our success has come and continues to come at the expense of all other species (except domesticated plants, animals, vermin, and microbes). The wise one has become nature's warden and executioner.

To adapt to climate change and eventually mitigate its related extinction crisis, that which we call Culture has to be integrated with that which we call Nature in a more mutually constructive manner. The philosophical prerequisite for this is to reconceptualize the two worlds as one. The practical challenge is to reorganize the landscape so that the urban world and its infrastructure becomes symbiotic with, instead of parasitic upon, the earth system.

As it approaches a population of *at least* ten billion people this century, the first challenge for the urbanized world will be to house another three billion or so people. This is the equivalent of building around 350 New York Cities in the next eighty years—that's four New Yorks every year. But making lots of buildings for lots of people in record time is not really the problem—servicing this growth with food, water, and energy is.

Although during construction, urbanization is in many ways a destructive process, one good thing about it is that it tends to eventually slow population growth. It is possible that as the world urbanizes—say, sometime in the twenty-second century—global population will then stabilize and even begin to decline, and pressure on the earth system will accordingly ease. That said, as their desires and access to goods expands, urban citizens also tend to have large ecological footprints. Much will then depend on the degree to which cities and their supply chains can be redesigned as ecological organisms, not just fossil-fueled machines. In this sense, it is not the end of the world at all, but the beginning of an ecological design revolution.

From a large-scale landscape perspective, the biggest problem for the urbanized world is the question of how it will feed its ten billion or more citizens. If those ten billion people consume food as citizens in the developed world do today (i.e., shopping in supermarkets and eating more or less whatever they want, whenever they want), then a back-of-the-envelope calculation at today's levels of agricultural yield suggests it will take around 90% of the earth's terrestrial surface to produce the crops. This means that deserts—which currently take up around 30% of earth's ice-free terrestrial area—would have to be converted into vast monocultures irrigated by desalination plants. Add to that the global footprint of urbanized areas (around 4% of global land area), then a mere 6% or so of the planet is all that is left for biodiversity. And this is to say nothing of land area needed for forestry, carbon sequestration, renewable energy production, and the need to not only preserve the existing estate of protected areas, but also expand them.

Which brings us to the second world of so-called Nature. At exactly the same time as we will need every square meter of land for food and energy production, the late biologist E.O. Wilson called for 50% of the earth to be set aside for biodiversity. And maybe, for a perfectly healthy planet, he is right, but he never really explained where this land would be, or how it would work as something ostensibly separate from humans. Instead of making two old worlds, Nature here and Culture there, our world is a hybrid of nature and culture at every turn. The problem is not its hybridity per se, it's that it was not consciously created to serve more than human interests. Biodiversity, a proxy for healthy ecosystems, is now a matter of human interest, and as such, every act of design, at all scales, has to foreground the well-being of the nonhuman as well as the human.

In the global political order of things, the key to this is the Convention on Biological Diversity (CBD), in particular Aichi Target 11, which stipulates that the 196 nations who are party to the Convention are obliged to secure 17% of their sovereign territory as protected areas [p. 186–187]. And it is likely that a majority of these nations will also soon agree to increasing the target to 30%. So, deducting 30% for biodiversity and 30% of current desert leaves 40% for food production, which is close to the current agricultural footprint. Since there is no space for agricultural expansion in this scenario, yields from existing farmland will have to increase, and large-scale protein production will have to advance almost to eliminate ruminants altogether. Alternatively, we must accept that billions of people will *not* be able to eat as citizens of the developed world today take for granted, and the injustices of the past will continue into the future.

Importantly, according to the small print of the CBD, the 17% protected area cannot just be anywhere. It must be "representative"—that is, the land should be representative of the world's 867 ecoregions. More challenging still, these representative protected areas should, according to the CBD, also be "connected." This means forging landscape corridors between patches of protected area so as to open pathways for species to migrate and adapt to climate change. Taken seriously, this means reorganizing land use on a planetary scale and doing so at a time when every square meter of land is also being sought for increased food and energy production. This is a planetary design problem, one that can't just be left to the tragedy of the commons.

When my research assistants and I began work on the *Atlas for the End of the World* in late 2014, the world's terrestrial protected area total was hovering at 13.5%. In 2022—including so-called Other

Effective Area-Based Conservation Measures—total protected area was 16.64%. The 0.36% required to reach the 17% target is, however, not nothing—in fact, it is equivalent to 150,000 Central Parks [p.188–189], and if we put these end-to-end, it would form a landscape corridor fifteen times the earth's circumference. The research question then becomes where, as a matter of priority, should these Central Parks be?

The commonsense answer to this question is, I think, in the world's thirty-six biodiversity hotspots. The biodiversity hotspots are more or less agreed upon by the scientific and conservation communities as the most important biological places on earth. What libraries are to culture, the hotspots are to nature. According to our audit of protected areas [p. 192–201], in the hotspots, a total twenty-one of thirty-six currently fall well short of reaching the 17% protected area target. More specifically, we find that 201 of their 391 constituent ecoregions fall short. The *Atlas* thus draws attention to this land, arguing that the conservation dollar be directed toward this territory as a matter of priority.

In addition to identifying these protected area shortfalls, the *Atlas* also identifies zones in the hotspots where there is conflict between resource extraction, food production, future urbanization, and biodiversity. It also zooms in on the 422 major hotspot cities [p. 202–203] (three hundred thousand people or more), and identifies where their 2050 growth trajectories conflict with remnant habitat and the range lands of threatened species. Not surprisingly, 383 (92%) of these 422 cities are growing on a direct collision course with unique and irreplaceable biodiversity, and most of them don't have any semblance of urban planning to help mitigate the situation.

Under the Convention on Biological Diversity, each nation is expected to develop a National Biodiversity Strategy and Action Plan. In practice, these tend to be platitudinous reports with scant spatial planning, and most fail to consider the 17% target for protected area. Most of the nations who are party to the Convention on Biological Diversity are also signatories to the Paris Agreement on Climate Change, which demands that they prepare national climate change plans. The *Atlas for the End of the World* lays the groundwork for the 142 nations who preside over the world's biodiversity hotspots to now view climate change, biodiversity, and urbanization as interrelated phenomena and plan for the future. Landscape architects can and should coordinate interdisciplinary teams in consultation with Indigenous custodians and other stakeholders to do this work.

The identification of conflict between urban growth and biodiversity in the *Atlas* has been taken further in a second phase of this research conducted under the rubric of the "Hotspot Cities Project" [p. 204–211]. In this phase we reduce the original sample set of 422 cities to 33. Exempting the hotspots of Polynesia-Micronesia, East Melanesia, and New Caledonia, which do not have cities that reach the UN definition of a city as 300,000 or more people, these 33 cities are the biggest and fastest growing in each of the hotspots. In 2019 I brought together at Penn representatives of many of these hotspot cities to formally discuss how they are attempting to mitigate conflict between biodiversity and urban sprawl. I have also conducted design studios and case studies regarding some of these cities. For example, in collaboration with David Gouverneur, an authority on informal (unplanned/self-constructed) urbanization, we have prepared a plan for the future of Bogotá [p. 212–215], the capital of Colombia—one of the world's most biodiverse nations. This plan combines social and economic values with environmental values to demonstrate what the future city would look like if the protection and connectivity of biodiversity was taken seriously in the urban planning process.

Bogotá was chosen as a case study because it sits in a particularly biodiverse region and also because its urban growth is taking place in both formal (planned) and informal ways. Adding to its relevance, Bogotá is also sprawling into its own food-bowl, the rich agricultural lands directly adjacent to the city known as the Sabana de Bogotá. Creating a regional plan that integrates formal and informal urban growth with biodiversity and agricultural lands could, we believe, not only contribute directly to Bogotá, but also serve as a model for other cities in biodiversity hotspots.

The plan for "Bogotá – La Sabana 2050" is organized around an ecological network [p. 212] determined by forging connectivity between patches of protected areas and buffering and restoring the hydrological system of the Sabana and the Río Bogotá. To achieve this, existing large-scale protected areas in the region are connected to peri-urban areas of remnant habitat, which in turn are connected to revegetated riparian zones and wetlands. The future urban growth of Bogotá is then integrated with and shaped by this ecological network and clustered along a new transit loop linking the old city to the new. These districts are mixed-use, walkable, transit-oriented developments that include and allow for a degree of informal urban development. The urban morphology [p. 213] is adjusted at its edges to meet the organic form of the ecological network. Housing and key institutions face onto the ecological network so as to help safeguard its integrity as public space and prevent informal spillover. By the same token, the ecological network has been tightened, and in parts realigned, so as to help ensure functional and legible urban form. At the heart of the new city of Bogotá [p 214–215] is a wetland system and biodiversity research park several times larger than Central Park, framed by a continuous urban boulevard abutted by high-density development. This project hopes to demonstrate that the old dichotomy between conservation and urbanization can be overcome by envisioning both as equal partners in a process of compromise.

As previously noted, the amount of land area necessary to reach the globally agreed target of 17% protected area is equivalent to around 150,000 Central Parks. The general answer to where these should be established is in the world's biodiversity hotspots, and while conservationists and Indigenous custodians are the best people to decide exactly which land should be placed under protection, simply adding more ad hoc fragments of protected areas is unlikely to achieve the required representation or connectivity. A different approach is that these 150,000 Central Parks should be amalgamated into a single vision: a World Park. The World Park Project [p. 216–227] begins with the simple principle of creating recreational trails (hiking and cycling) that pass through as many biodiversity hotspots, existing protected areas, UNESCO World Heritage sites and Biosphere Reserves as possible. Applying this principle at a global scale leads to three primary trails: the first from Australia to Morocco (the Aus-roc trail) [p. 218–219], the second from Turkey to Namibia (the Tur-ibia trail) [p. 220–221], and the third from Patagonia to Alaska (the Pat-aska trail) [p. 222–223].

Most importantly, the trails pass through some 163,000 square kilometers of degraded land *in between* the existing protected areas. If continuous corridors of habitat are to be created so as to facilitate species migration, then these lands need to be ecologically restored and connected to the existing protected areas. This massive restoration project is the World Park's main purpose, and would come under the umbrella of a "World Park Rangers" program operating akin to the way in which the US Peace Corps does today and in which the US Conservation Corps did during the Roosevelt administration's New Deal regime in the 1930s. With the support of the fifty-five nations whose sovereign territory the World Park includes, as well as other nations who may wish to invest on behalf of their citizens, the World Park's potential to employ people in the work of landscape restoration is vast.

The World Park might seem to some like neocolonial megalomania. It isn't. Humans have created numerous systems of connectivity at a planetary scale, but all of this has been at the expense of other species. It is high time to create a planetary network of green infrastructure that serves all species. While the World Park would become a global institution and galvanize global funding, it is not conceived as a top-down, one-size-fits-all master plan for a "park." Although it aims to achieve connectivity at a planetary scale, the World Park is not one project, it is constituted by many small-scale restoration projects that must be attuned to local cultural and ecological conditions. Every piece of land is a complex interweaving of culture and biology; every piece of land is laden with vested interests; every piece of land has a deep history; and every piece of land has multiple potential futures that need to be articulated and negotiated to balance benefits to both local and global culture. The ethos of the park is not that it is a quick-fix, nature-based solution, but rather an ecological and sociopolitical experiment in designing and managing ecosystems about which we still have much to learn. The World Park is a landscape experiment that would become the first citizen-science program coordinated on a planetary scale. World Park: Phase 2 [p. 226–227] shows how the three primary trails could be expanded so as to increase the number of hotspots and nations brought within the park's jurisdiction.

The World Park concept is not a pipe dream, it is part of a new wave of large-scale conservation-related projects taking place worldwide today. My current research partner, Rob Levinthal, and I call these mega-eco projects. As part of an ongoing research project, we have identified over 200 mega-eco projects [p. 228–229] taking place around the world today and organized them into four categories: landscape connectivity projects, watershed plans, antidesertification initiatives, and metropolitan green and blue infrastructure. Examples of each category are the Yellowstone to Yukon Conservation Initiative, the Four Major Rivers Restoration Project in Korea, the Great Green Wall across sub-Saharan Africa, and the São Paulo Green Belt Biosphere Reserve.

The term "megaproject" first appeared in the 1970s after a plethora of billion-dollar public infrastructure works such as dams, seawalls, canals, tunnels, and bridges were built in the previous two decades. Generally speaking, megaprojects have a bad reputation, not only for their insensitivity to local cultural and ecological conditions, but also because they often blow their budgets. The mega-eco project can be understood as different to the megaproject in several significant ways. First, where megaprojects largely resist natural forces, the mega-eco project seeks to achieve resilience by working *with* such forces. Second, instead of being couched in terms of nation building and modern progress, mega-eco projects are framed as works of resilience, environmental restoration, and sustainability. Third, whereas the megaproject is typically singular in its function and designed exclusively for humans, the mega-eco project is multifunctional and designed for humans *and* nonhumans. Fourth, where the megaproject is typically built of inert materials such as concrete and steel, mega-eco projects comprise mainly living materials. Fifth, unlike megaprojects planned by governments and international banks and corporations, the mega-eco project typically makes a point of engaging with local communities in the planning and implementation phase of the project. And finally, instead of being motivated by profit and delivered to a deadline, the mega-eco project often utilizes not-for-profit funding and has an open-ended timeline.

At a time when the sociopolitical and environmental crisis of climate change seems overwhelming, it is tempting to hail the mega-eco project as a form of environmental salvation. Certainly, the advent of such projects around the world represents a significant historical shift in how industrialized humans perceive and care for their environment. And yes, within the good mega-eco project there are surely signs that humans can work together for the greater good, but the reason we are situating them within the tradition of the modern megaproject is to approach them with a degree of critical circumspection. Most mega-eco projects today have long timelines and are still under construction, making it hard to evaluate their real merits, but historical precedents, particularly antidesertification projects, indicate that mega-eco projects are not without their own social and ecological problems. The purpose then of our ongoing analysis of these mega-eco projects is to try to separate emerging best practice from greenwashing and avoid the mistakes of twentieth-century megaprojects.

And Back Again

While the work in the second section of this book gathered under the rubric of instrumentality primarily concerns more plannerly projects, the work has always been conceived, to some degree, in aesthetic terms. Though not artworks per se, the five major research projects in this section—Boomtown 2050, Made in Australia, the Atlas for the End of the World, the Hotspot Cities Project, and the World Park—all use aesthetics to present empirical data and make coherent arguments in legible, credible, and compelling ways. The way information is visualized and organized is crucial to the success or otherwise of these projects in reaching academic, government, and public audiences. More than this, although these research projects all broach critical issues, they strive never to lose sight of the fact that these issues are not just problems in need of solutions, but also questions of a philosophical nature.

As well as publications, these research projects have all been exhibited in art galleries and museums where their instrumental aspects are combined with aesthetic tropes. For example, in 2023, the mega-eco projects we are studying were installed in the *Eco-Vision* exhibition at the China Central Academy of Fine Art in Beijing under the title *The Butterfly and the Locust* [p. 232–233]. An aerial image of each mega-eco project is printed in color on mylar and framed with a laser cut wooden edge, then pinned to the wall of the gallery in the manner of butterfly wings in natural history collections. The World Park Project was exhibited at the 2021 Venice Biennale of Architecture [p. 230–231] as a topographic "fly-through" printed on acrylic sheets. Also at Venice, the Hotspot Cities Project was explained through 33 maps, each accompanied by a trophy etched with the names of endangered species endemic to the map, and a collection of chicken bones. These works were also exhibited at the 2022 Rotterdam Architecture Biennale.

Along with these research projects at both Biennales was an additional artwork titled *Not the Blue Marble* [p. 236–239]. This piece is based on an exact copy of the Apollo 11 command module hatch. This is not the hatch through which Neil Armstrong and Buzz Aldrin exited the lunar module (the "Eagle") to walk on the moon, it is the one that had to be wrenched open [p. 234–235] so they could reenter earth. Through the window in this replica of the hatch is an animation of a future earth [p. 238–239]. Except for a few traces of what appears to be some vegetation and water (coinciding with today's protected areas), this future earth is essentially barren. This is a planet caught in the positive feedback loop of global warming, an image of what earth might be like in a million years or so. In two small black squares (exactly where the instructions for opening the hatch were on the original), new landing instructions are provided. These instructions indicate that the mission of whomever (or whatever) is about to open the hatch this time is to release forms of microbial and plant life into the earth system in order to begin to resuscitate its metabolism.

This artwork suggests, pessimistically, that climate change will be devastating. More optimistically, it also suggests that the work of earthly cultivation *will* one day come to supersede the three worldviews that led to climate change in the first place—namely, the economic dogma of endless capitalist growth, the theological farce that paradise is otherworldly, and the technological fantasy of colonizing space. Alternatively, the narrative of cultivating the earth provides humanity with a shared and peaceable purpose grounded in meaningful work. This recultivated earth is not some boring, sanctimonious, doctrinaire, new age ecotopia: it is a highly scientific, aesthetic, inventive, diverse, and experimental project. It is a landscape architectural project.

This essay could finish right here. But instead of closing with such grandiloquent prognostications, I want to close by coming back to today and acknowledging just how far the profession of landscape architecture has come in the last forty years. At the beginning of this essay, I noted that Central Park is routinely lauded for its artistry and its instrumentality. This much is true, but veneration of the park as *the* preeminent work of modern landscape architecture is an exaggeration that overshadows the fact that there are works of contemporary landscape architecture that combine art and instrumentality in new and important ways.

For example, despite accusations of gentrification, the High Line in New York by James Corner Field Operations is a beautifully crafted catwalk that brings the theater of the garden into the twenty-first century. More directly related to an emerging aesthetic of the Anthropocene, and also by Field Operations, is Fresh Kills [p. 240] on Staten Island. As the world's largest former rubbish dump, Fresh Kills is an ongoing restorative experiment. The initial renders for this project didn't promise the eco-paradisiacal nor did they overindulge in the grotesque nature of toxicity. Instead, with modesty and honesty, they showed that breathing life into dead land is not easy. That this work is hard is an understatement. As Keith Bowers and his team at Biohabitats in the USA show, it requires a whole-of-office commitment and genuine interdisciplinarity.

In this vein, given the state of the world, the argument could now be made that landscape architects should only focus on and specialize in ecological restoration and that schools should produce what James Lovelock referred to as "earth doctors", not "designers". Yes, but this (old) argument needn't be posed as either/or (i.e., instrumentality or art.) The promise of landscape architecture is that it is both. Where we see this coming together is in projects where communities and ecosystems are brought together under the rubric of resiliency, through design processes led by landscape architects. Projects such as the Big U by One Architecture, Scape's Oyster-tecture, and work for the Army Corps of Engineers by Sean Burkholder are significant early experiments in resilience. Even though not formally concerned with aesthetics per se, these projects can be read as anti-monuments to the Anthropocene. On the other side of the US, OLIN's LA River project, though yet to break ground, is also taking landscape architecture's level of engagement with technical, ecological, and social complexity to new heights.

In Europe, Martí Franch's Tudela-Culip restoration at Cap de Creus on the Costa Brava in Spain (2009) is exemplary because it finds *genius loci* through subtraction rather than addition. Catherine Mosbach's Louvre Lens Museum Park in France is important because the landscape is not constructed as a scene—over there—but as a collection of microcuriosities in the ground plane. So too, Georges Descombes's River Aire renaturation outside Geneva is important because, picking up where Smithson left off, it links entropy with ecology and the poetics of the locale. In Copenhagen, Martin Rein-Cano of Topotek 1's Superkilen stands out because it refuses to smooth social tensions with sweet nature or faux ecology. In the Ruhrgebiet, Emscher Landscape Park is a huge achievement in terms of triangulating community, economics, and environmental values. In China, Kongjian Yu's National Ecological Security Pattern Plan and Sponge Cities initiative have gained the attention of government and become national priorities. Finally, the work of Dutch landscape architects H+N+S on projects such as the Sand Motor [p. 241] and Room for the River move boldly toward an aesthetic of the Anthropocene because their organic functionality (coastal reinforcement and flood mitigation respectively) is so clearly reflected in their engineered form. All these projects are rooted in instrumentality and yet they can also be read as artworks that capture aspects of their zeitgeist and reveal the frightening beauty of landscape processes now being engineered by humans on a planetary scale.

LANDSCAPE AS INSTRUMENT

Typical new suburban development in Perth, Western Australia, erasing habitat in the Southwest Australia biodiversity hotspot (*left*). Diagram (*right*) showing a matrix of linear green spaces, which would force orthodox suburban development into a more rational urban form [137–139].

Wungong (Perth, 2009). Master plan for a new 1,500-hectare suburban development for 40,000 people. Blue lines represent linear open spaces, and green areas represent existing remnant habitat and buffered riparian corridors. The built project is located (red square, *right*) within a larger landscape structure plan of habitat patches and corridors for the region [138–139].

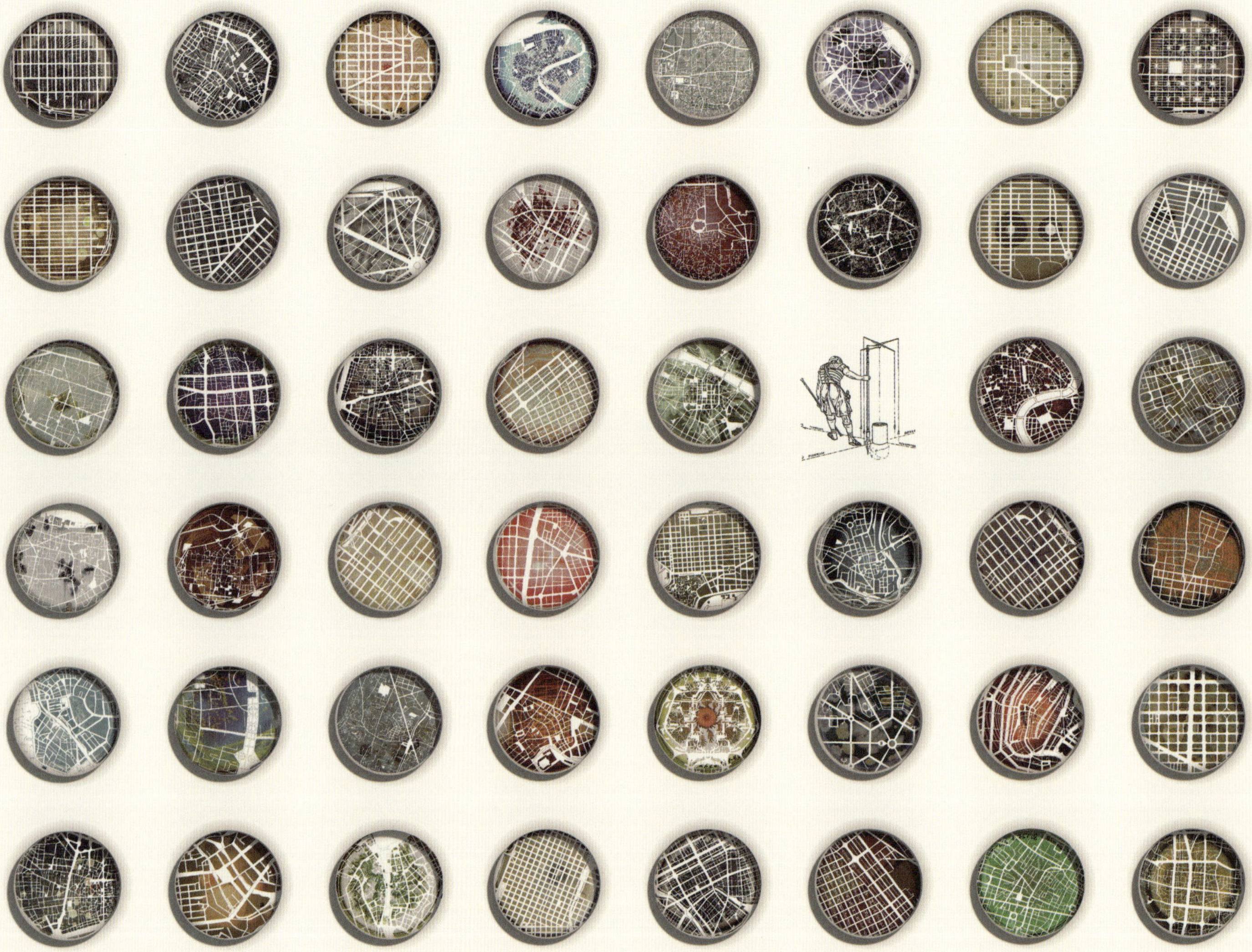

"POD City" (Perth, 2009). Scenario from *Boomtown 2050* for 48 medium-density performance-oriented developments (PODs) to absorb 1.5 million additional people in the city of Perth by 2050 [140].

"Food City" and "Car Free City" (Perth, 2009). Scenarios from *Boomtown 2050* of a city designed with enough space for food production to meet the needs of the adjacent population (*left*); and combined with a grid of public transport (*right*) [141].

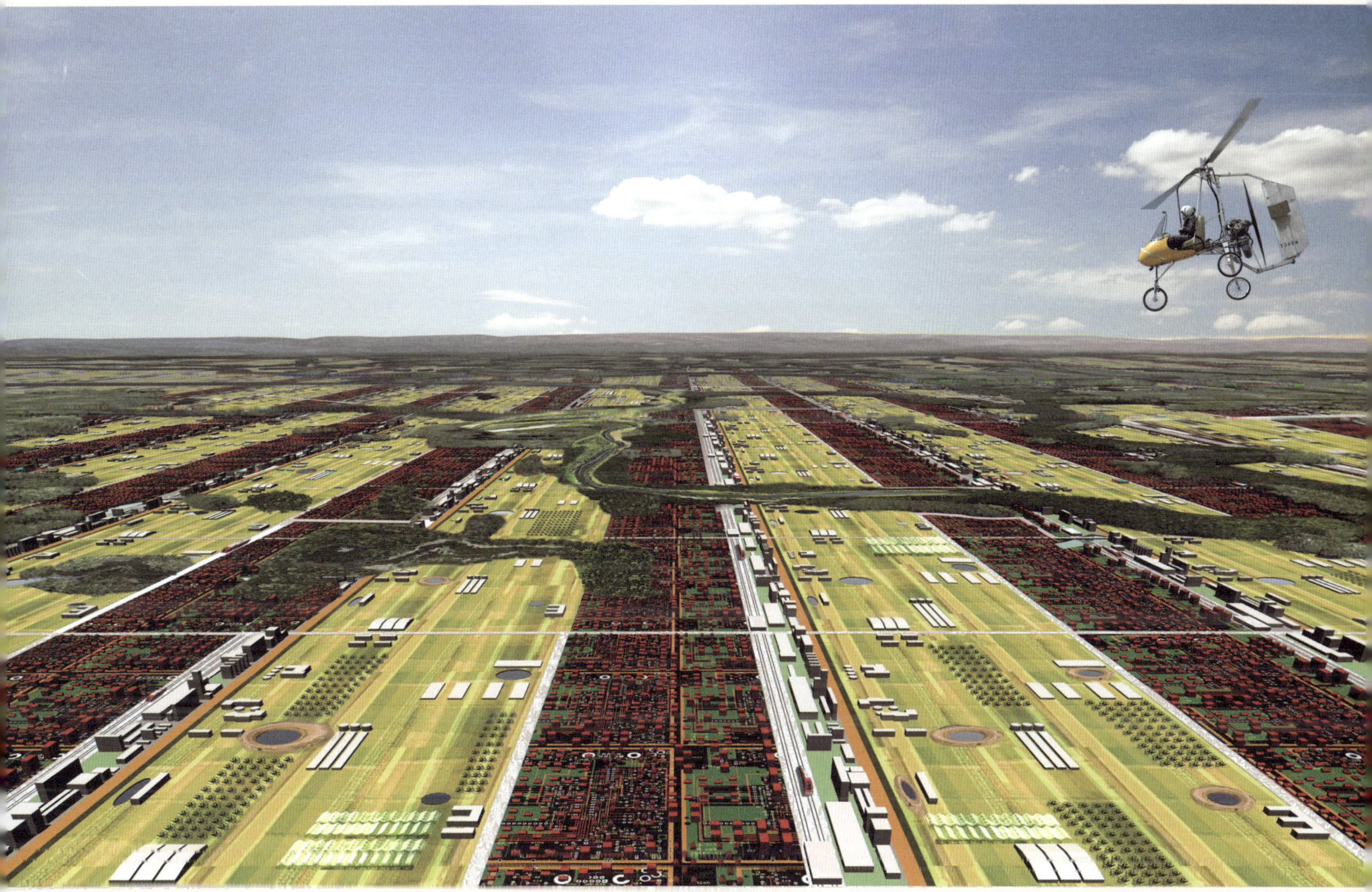

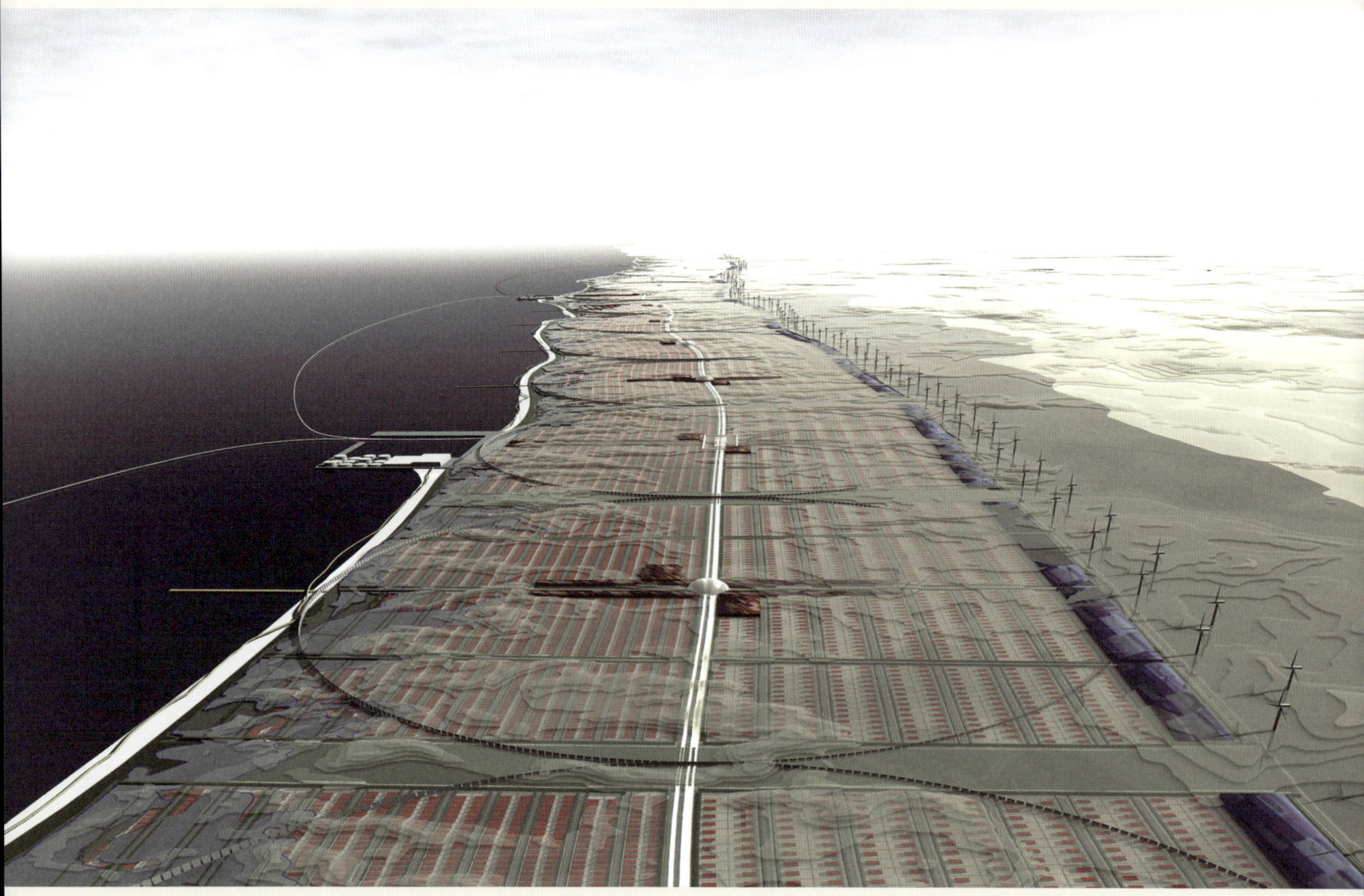

"Seachange City" and "Treechange City" (Perth, 2009). Scenarios from *Boomtown 2050* of a city where population growth is accommodated in low-density development within walkable distance of the beach (*left*); and a city with a semirural level of low-density development integrated with solar energy production and forestry (*right*) [141].

"Sky City" (*left*), "River City" and "Surf City" (*right*) (Perth, 2008). Scenarios from *Boomtown 2050* for high-density infill development in areas of high cultural amenity and public transportation so as to accommodate 2050 population projections [141].

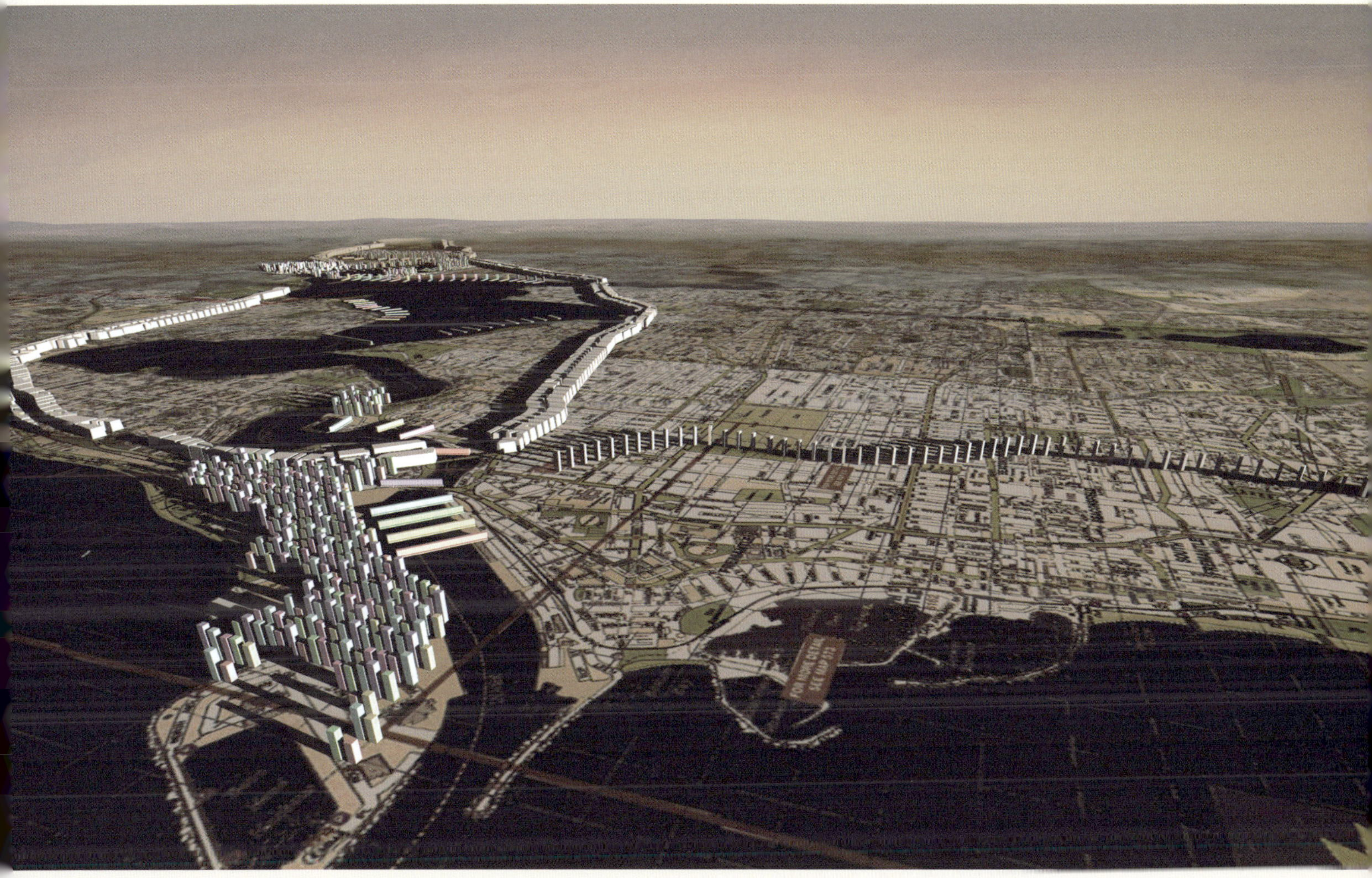

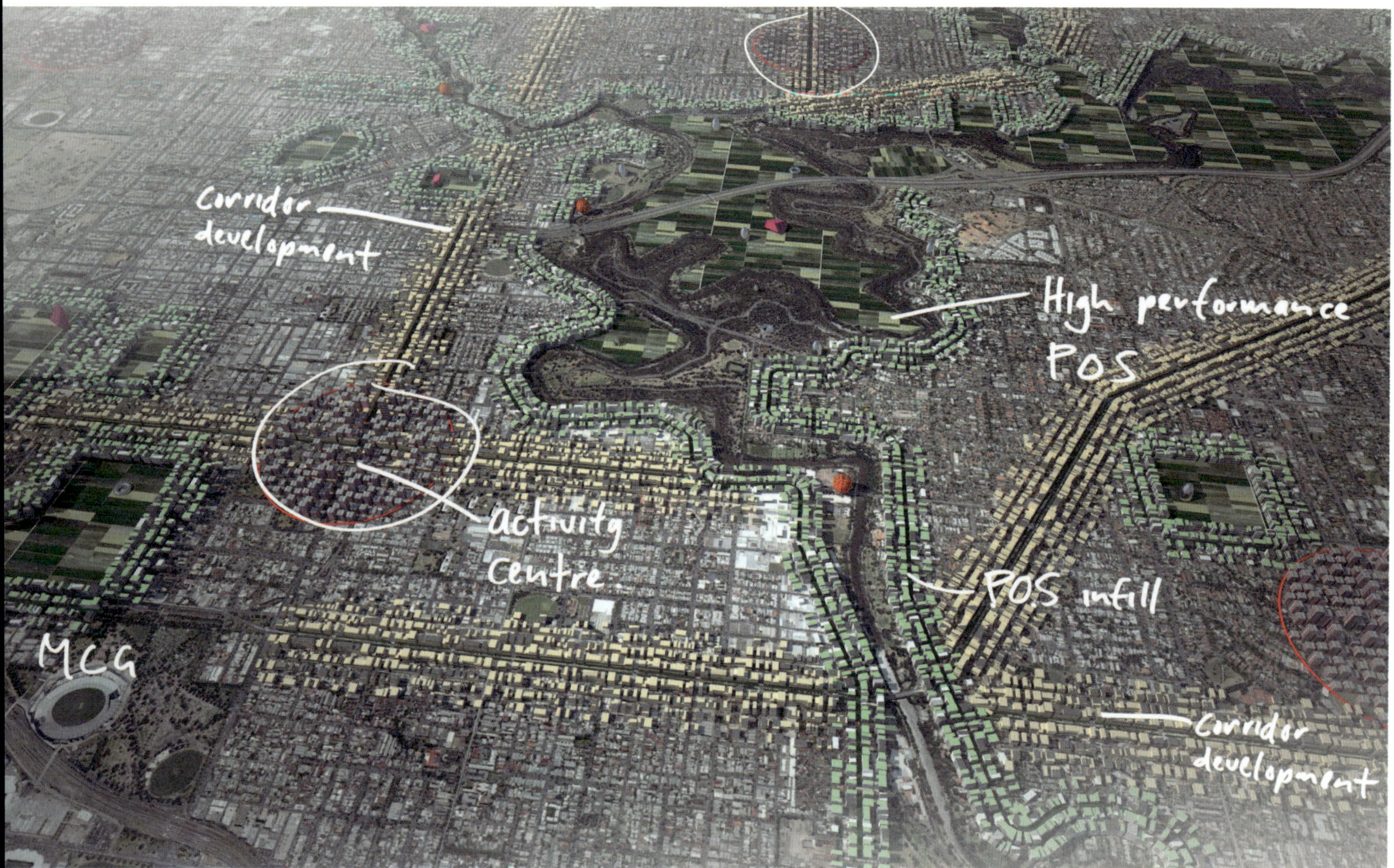

"GOD: Green Oriented Development" (Melbourne and Adelaide, 2013). Scenarios from *Made in Australia* showing how the growing population of Australian cities can be accommodated through increased density adjacent to public open space [142].

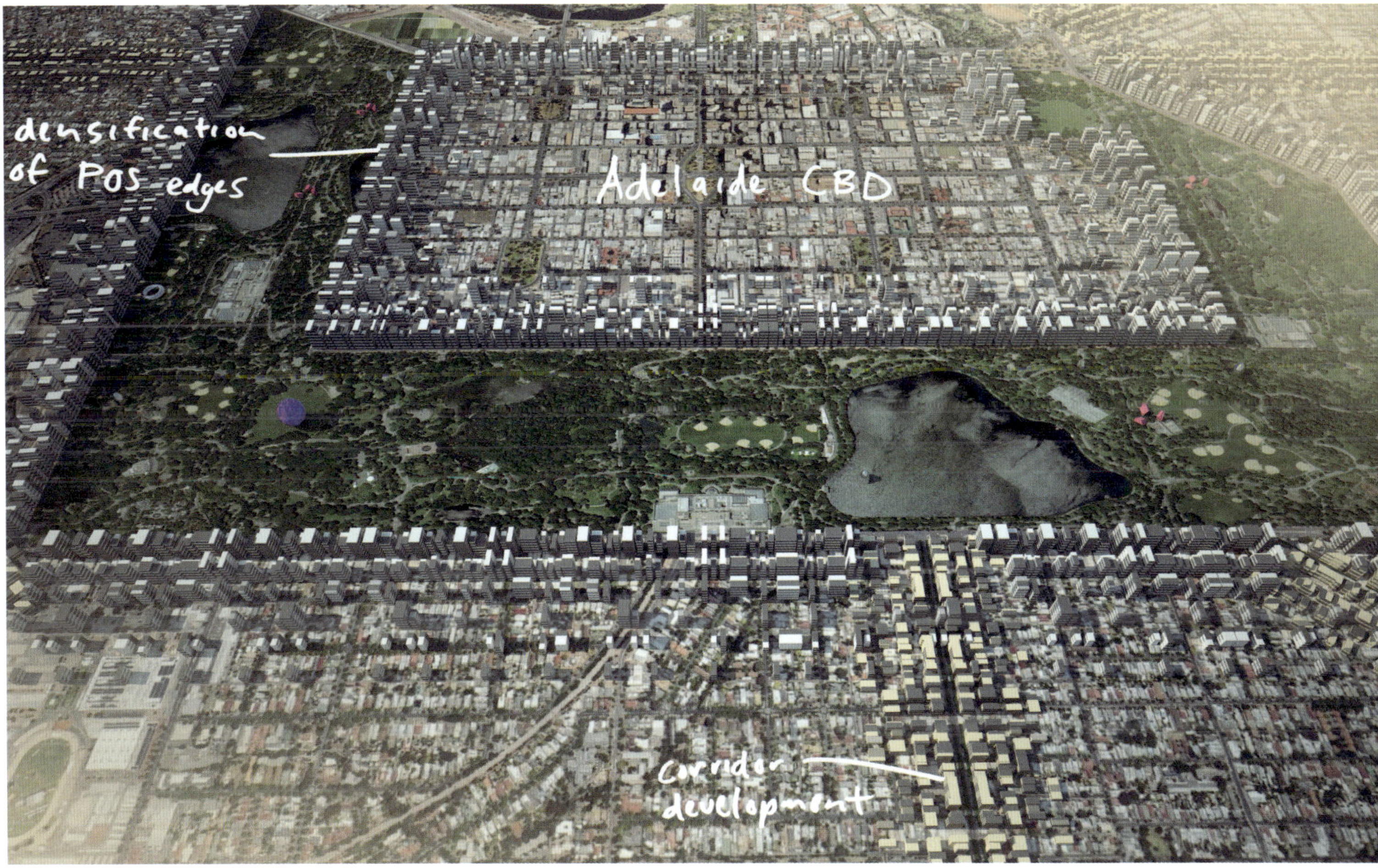
densification
of POS edges
Adelaide CBD
corridor
development

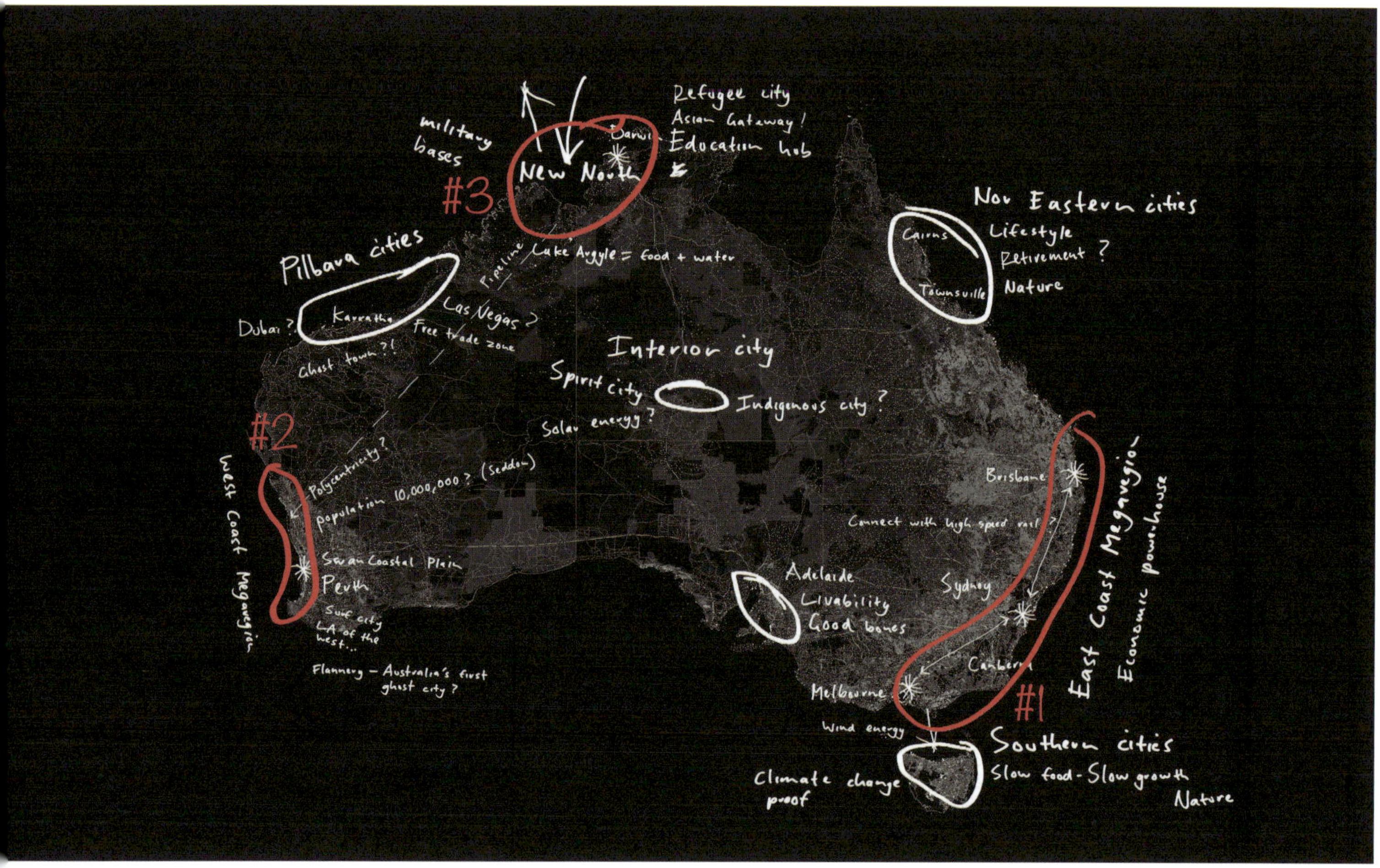

Sketch concept from *Made in Australia* (2013) summarizing the possibility of decentralizing Australia's projected 2050 population growth into emerging megaregions and new regional centers [142].

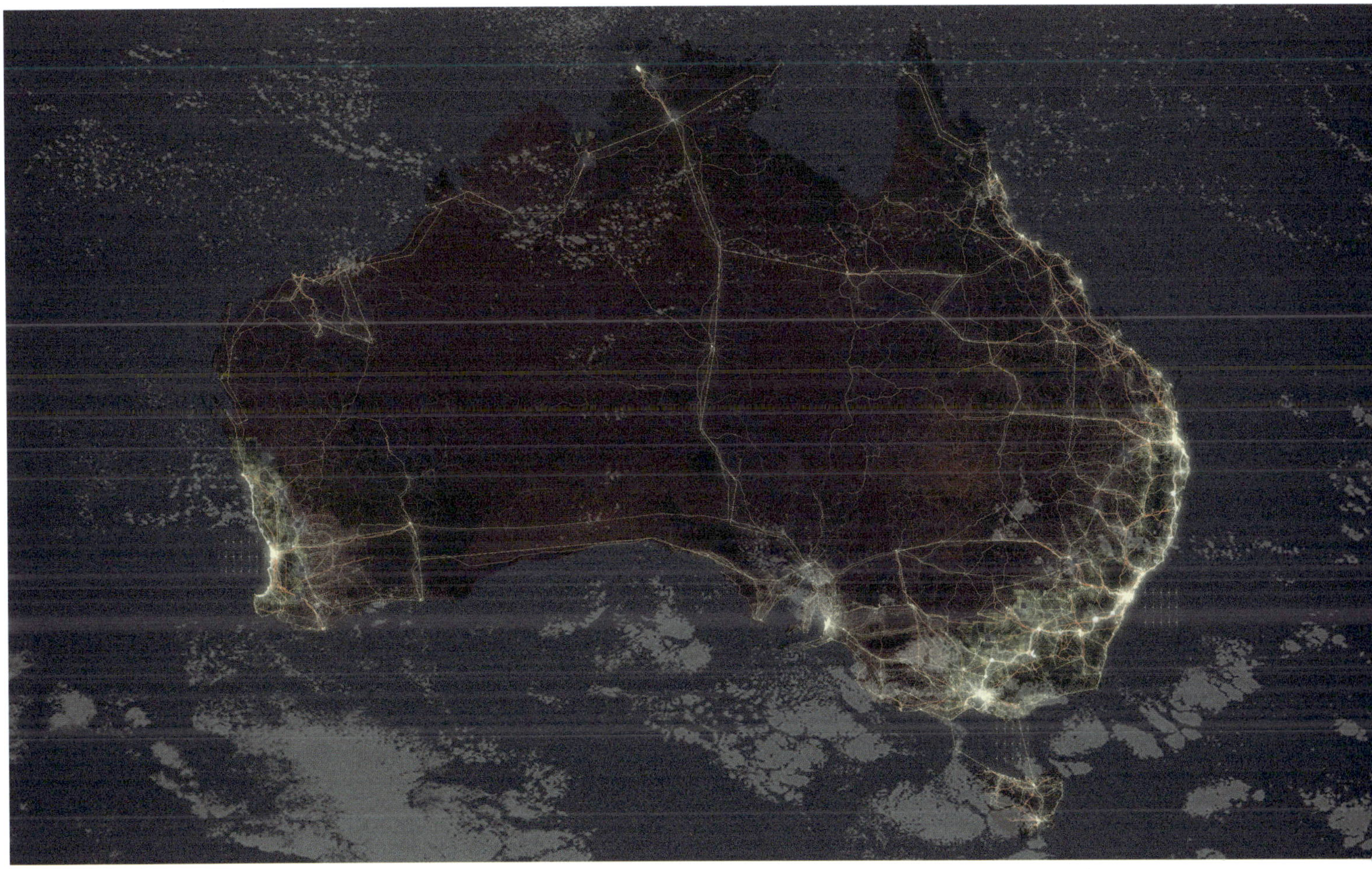

Scenarios from *Made in Australia* (2013) creating west and east coast megaregions incentivized by high-speed rail and new regional cities to accommodate Australia's projected 2050 population growth [143].

Scenarios from *Made in Australia* (2013) showing views over hypothetical new cities in the west and east coast megaregions. The new development is grafted onto existing settlements and connected to high-speed rail [143].

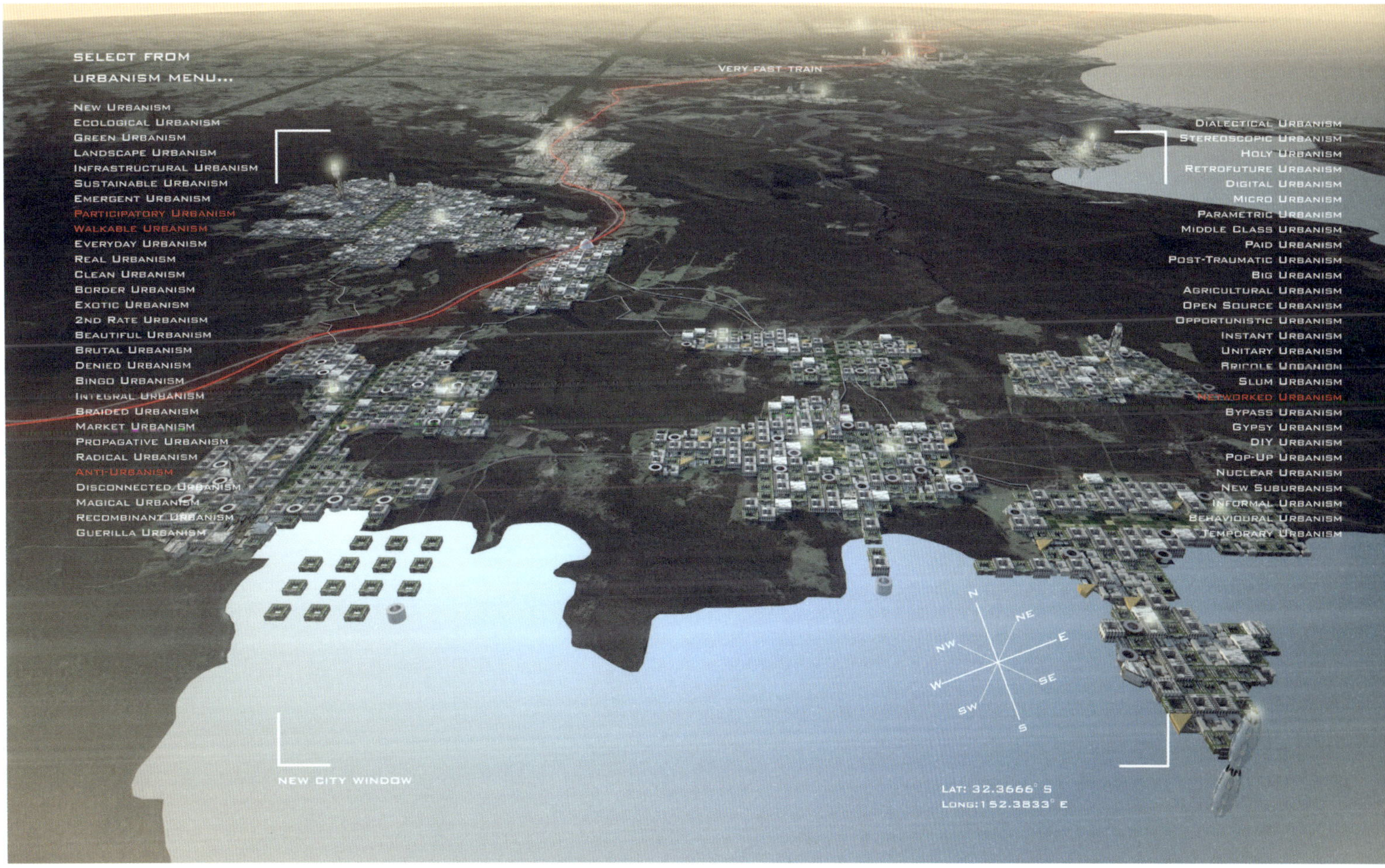
SELECT FROM
URBANISM MENU...
New Urbanism
Ecological Urbanism
Green Urbanism
Landscape Urbanism
Infrastructural Urbanism
Sustainable Urbanism
Emergent Urbanism
Participatory Urbanism
Walkable Urbanism
Everyday Urbanism
Real Urbanism
Clean Urbanism
Border Urbanism
Exotic Urbanism
2nd Rate Urbanism
Beautiful Urbanism
Brutal Urbanism
Denied Urbanism
Bingo Urbanism
Integral Urbanism
Braided Urbanism
Market Urbanism
Propagative Urbanism
Radical Urbanism
Anti-Urbanism
Disconnected Urbanism
Magical Urbanism
Recombinant Urbanism
Guerilla Urbanism
VERY FAST TRAIN
Dialectical Urbanism
Stereoscopic Urbanism
Holy Urbanism
Retrofuture Urbanism
Digital Urbanism
Micro Urbanism
Parametric Urbanism
Middle Class Urbanism
Paid Urbanism
Post-Traumatic Urbanism
Big Urbanism
Agricultural Urbanism
Open Source Urbanism
Opportunistic Urbanism
Instant Urbanism
Unitary Urbanism
Bricole Urbanism
Slum Urbanism
Networked Urbanism
Bypass Urbanism
Gypsy Urbanism
DIY Urbanism
Pop-Up Urbanism
Nuclear Urbanism
New Suburbanism
Informal Urbanism
Behavioural Urbanism
Temporary Urbanism
N
NE
E
SE
S
SW
W
NW
NEW CITY WINDOW
Lat: 32.3666° S
Long: 152.3833° E

Installation image from the *Roma 20-25: Lifecycles of the Metropolis* (MAXXI Gallery, Rome, 2015), addressing the future of peri-urban Rome. The proposal is for a citywide composting system sponsored by the Vatican and Rome's fashion industry as a catalyst for development and improved land use [144].

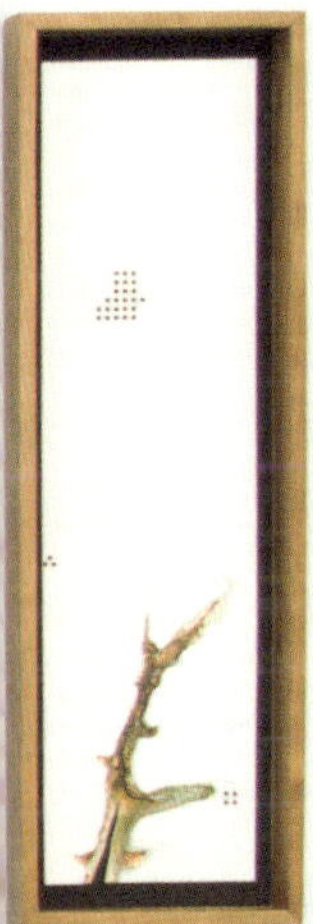

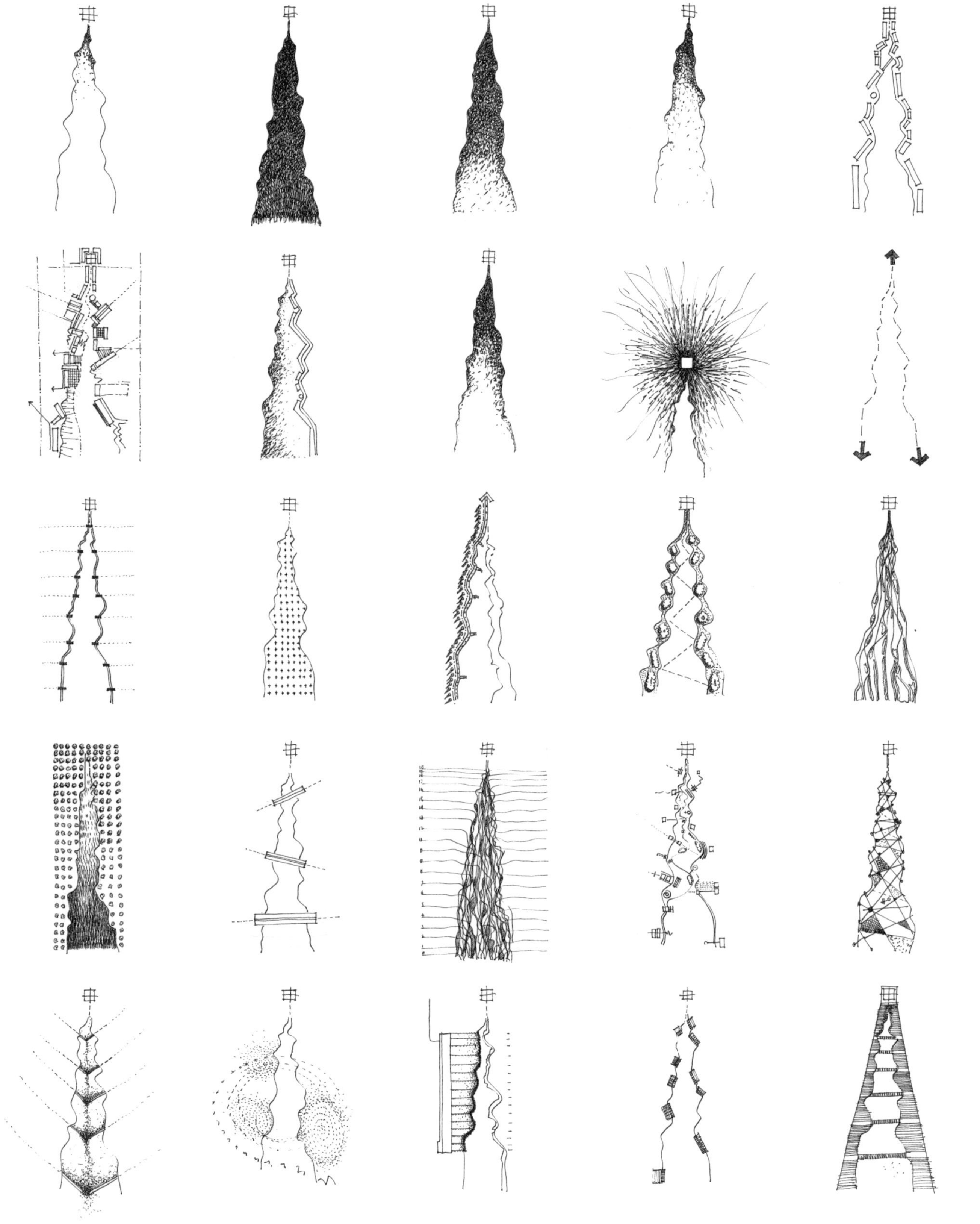

Concept images for *Roma 20-25: Lifecycles of the Metropolis* (MAXXI Gallery, Rome, 2015) indicating new programming of Rome's peri-urban landscape focusing on the existing ravines [144].

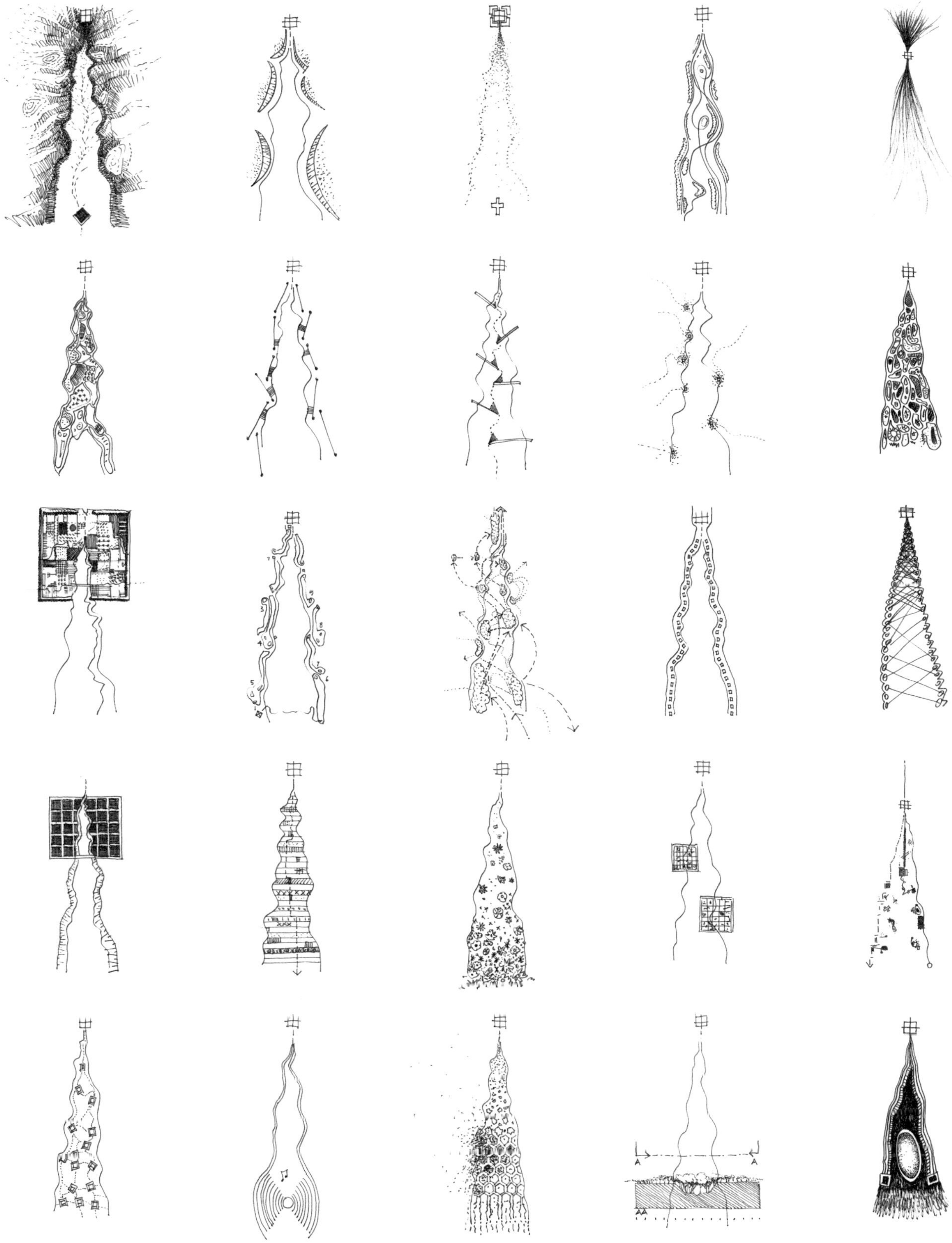
A
A

World map from the first modern atlas, *Theatrum Orbis Terrarum* (1570), by Abraham Ortelius, merged with names from the IUCN red list of endangered species [145].

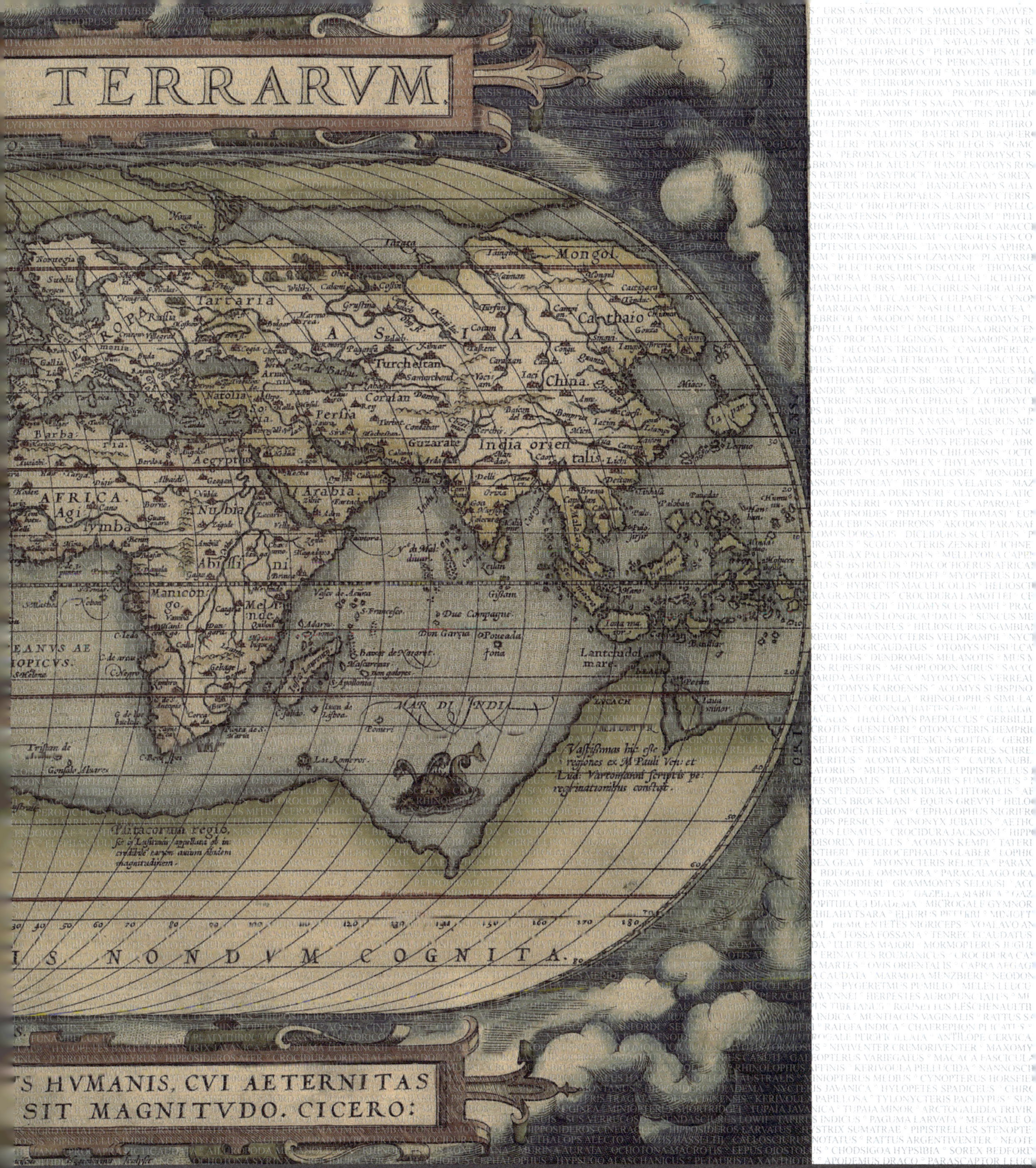
TERRARVM
IS NONDVM COGNITA.
TS HVMANIS, CVI AETERNITAS
SIT MAGNITVDO. CICERO:

"The Problem of the Two Worlds" from the *Atlas for the End of the World* (2014). The world on the left shows only the planetary mesh of urbanization and related infrastructure, while the world on the right shows only protected areas. Mitigation of the sixth extinction depends on how these two worlds relate [145].

NATURE

The "World's Protected Areas" from the *Atlas for the End of the World* (updated 2022). This territory currently amounts to 16.64% of global terrestrial area, falling short of the 17% target agreed to by 196 nations under the Convention on Biological Diversity. This target is set to increase to 30% by 2030 [147].

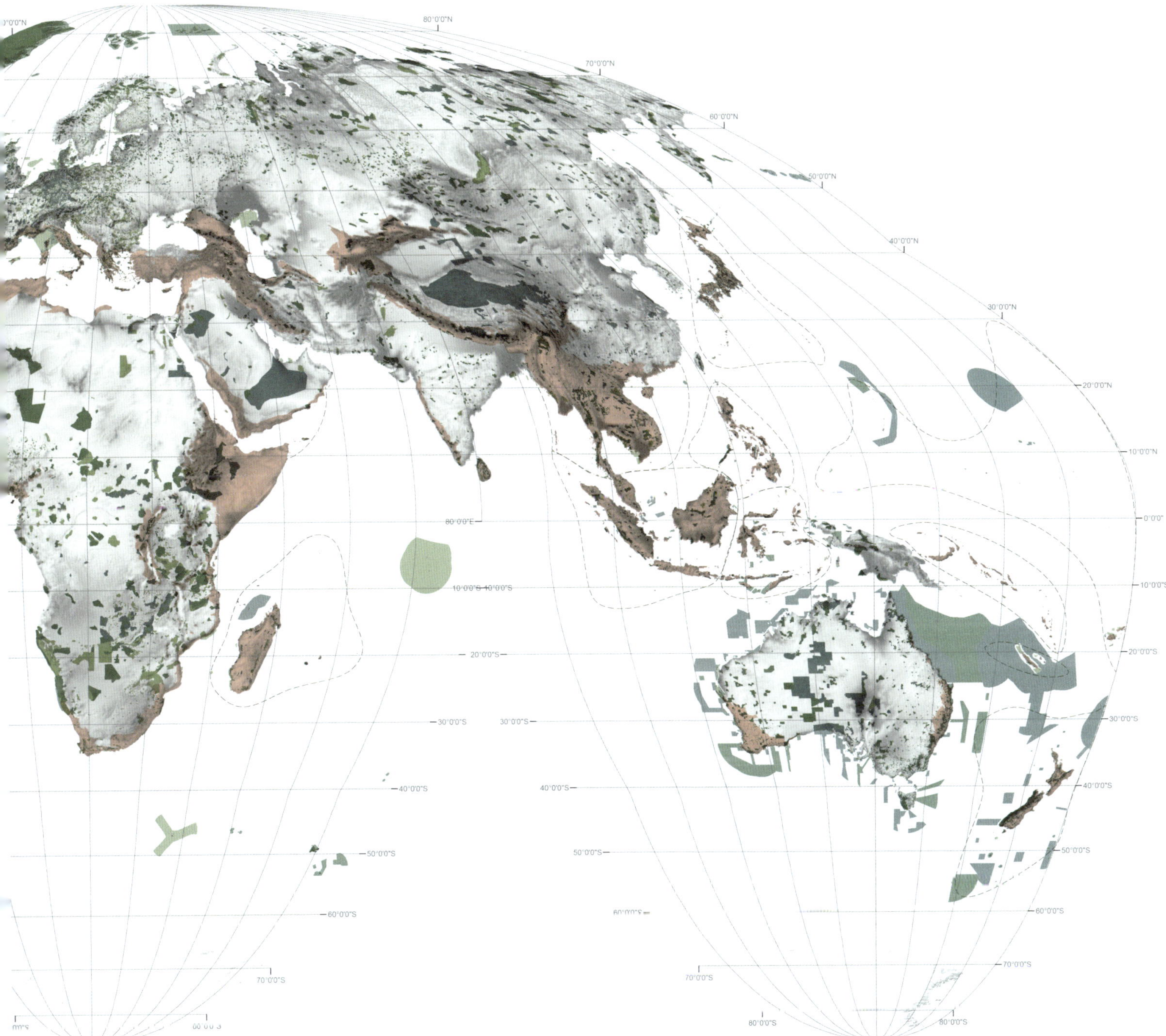
80°0'0"N
70°0'0"N
60°0'0"N
50°0'0"N
40°0'0"N
30°0'0"N
20°0'0"N
10°0'0"N
0°0'0"
80°0'0"E
10°0'0"S
20°0'0"S
30°0'0"S
40°0'0"S
50°0'0"S
60°0'0"S
70°0'0"S
80°0'0"S

For the world to reach the agreed target of 17% global terrestrial protected area, the equivalent of 150,000 Central Parks needs to be formally placed under protection [148].

,000

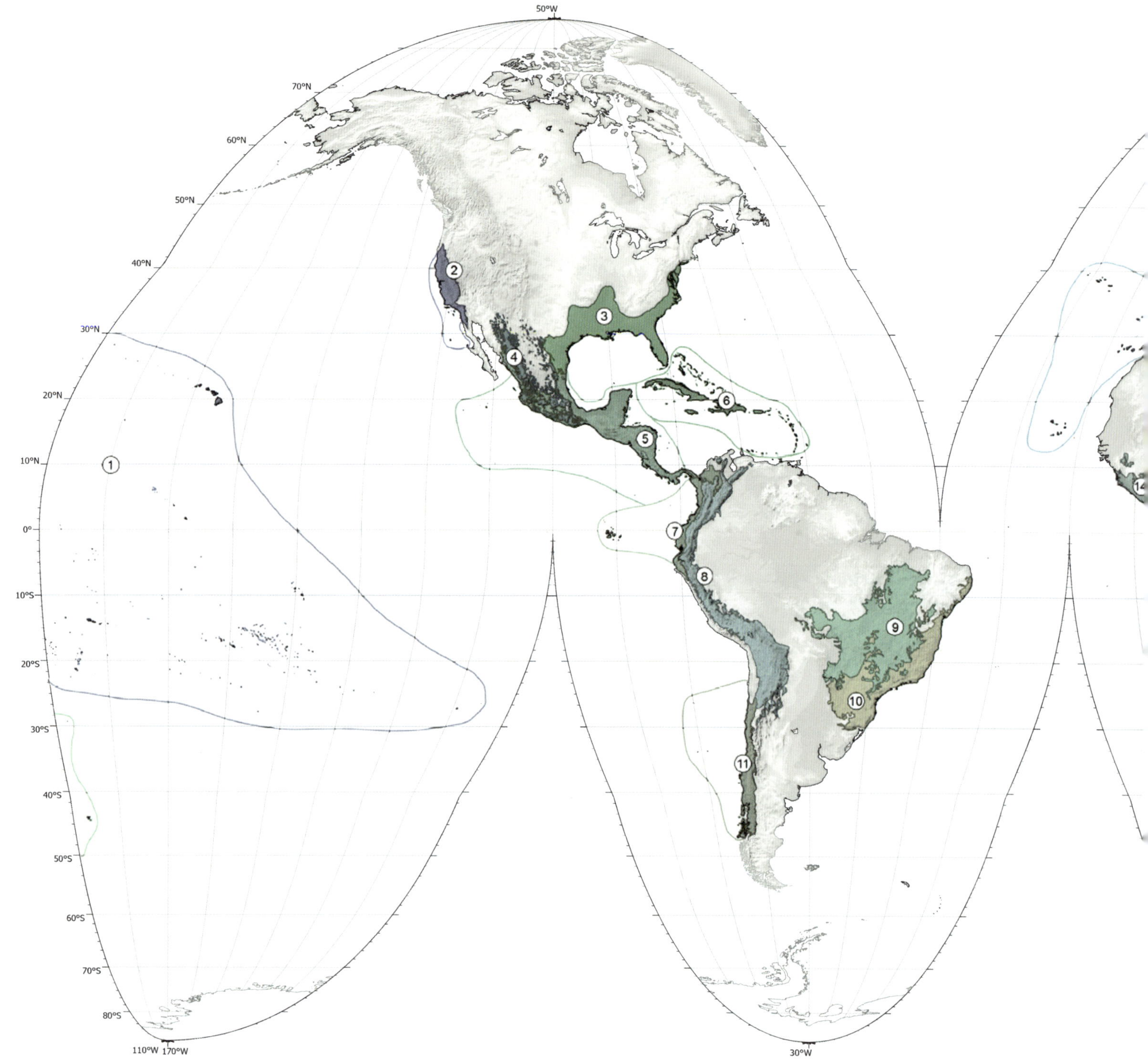

1. Polynesia – Micronesia
2. California Floristic Province
3. North America Coastal Plain
4. Madrean Pine – Oak Woodlands
5. Mesoamerican
6. Caribbean
7. Tumbes-Choco-Magdalena
8. Tropical Andes
9. Cerrado
10. Atlantic Forest
11. Chilean Winter Rainfall – Valdivian Forests
12. Mediterranean Basin
13. Caucasus
14. Guinean Forests of West Africa
15. Eastern Afromontane
16. Horn of Africa
17. Coastal Forests of East Africa
18. Madagascar

The shaded areas represent the world's 36 recognized biodiversity hotspots, regions where much of the world's irreplaceable biodiversity is threatened with extinction [145].

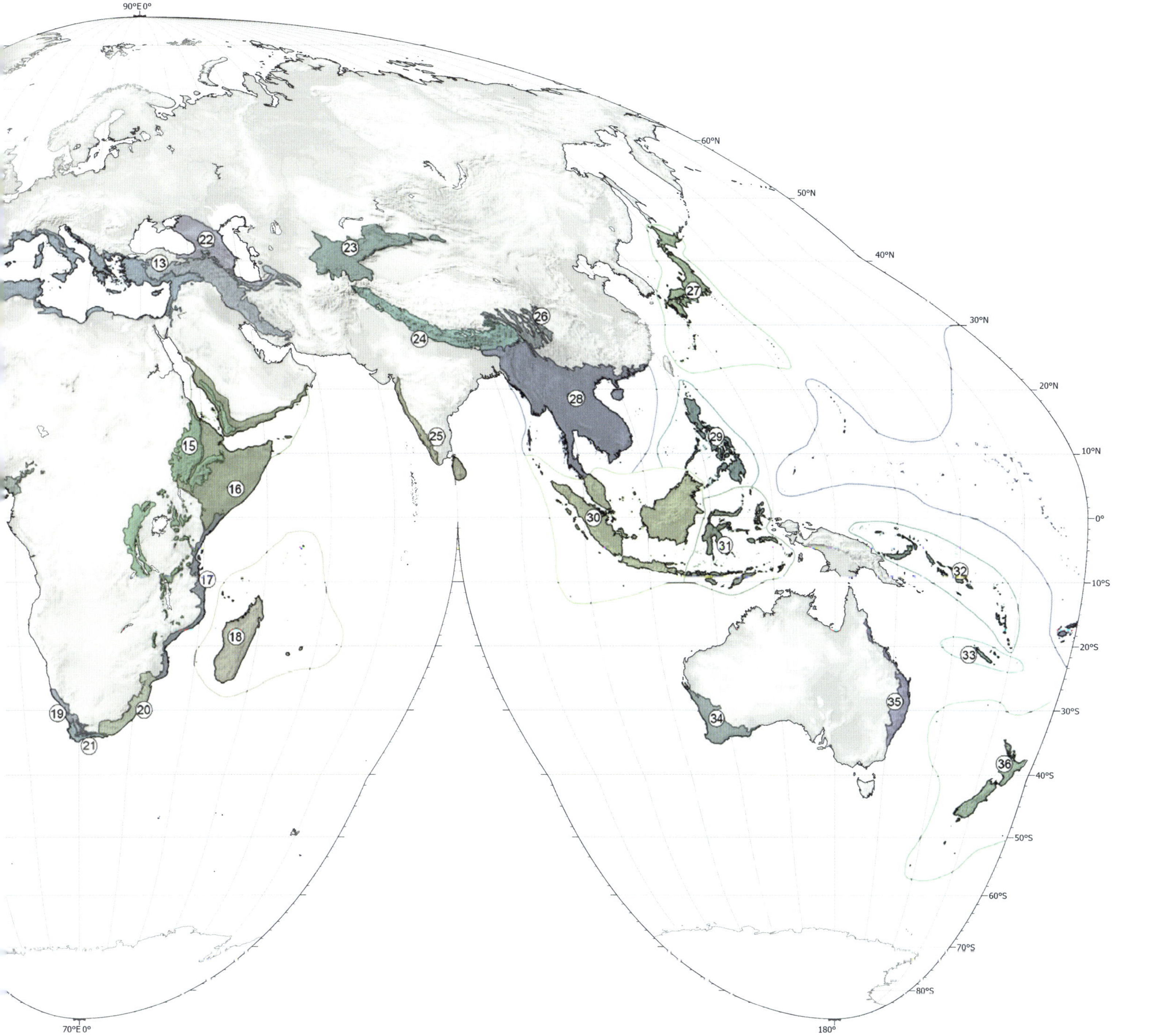

19. Succulent Karoo
20. Maputaland-Pondoland-Albany
21. Cape Floristic Region
22. Irano-Anatolian
23. Mountains of Central Asia
24. Himalaya
25. Western Ghats + Sri Lanka
26. Mountains of Southwest China
27. Japan
28. Indo-Burma
29. Philippines
30. Sundaland
31. Wallacea
32. East Melanesian Islands
33. New Caledonia
34. South West Australia
35. Forests of Eastern Australia
36. New Zealand

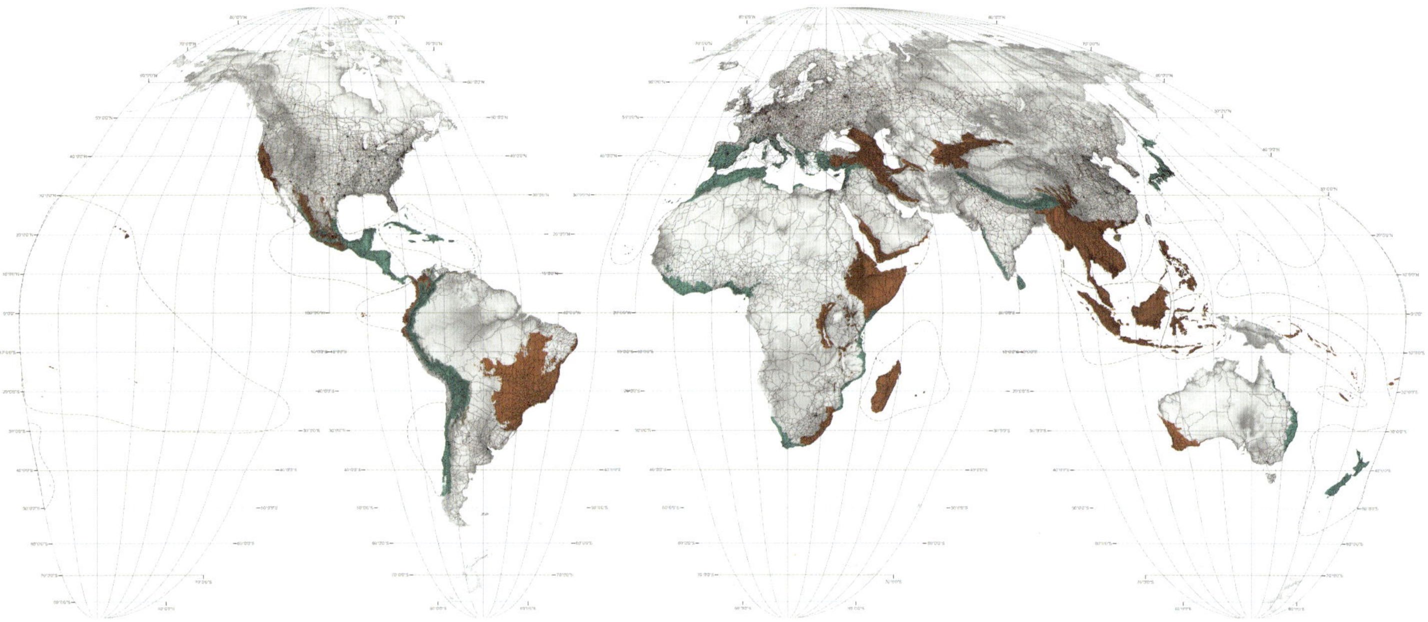

World map (*left*) showing the 21 biodiversity hotspots that currently fall well short of reaching protected area targets in brown; an example of hotspot mapping from the *Atlas for the End of the World* (*right*) auditing the degree to which each of the world's 36 hotspots meets UN protected area targets [148].

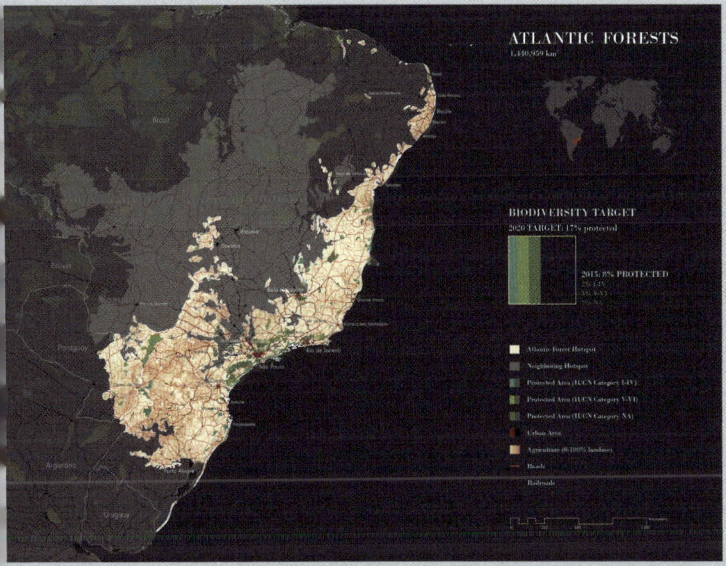

ATLANTIC FORESTS
1,440,959 km²
BIODIVERSITY TARGET
2020 TARGET: 17% protected
2015: 8% PROTECTED
Atlantic Forest Hotspot
Neighboring Hotspot
Protected Area (IUCN Category I-IV)
Protected Area (IUCN Category V-VI)
Protected Area (IUCN Category NA)
Urban Area
Agriculture (0-100% landuse)
Roads
Railroads

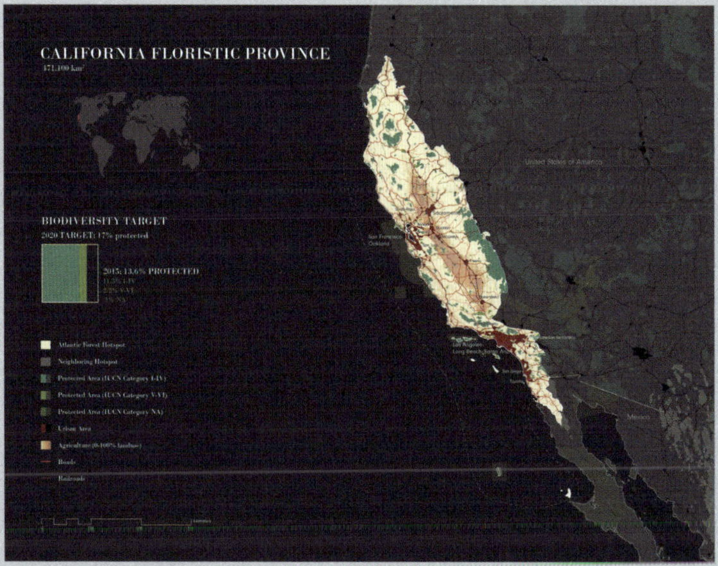

CALIFORNIA FLORISTIC PROVINCE
471,100 km²
BIODIVERSITY TARGET
2020 TARGET: 17% protected
2015: 13.6% PROTECTED
Atlantic Forest Hotspot
Neighboring Hotspot
Protected Area (IUCN Category I-IV)
Protected Area (IUCN Category V-VI)
Protected Area (IUCN Category NA)
Urban Area
Agriculture (0-100% landuse)
Roads
Railroads

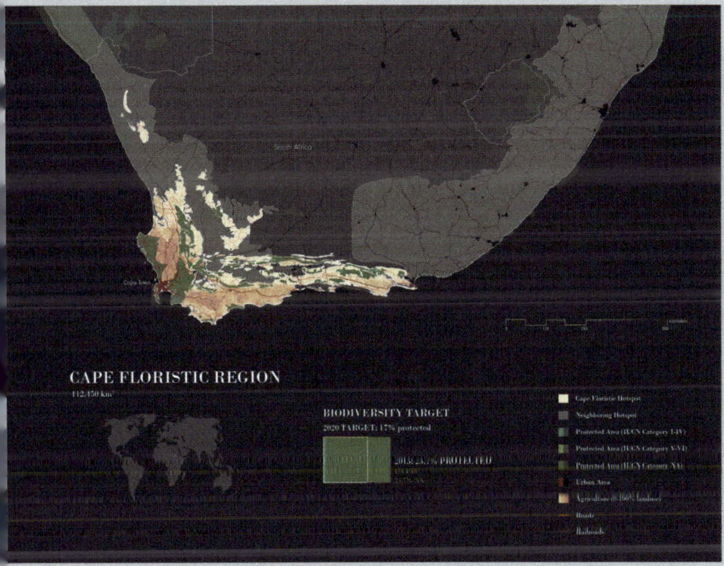

CAPE FLORISTIC REGION
112,450 km²
BIODIVERSITY TARGET
2020 TARGET: 17% protected
Cape Floristic Hotspot
Neighboring Hotspot
Protected Area (IUCN Category I-IV)
Protected Area (IUCN Category V-VI)
Urban Area
Agriculture (0-100% landuse)
Roads
Railroads

CARIBBEAN ISLANDS
260,671 km²
BIODIVERSITY TARGET
2015: 17.6% PROTECTED
Caribbean Islands Hotspot
Neighboring Hotspot
Protected Area (IUCN Category I-IV)
Protected Area (IUCN Category NA)
Agriculture (0-100% landuse)
Railroads

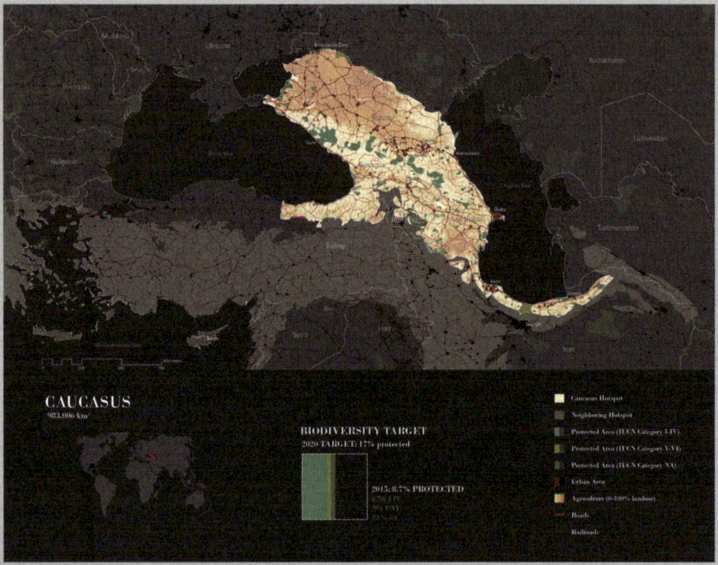
CAUCASUS
933,006 km²
BIODIVERSITY TARGET
2020 TARGET: 17% protected
2015: 8.7% PROTECTED
Caucasus Hotspot
Neighboring Hotspot
Protected Area (IUCN Category I-IV)
Protected Area (IUCN Category V-VI)
Protected Area (IUCN Category NA)
Urban Area
Agriculture (0-100% landuse)
Roads
Railroads

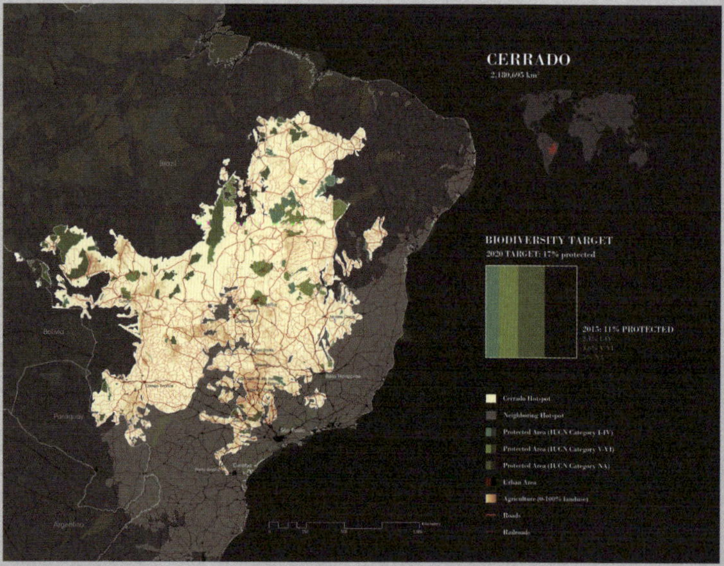
CERRADO
2,180,695 km²
BIODIVERSITY TARGET
2020 TARGET: 17% protected
2015: 11% PROTECTED
Cerrado Hotspot
Neighboring Hotspot
Protected Area (IUCN Category I-IV)
Protected Area (IUCN Category V-VI)
Protected Area (IUCN Category NA)
Urban Area
Agriculture (0-100% landuse)
Roads
Railroads

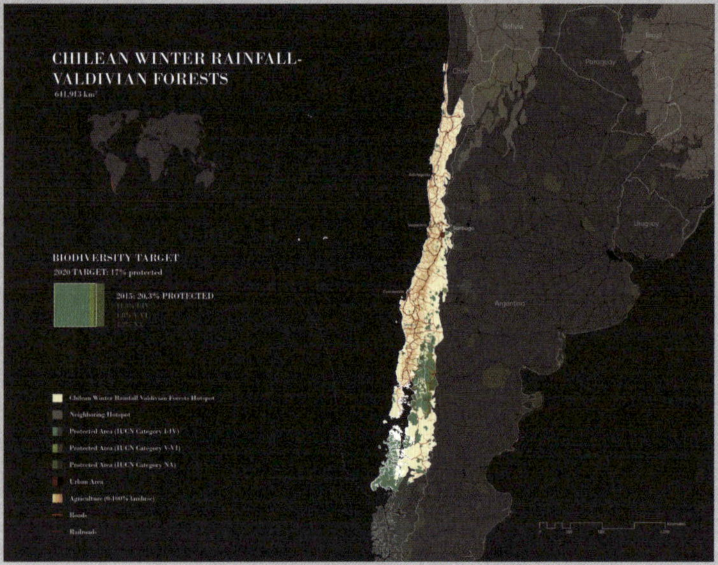
CHILEAN WINTER RAINFALL-
VALDIVIAN FORESTS
641,913 km²
BIODIVERSITY TARGET
2020 TARGET: 17% protected
2015: 20.3% PROTECTED
Chilean Winter Rainfall Valdivian Forests Hotspot
Neighboring Hotspot
Protected Area (IUCN Category I-IV)
Protected Area (IUCN Category V-VI)
Protected Area (IUCN Category NA)
Urban Area
Agriculture (0-100% landuse)
Roads
Railroads

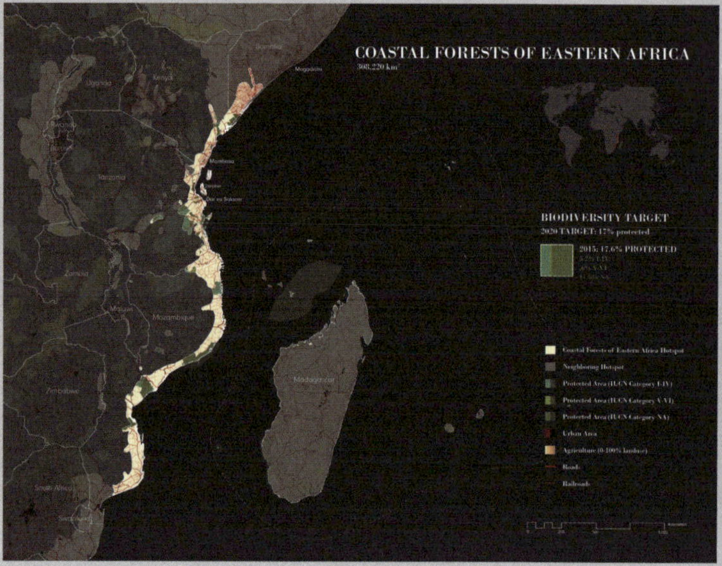
COASTAL FORESTS OF EASTERN AFRICA
308,220 km²
BIODIVERSITY TARGET
2020 TARGET: 17% protected
2015: 17.6% PROTECTED
Coastal Forests of Eastern Africa Hotspot
Neighboring Hotspot
Protected Area (IUCN Category I-IV)
Protected Area (IUCN Category V-VI)
Protected Area (IUCN Category NA)
Urban Area
Agriculture (0-100% landuse)
Roads
Railroads

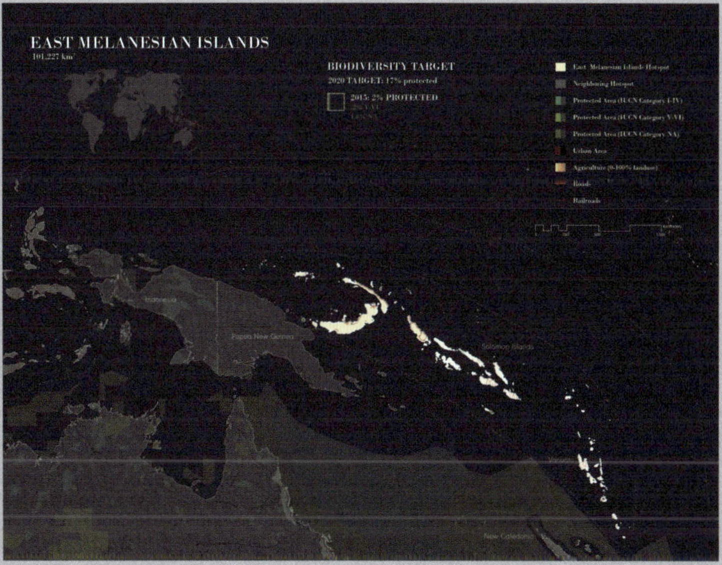
EAST MELANESIAN ISLANDS
101,227 km²
BIODIVERSITY TARGET
2020 TARGET: 17% protected
2015: 2% PROTECTED
East Melanesian Islands Hotspot
Neighboring Hotspot
Protected Area (IUCN Category I-IV)
Protected Area (IUCN Category V-VI)
Protected Area (IUCN Category NA)
Urban Area
Agriculture (0-100% landuse)
Roads
Railroads

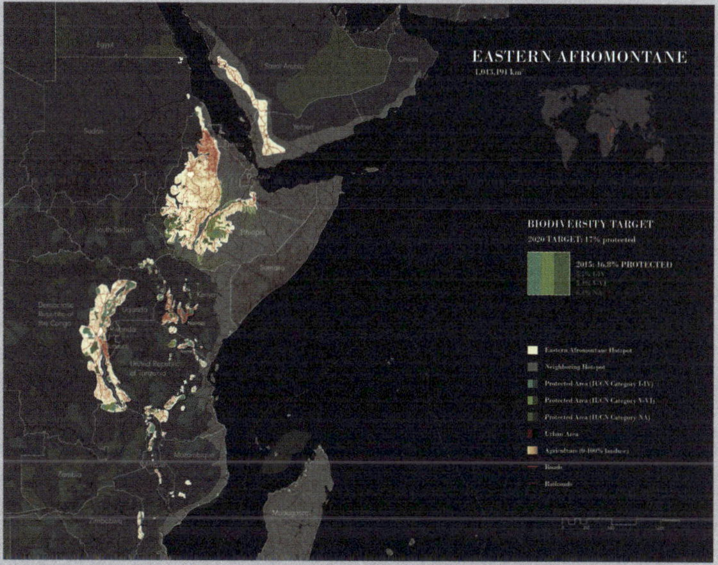
EASTERN AFROMONTANE
1,015,191 km²
BIODIVERSITY TARGET
2020 TARGET: 17% protected
2015: 16.8% PROTECTED
Eastern Afromontane Hotspot
Neighboring Hotspot
Protected Area (IUCN Category I-IV)
Protected Area (IUCN Category V-VI)
Protected Area (IUCN Category NA)
Urban Area
Agriculture (0-100% landuse)
Roads
Railroads

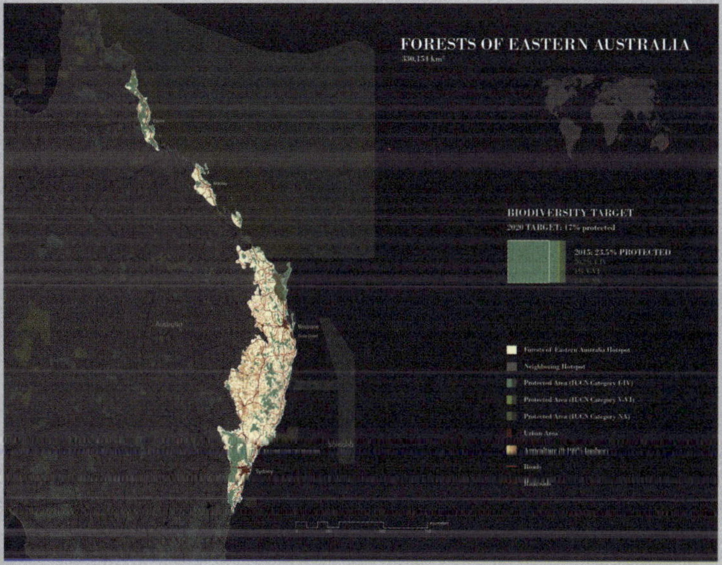
FORESTS OF EASTERN AUSTRALIA
330,154 km²
BIODIVERSITY TARGET
2020 TARGET: 17% protected
2015: 23.5% PROTECTED
Forests of Eastern Australia Hotspot
Neighboring Hotspot
Protected Area (IUCN Category I-IV)
Protected Area (IUCN Category V-VI)
Protected Area (IUCN Category NA)
Urban Area
Roads

GUINEAN FORESTS OF WEST AFRICA
626,397 km²
2015: 17.7% PROTECTED
Neighboring Hotspot
Protected Area (IUCN Category I-IV)
Protected Area (IUCN Category NA)
Agriculture (0-100% landuse)
Railroads

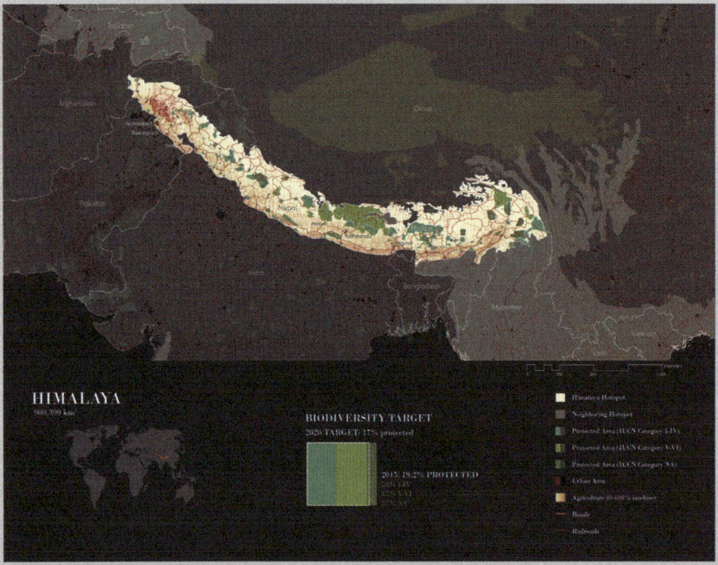
HIMALAYA
BIODIVERSITY TARGET
2020 TARGET: 17% protected
2015: 19.2% PROTECTED
Himalaya Hotspot
Neighboring Hotspot
Protected Area (IUCN Category I-IV)
Protected Area (IUCN Category V-VI)
Protected Area (IUCN Category NA)
Urban Area
Roads
Railroads

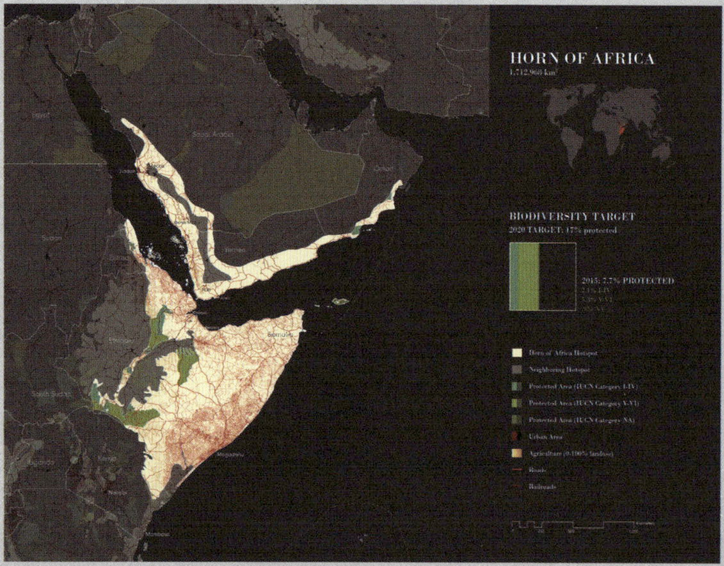
HORN OF AFRICA
BIODIVERSITY TARGET
2020 TARGET: 17% protected
2015: 7.7% PROTECTED
Horn of Africa Hotspot
Neighboring Hotspot
Protected Area (IUCN Category I-IV)
Protected Area (IUCN Category V-VI)
Protected Area (IUCN Category NA)
Urban Area
Agriculture (0-100% landuse)
Roads
Railroads

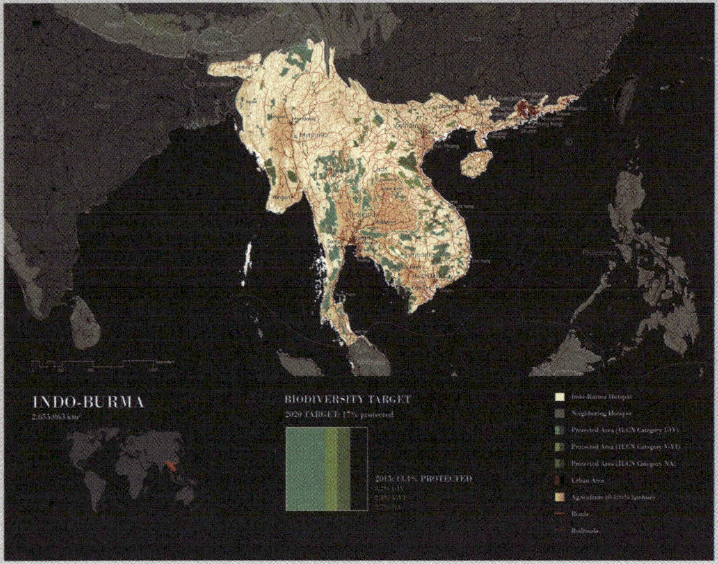
INDO-BURMA
BIODIVERSITY TARGET
2020 TARGET: 17% protected
2015: 13.1% PROTECTED
Neighboring Hotspot
Protected Area (IUCN Category I-IV)
Protected Area (IUCN Category V-VI)
Protected Area (IUCN Category NA)
Urban Area
Roads
Railroads

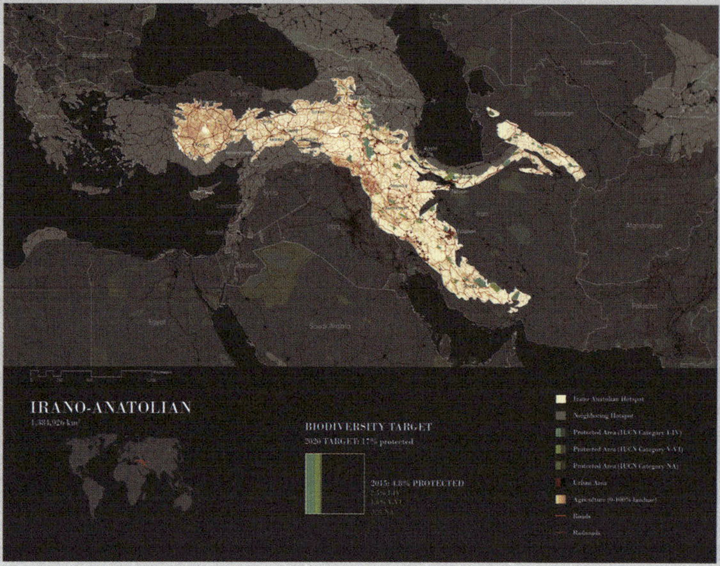
IRANO-ANATOLIAN
BIODIVERSITY TARGET
2020 TARGET: 17% protected
2015: 4.8% PROTECTED
Irano-Anatolian Hotspot
Neighboring Hotspot
Protected Area (IUCN Category I-IV)
Protected Area (IUCN Category V-VI)
Protected Area (IUCN Category NA)
Urban Area
Agriculture (0-100% landuse)
Roads
Railroads

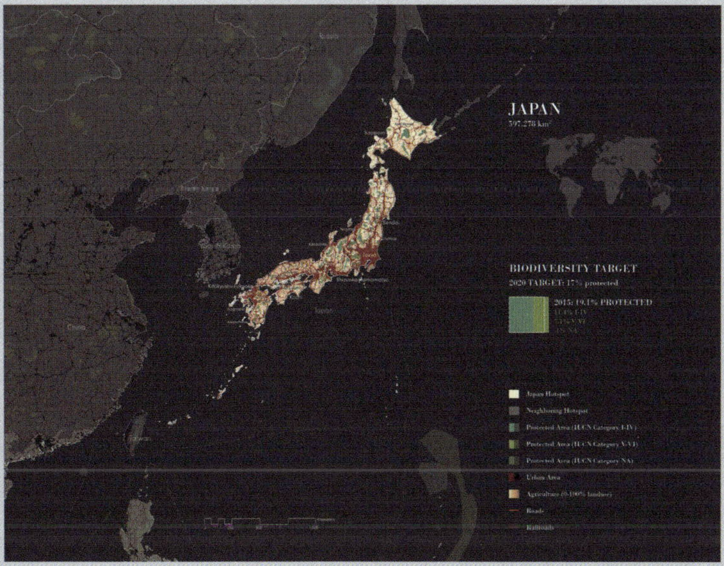
JAPAN
597,278 km²
BIODIVERSITY TARGET
2020 TARGET: 17% protected
2015: 19.1% PROTECTED
Japan Hotspot
Neighboring Hotspot
Protected Area (IUCN Category I-IV)
Protected Area (IUCN Category V-VI)
Protected Area (IUCN Category NA)
Urban Area
Agriculture (0-100% landuse)
Roads
Railroads

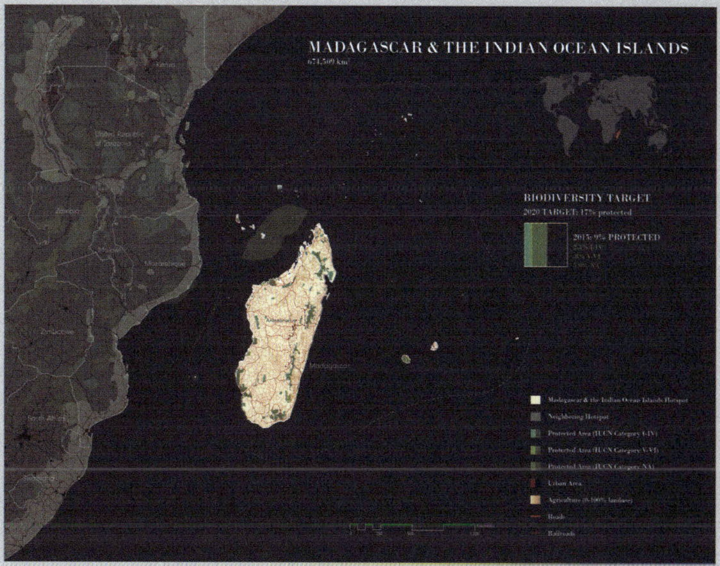
MADAGASCAR & THE INDIAN OCEAN ISLANDS
674,509 km²
BIODIVERSITY TARGET
2020 TARGET: 17% protected
2015: 9% PROTECTED
Madagascar & the Indian Ocean Islands Hotspot
Neighboring Hotspot
Protected Area (IUCN Category I-IV)
Protected Area (IUCN Category V-VI)
Protected Area (IUCN Category NA)
Urban Area
Agriculture (0-100% landuse)
Roads
Railroads

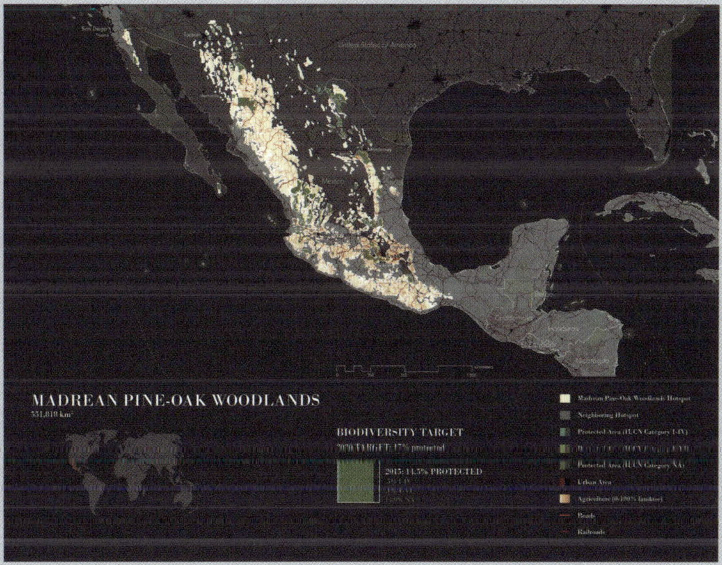
MADREAN PINE-OAK WOODLANDS
531,818 km²
BIODIVERSITY TARGET
2020 TARGET: 17% protected
2015: 14.5% PROTECTED
Madrean Pine-Oak Woodlands Hotspot
Neighboring Hotspot
Protected Area (IUCN Category I-IV)
Protected Area (IUCN Category NA)
Urban Area
Agriculture (0-100% landuse)
Roads
Railroads

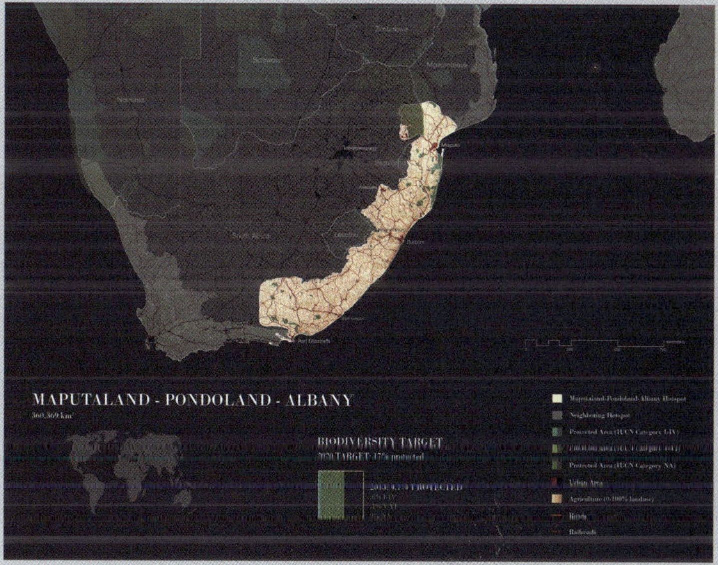
MAPUTALAND - PONDOLAND - ALBANY
360,369 km²
BIODIVERSITY TARGET
2020 TARGET: 17% protected
Maputaland-Pondoland-Albany Hotspot
Neighboring Hotspot
Protected Area (IUCN Category I-IV)
Protected Area (IUCN Category NA)
Urban Area
Agriculture (0-100% landuse)
Roads
Railroads

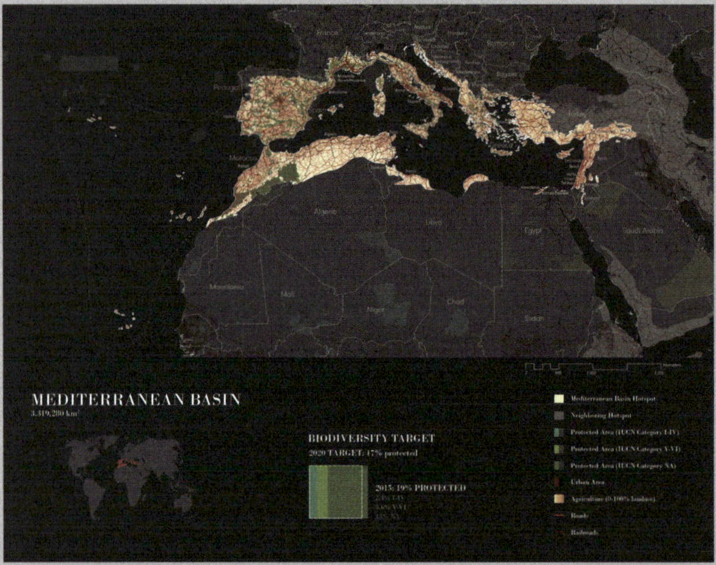

MEDITERRANEAN BASIN
3,319,280 km²
BIODIVERSITY TARGET
2020 TARGET: 17% protected
2015: 19% PROTECTED
Mediterranean Basin Hotspot
Neighboring Hotspot
Protected Area (IUCN Category I-IV)
Protected Area (IUCN Category V-VI)
Protected Area (IUCN Category NA)
Urban Area
Agriculture (0-100% landuse)
Roads
Railroads

MESOAMERICA
1,236,453 km²
BIODIVERSITY TARGET
2020 TARGET: 17% protected
2015: 19.3% PROTECTED
Mesoamerica Hotspot
Neighboring Hotspot
Protected Area (IUCN Category I-IV)
Protected Area (IUCN Category V-VI)
Protected Area (IUCN Category NA)
Urban Area
Agriculture (0-100% landuse)
Roads
Railroads

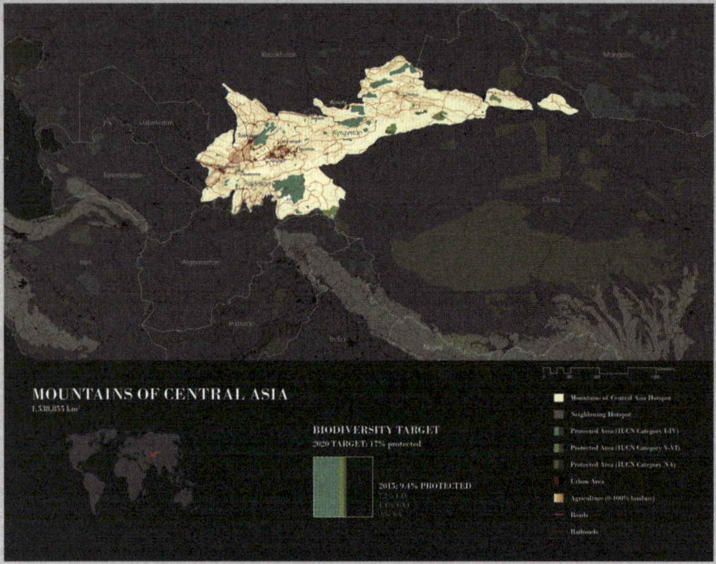

MOUNTAINS OF CENTRAL ASIA
1,538,855 km²
BIODIVERSITY TARGET
2020 TARGET: 17% protected
2015: 9.4% PROTECTED
Mountains of Central Asia Hotspot
Neighboring Hotspot
Protected Area (IUCN Category I-IV)
Protected Area (IUCN Category V-VI)
Protected Area (IUCN Category NA)
Urban Area
Agriculture (0-100% landuse)
Roads
Railroads

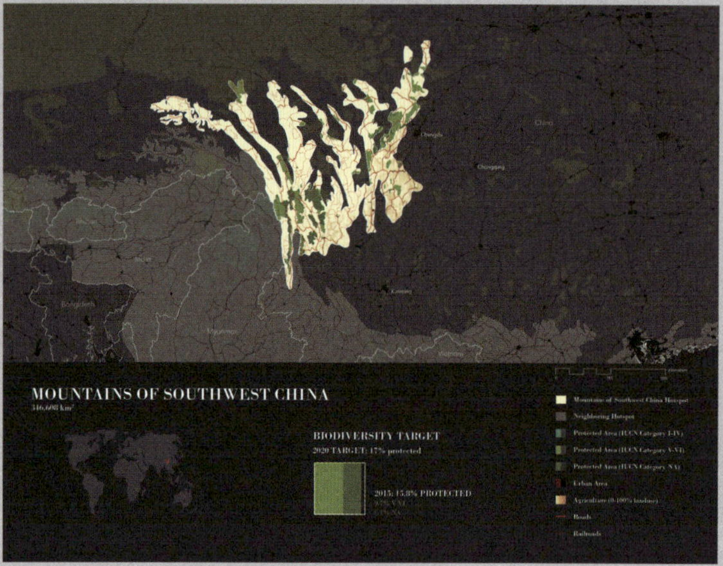

MOUNTAINS OF SOUTHWEST CHINA
346,608 km²
BIODIVERSITY TARGET
2020 TARGET: 17% protected
2015: 15.8% PROTECTED
Mountains of Southwest China Hotspot
Neighboring Hotspot
Protected Area (IUCN Category I-IV)
Protected Area (IUCN Category V-VI)
Protected Area (IUCN Category NA)
Urban Area
Agriculture (0-100% landuse)
Roads
Railroads

NEW CALEDONIA
21,779 km²
BIODIVERSITY TARGET
2020 TARGET: 17% protected
2015: 15.1% PROTECTED
New Caledonia Hotspot
Neighboring Hotspot
Protected Area (IUCN Category I-IV)
Protected Area (IUCN Category V-VI)
Protected Area (IUCN Category NA)
Urban Area
Agriculture (0-100% landuse)
Roads
Railroads

NEW ZEALAND
488,327 km²
BIODIVERSITY TARGET
2020 TARGET: 17% protected
2015: 33.4% PROTECTED
New Zealand Hotspot
Neighboring Hotspot
Protected Area (IUCN Category I-IV)
Protected Area (IUCN Category V-VI)
Protected Area (IUCN Category NA)
Urban Area
Agriculture (0-100% landuse)
Roads
Railroads

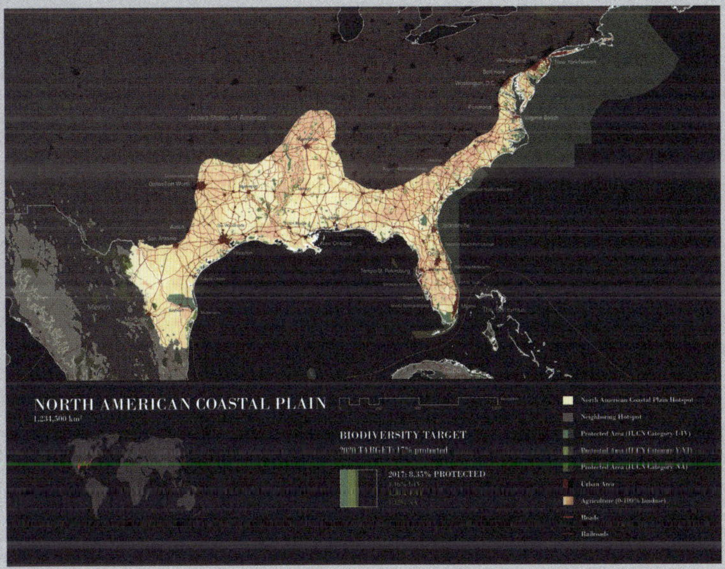
NORTH AMERICAN COASTAL PLAIN
1,234,500 km²
BIODIVERSITY TARGET
2020 TARGET: 17% protected
2017: 8.35% PROTECTED
North American Coastal Plain Hotspot
Neighboring Hotspot
Protected Area (IUCN Category I-IV)
Protected Area (IUCN Category NA)
Urban Area
Agriculture (0-100% landuse)
Roads
Railroads

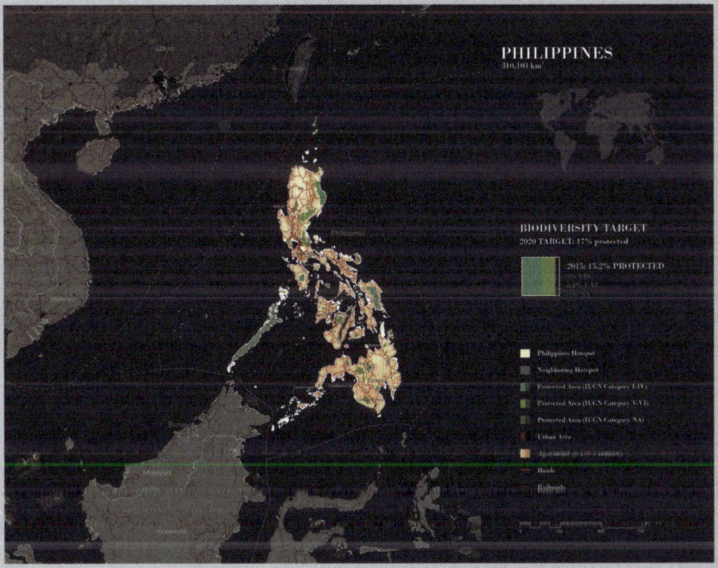
PHILIPPINES
310,103 km²
BIODIVERSITY TARGET
2020 TARGET: 17% protected
2015: 15.2% PROTECTED
Philippines Hotspot
Neighboring Hotspot
Protected Area (IUCN Category I-IV)
Protected Area (IUCN Category V-VI)
Protected Area (IUCN Category NA)
Urban Area
Roads
Railroads

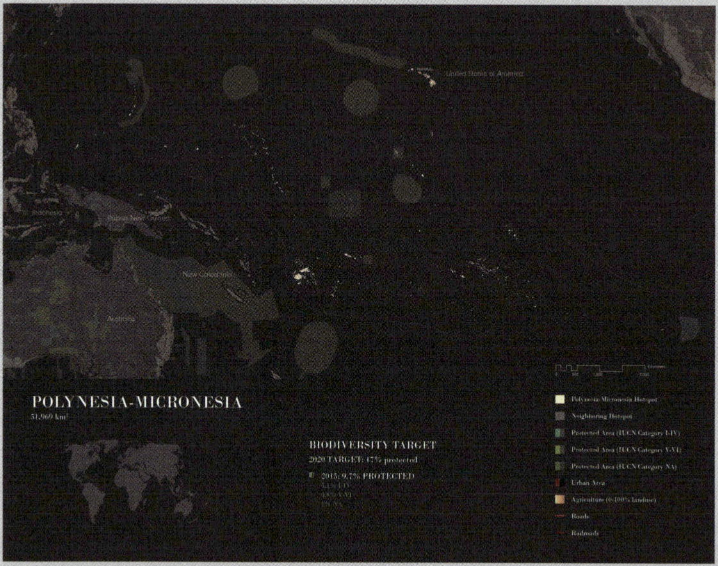
POLYNESIA-MICRONESIA
51,969 km²
BIODIVERSITY TARGET
2020 TARGET: 17% protected
2015: 9.7% PROTECTED
Polynesia-Micronesia Hotspot
Neighboring Hotspot
Protected Area (IUCN Category I-IV)
Protected Area (IUCN Category V-VI)
Protected Area (IUCN Category NA)
Urban Area
Agriculture (0-100% landuse)
Roads
Railroads
New Caledonia
Australia

SOUTHWEST AUSTRALIA
492,455 km²
BIODIVERSITY TARGET
2020 TARGET: 17% protected
2015: 16.4% PROTECTED
Southwest Australia Hotspot
Neighboring Hotspot
Protected Area (IUCN Category I-IV)
Protected Area (IUCN Category V-VI)
Protected Area (IUCN Category NA)
Urban Area
Agriculture (0-100% landuse)
Roads
Railroads

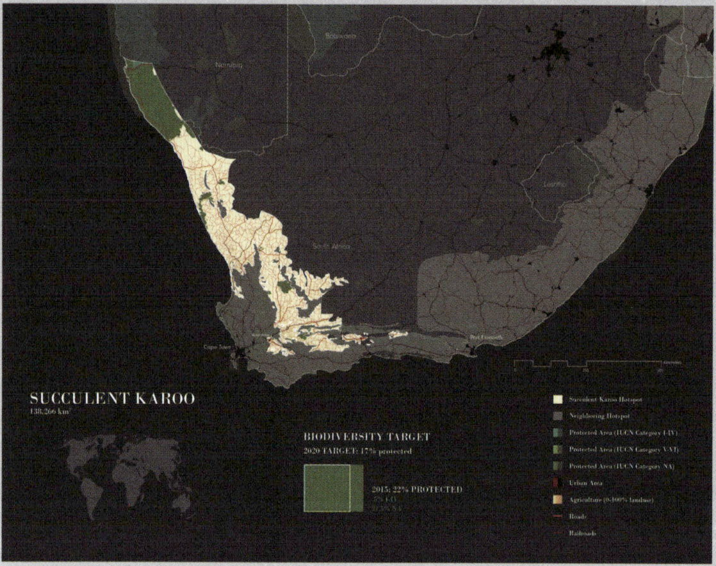
SUCCULENT KAROO
138,266 km²
BIODIVERSITY TARGET
2020 TARGET: 17% protected
2015: 22% PROTECTED
Succulent Karoo Hotspot
Neighboring Hotspot
Protected Area (IUCN Category I-IV)
Protected Area (IUCN Category V-VI)
Protected Area (IUCN Category NA)
Urban Area
Agriculture (0-100% landuse)
Roads
Railroads
Cape Town
Port Elizabeth

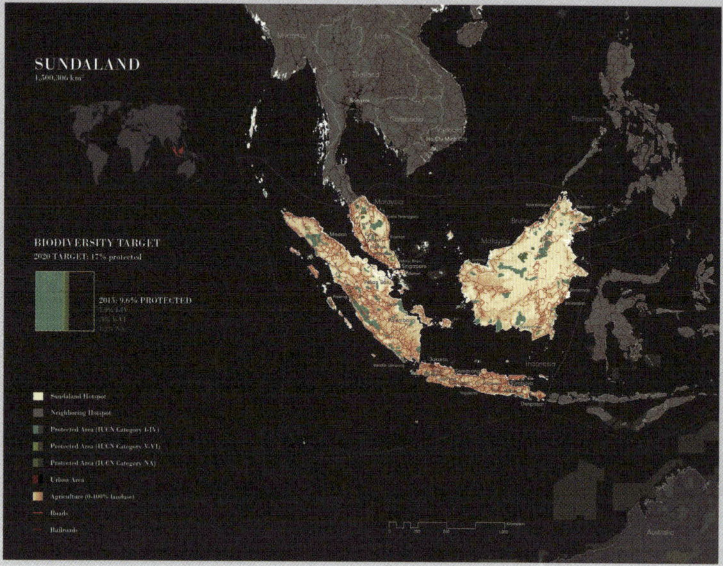
SUNDALAND
1,500,306 km²
BIODIVERSITY TARGET
2020 TARGET: 17% protected
2015: 9.6% PROTECTED
Sundaland Hotspot
Neighboring Hotspot
Protected Area (IUCN Category I-IV)
Protected Area (IUCN Category V-VI)
Protected Area (IUCN Category NA)
Urban Area
Agriculture (0-100% landuse)
Roads
Railroads
Malaysia
Indonesia
Philippines
Singapore
Jakarta
Australia

TROPICAL ANDES
1,656,935 km²
BIODIVERSITY TARGET
2020 TARGET: 17% protected
2015: 23.8% PROTECTED
Tropical Andes Hotspot
Neighboring Hotspot
Protected Area (IUCN Category I-IV)
Protected Area (IUCN Category V-VI)
Protected Area (IUCN Category NA)
Urban Area
Agriculture (0-100% landuse)
Roads
Railroads

TUMBES - CHOCO - MAGDALENA
276,395 km²
BIODIVERSITY TARGET
2020 TARGET: 17% protected
2015: 11.9% PROTECTED
Tumbes-Choco-Magdalena Hotspot
Neighboring Hotspot
Protected Area (IUCN Category I-IV)
Protected Area (IUCN Category V-VI)
Protected Area (IUCN Category NA)
Urban Area
Agriculture (0-100% landuse)
Roads
Railroads

WALLACEA
BIODIVERSITY TARGET
2020 TARGET: 17% protected
2015: 9.5% PROTECTED
Wallacea Hotspot
Neighboring Hotspot
Protected Area (IUCN Category I-IV)
Protected Area (IUCN Category V-VI)
Urban Area
Agriculture (0-100% landuse)
Roads
Railroads

WESTERN GHATS & SRI LANKA
BIODIVERSITY TARGET
2020 TARGET: 17% protected
2015: 20.2% PROTECTED
Western Ghats & Sri Lanka Hotspot
Neighboring Hotspot
Protected Area (IUCN Category I-IV)
Urban Area
Agriculture (0-100% landuse)
Roads
Railroads

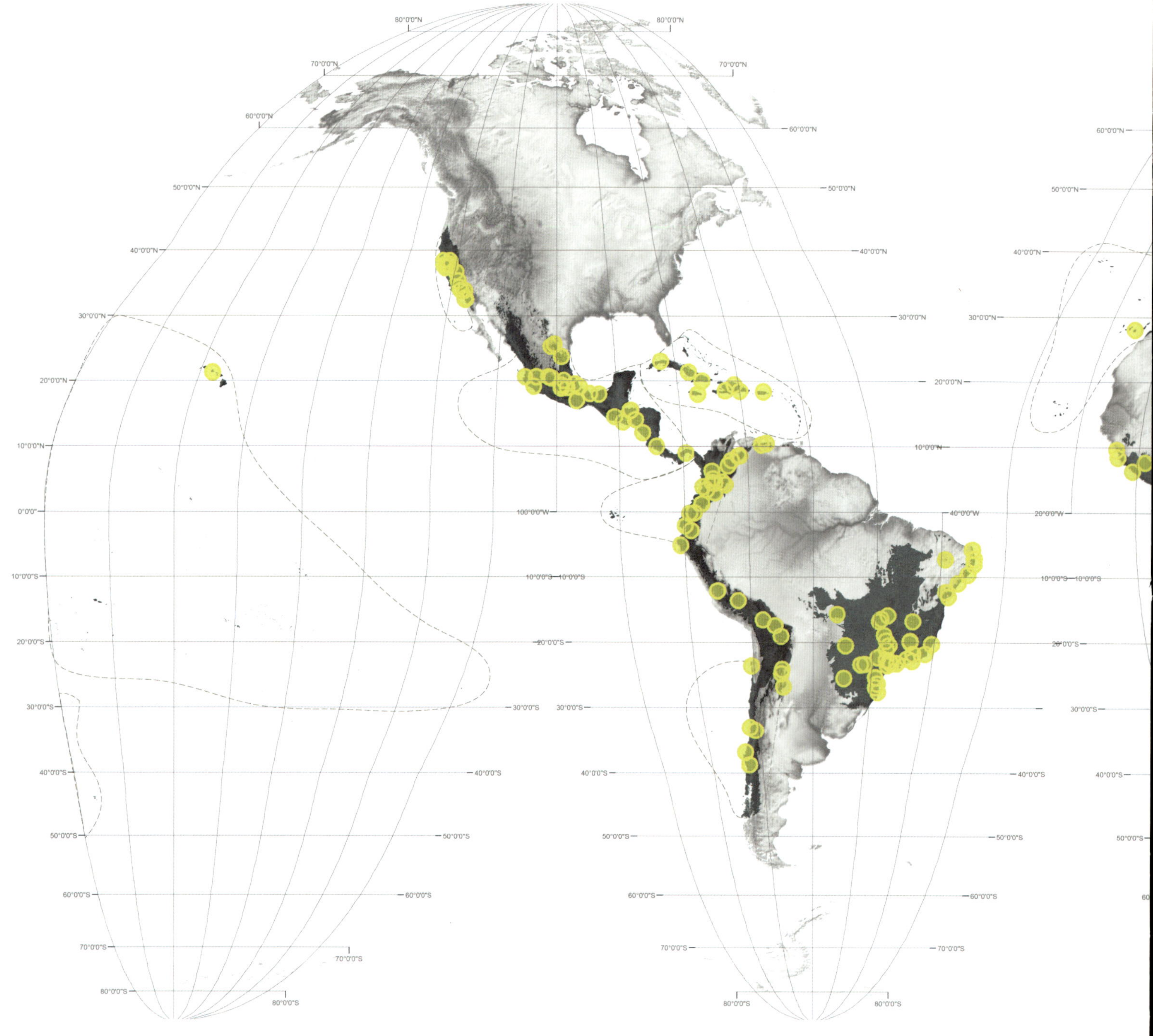

World map from "The Hotspots Cities Project" (2017–2021) showing that 383 of 422 cities in the world's biodiversity hotspots are growing on a direct collision course with remnant habitat and endangered species [149].

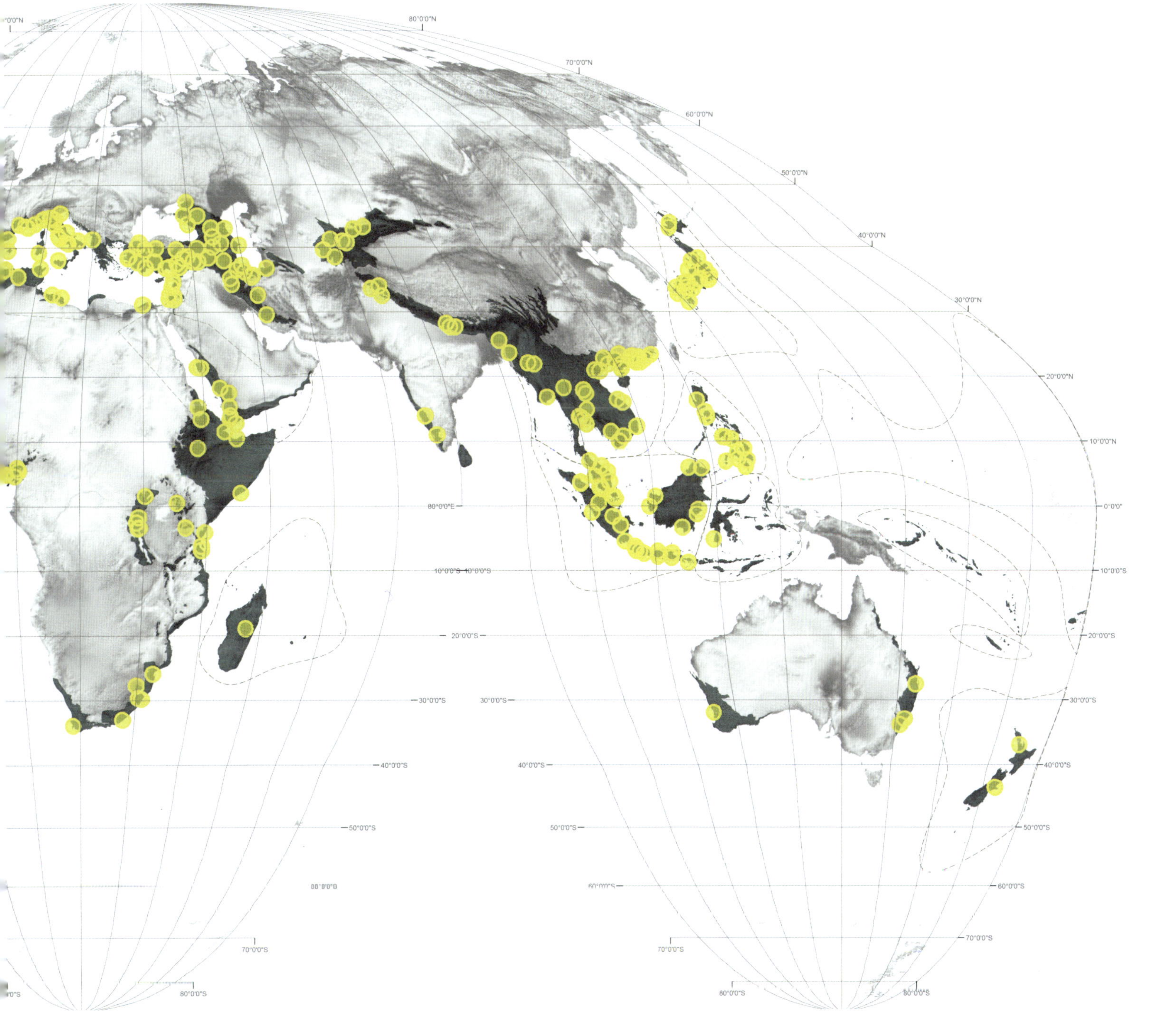

80°0'0"N
70°0'0"N
60°0'0"N
50°0'0"N
40°0'0"N
30°0'0"N
20°0'0"N
10°0'0"N
0°0'0"
80°0'0"E
10°0'0"S
20°0'0"S
30°0'0"S
40°0'0"S
50°0'0"S
60°0'0"S
70°0'0"S
80°0'0"S

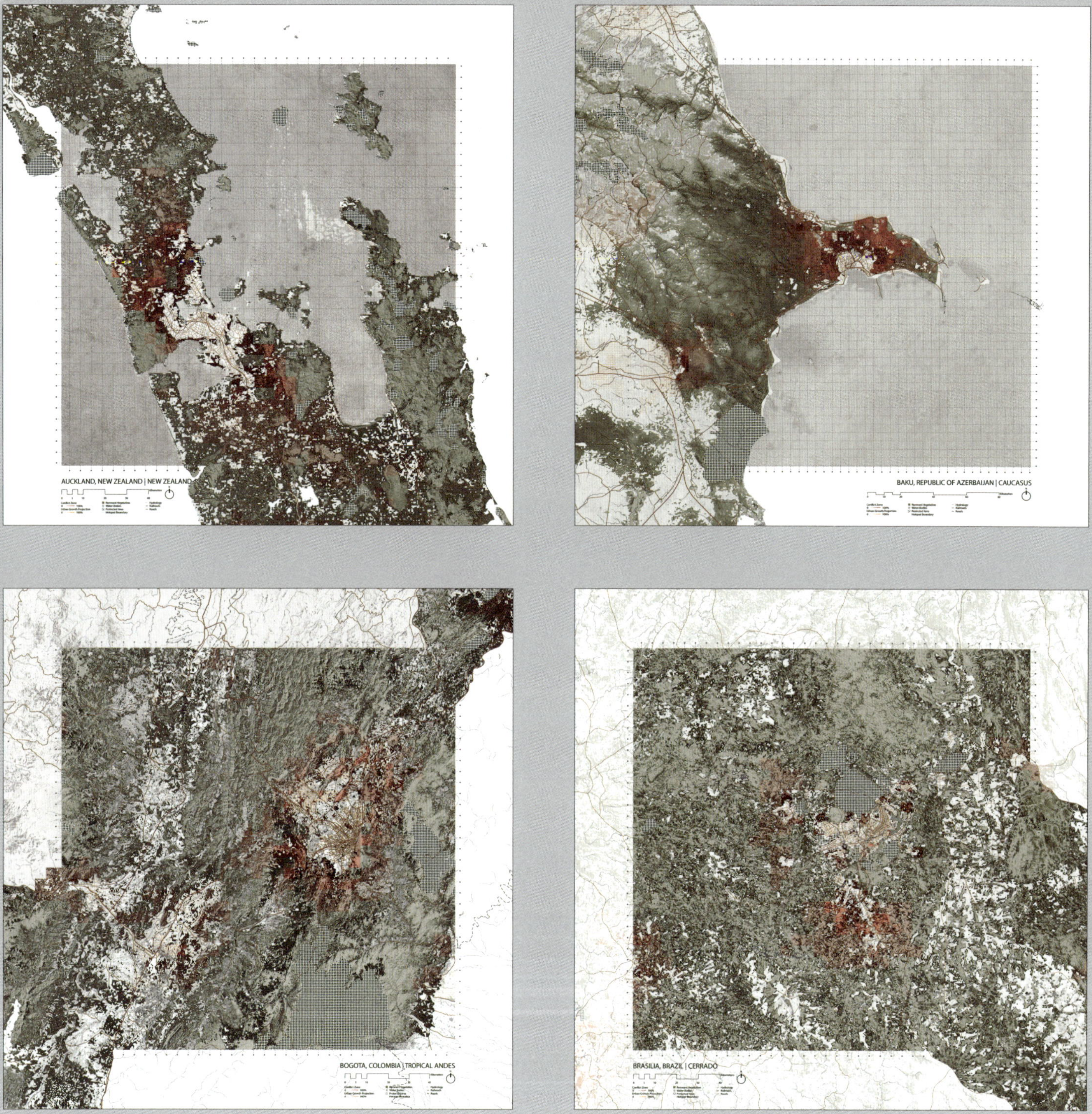

Mapping from "The Hotspots Cities Project" showing the fastest-growing cities in the world's biodiversity hotspots. These maps show (in red) areas of imminent conflict between urban growth projected to 2050 and endangered species [149].

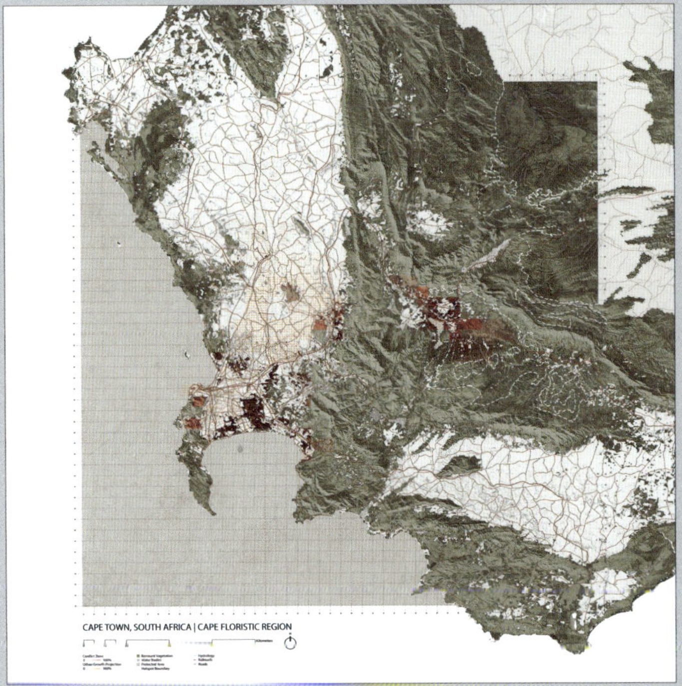
CAPE TOWN, SOUTH AFRICA | CAPE FLORISTIC REGION

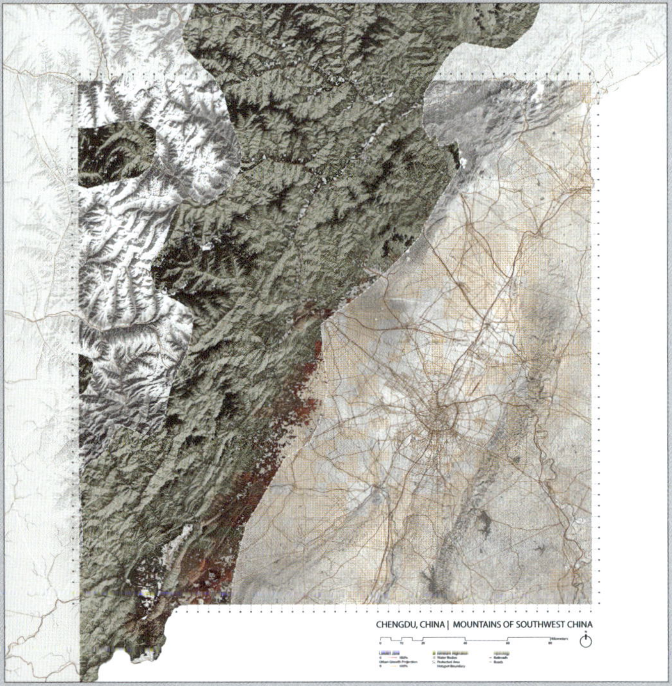
CHENGDU, CHINA | MOUNTAINS OF SOUTHWEST CHINA

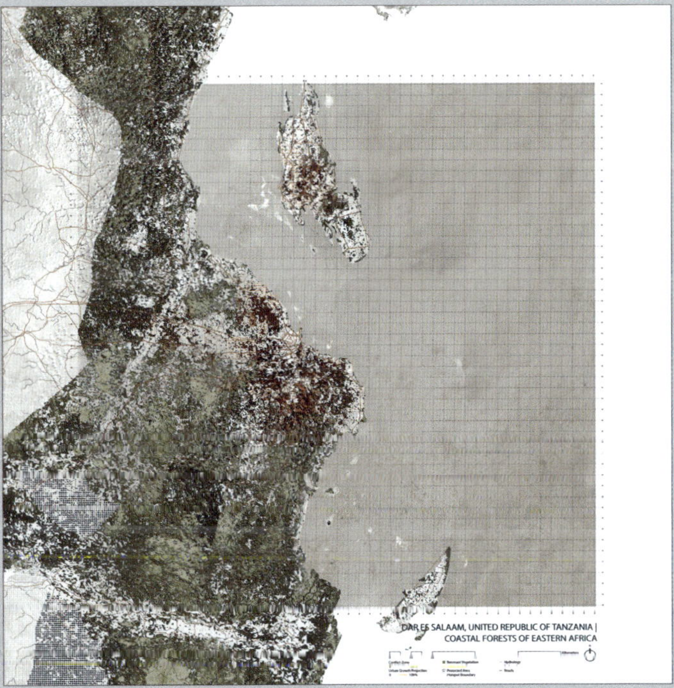
DAR ES SALAAM, UNITED REPUBLIC OF TANZANIA |
COASTAL FORESTS OF EASTERN AFRICA

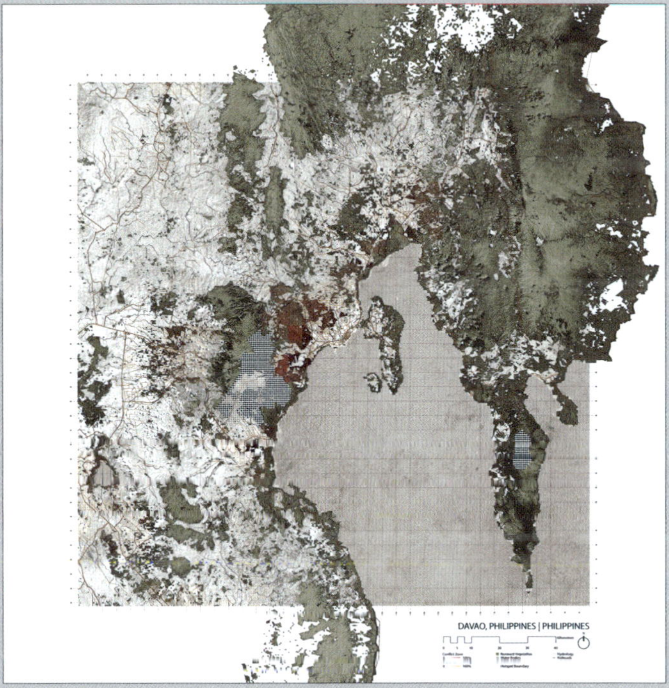
DAVAO, PHILIPPINES | PHILIPPINES

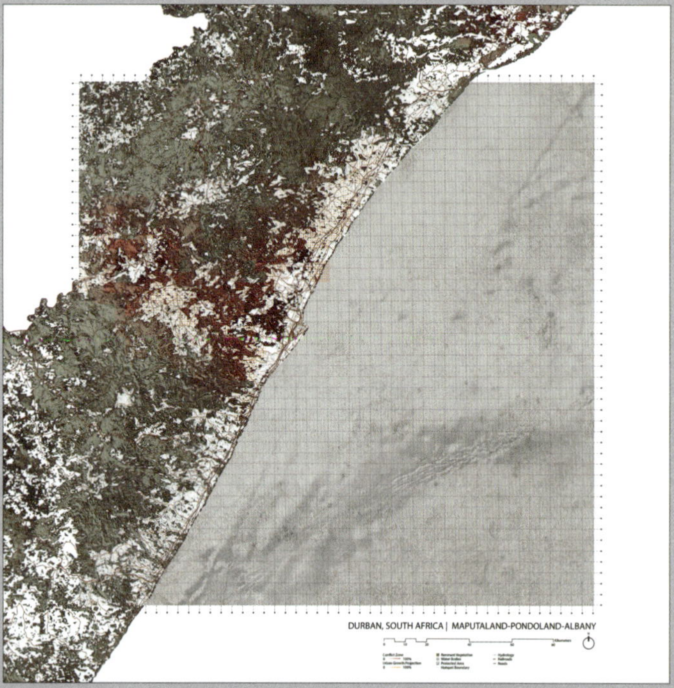
DURBAN, SOUTH AFRICA | MAPUTALAND-PONDOLAND-ALBANY

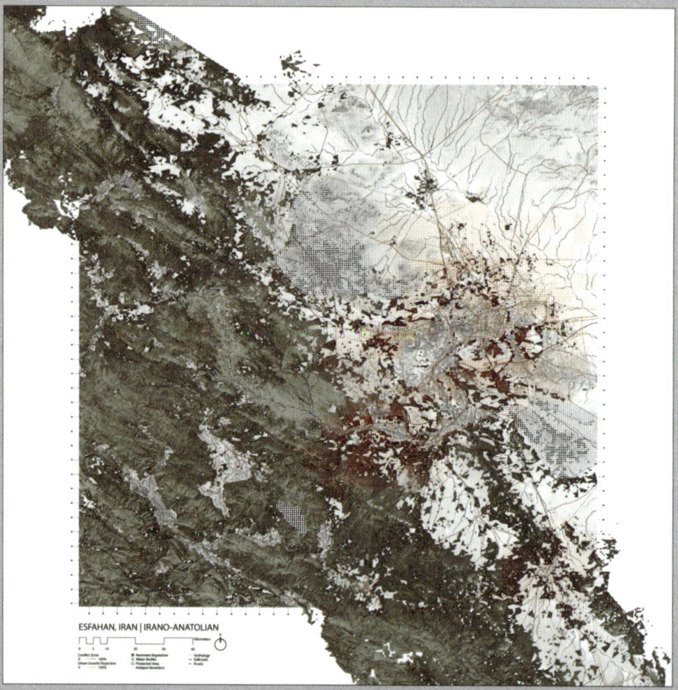
ESFAHAN, IRAN | IRANO-ANATOLIAN

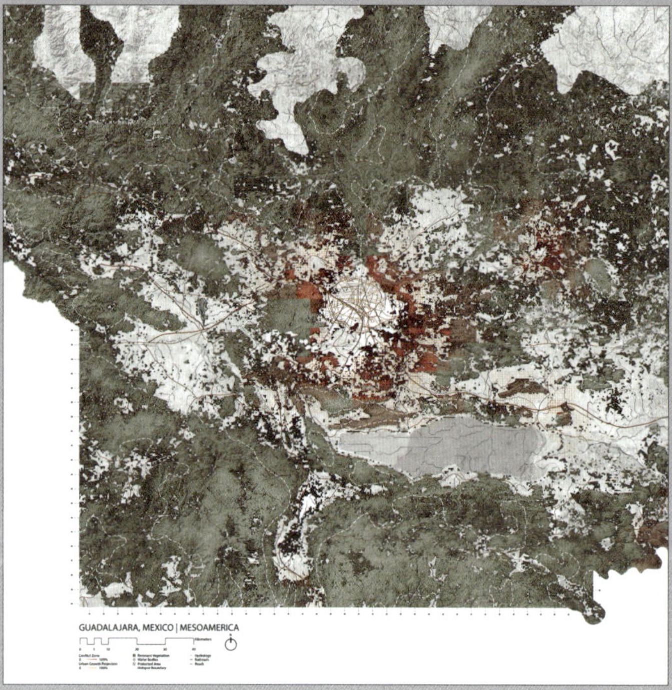
GUADALAJARA, MEXICO | MESOAMERICA

GUAYAQUIL, ECUADOR | TUMBES-CHOCO-MAGDALENA

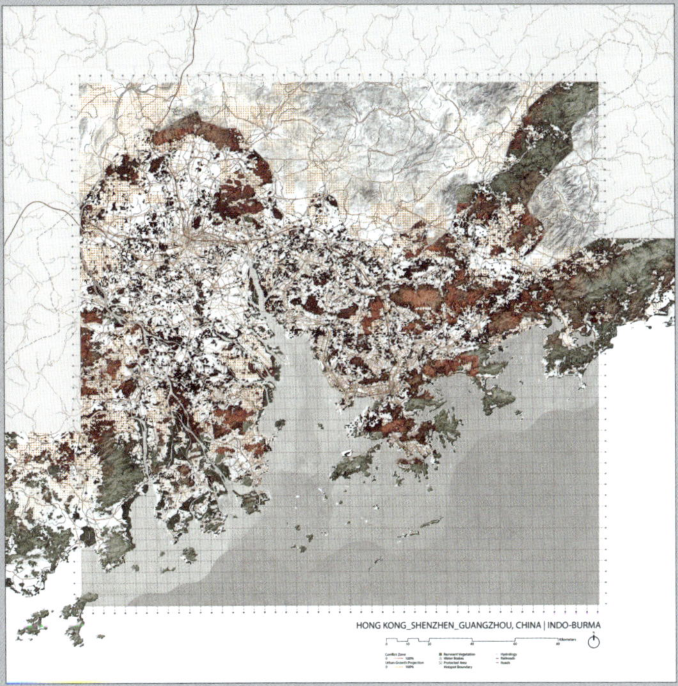
HONG KONG_SHENZHEN_GUANGZHOU, CHINA | INDO-BURMA

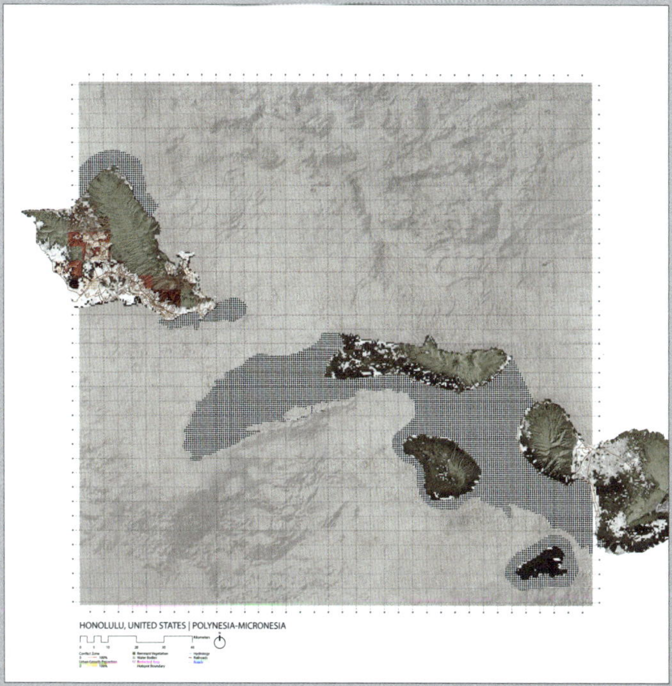
HONOLULU, UNITED STATES | POLYNESIA-MICRONESIA

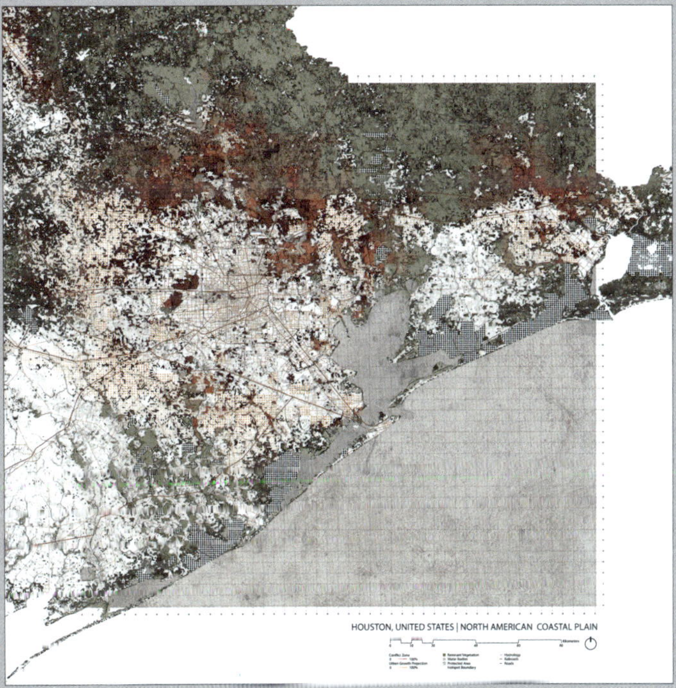
HOUSTON, UNITED STATES | NORTH AMERICAN COASTAL PLAIN

JAKARTA, INDONESIA | SUNDALAND

LAGOS, NIGERIA | GUINEAN FORESTS OF WEST AFRICA

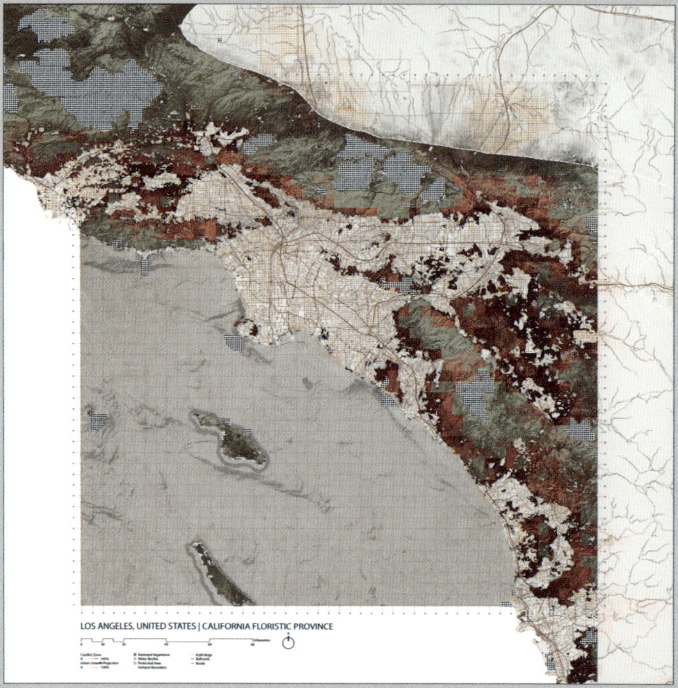
LOS ANGELES, UNITED STATES | CALIFORNIA FLORISTIC PROVINCE

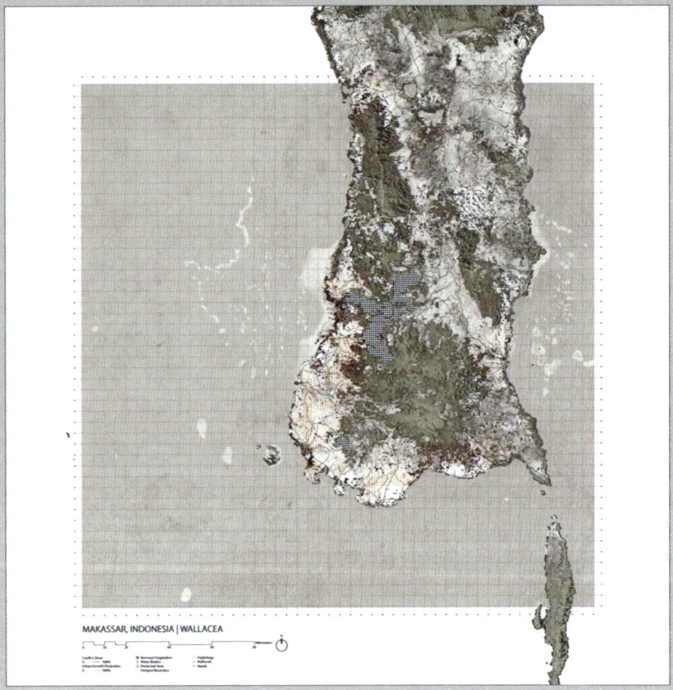
MAKASSAR, INDONESIA | WALLACEA

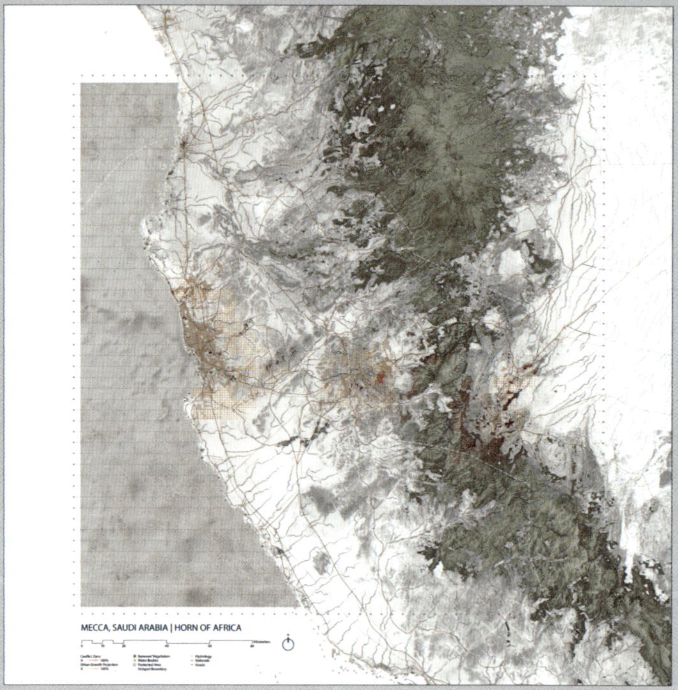
MECCA, SAUDI ARABIA | HORN OF AFRICA

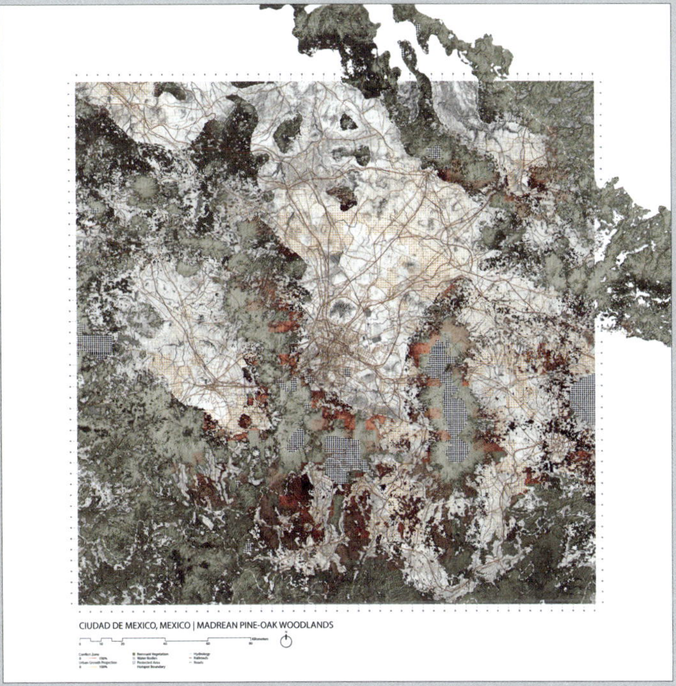
CIUDAD DE MEXICO, MEXICO | MADREAN PINE-OAK WOODLANDS

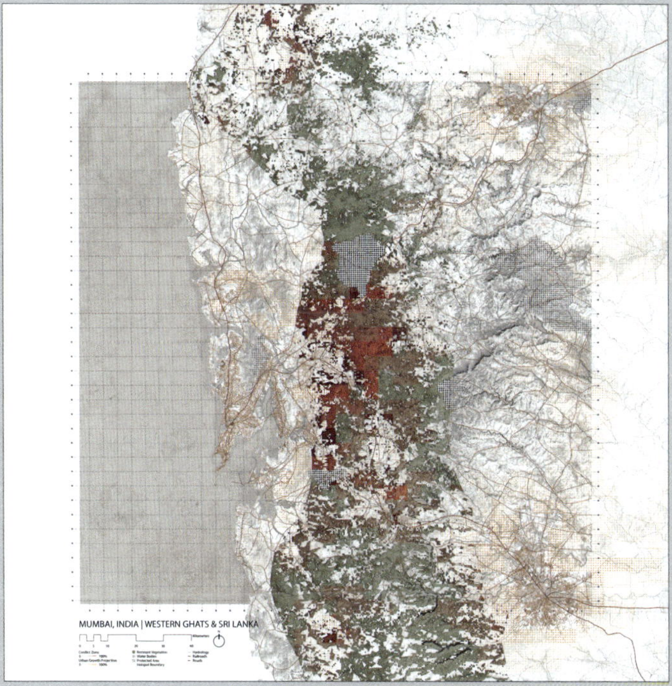
MUMBAI, INDIA | WESTERN GHATS & SRI LANKA

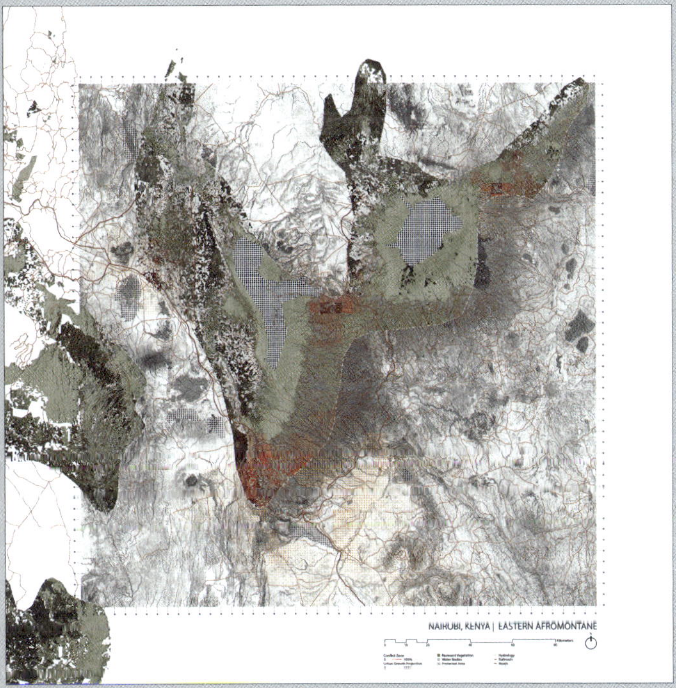
NAIROBI, KENYA | EASTERN AFROMONTANE

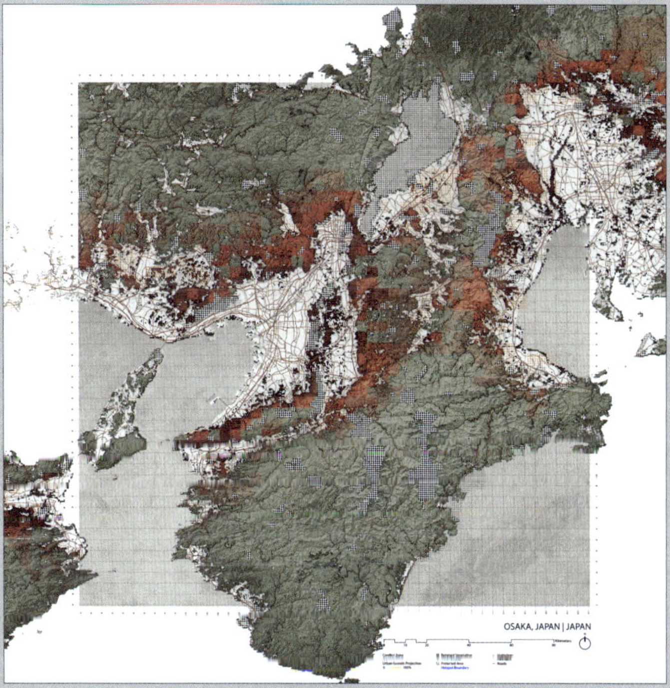
OSAKA, JAPAN | JAPAN

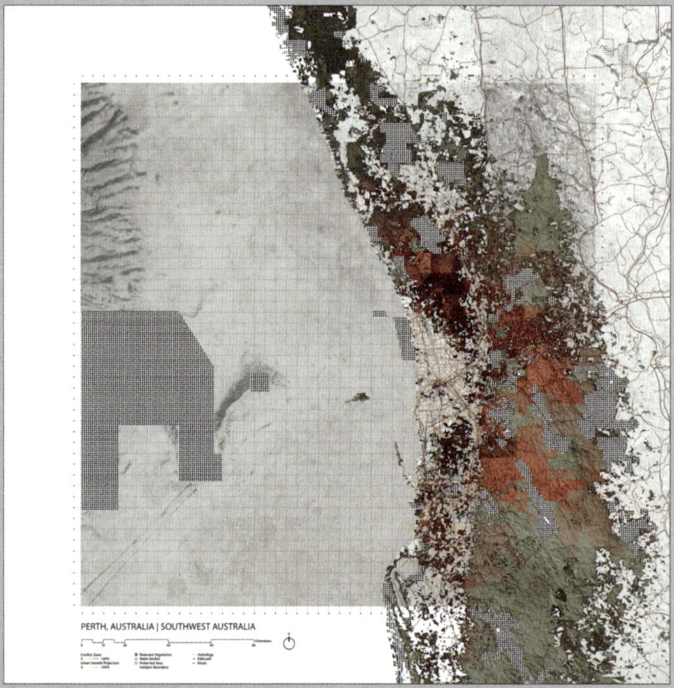
PERTH, AUSTRALIA | SOUTHWEST AUSTRALIA

PORT-AU-PRINCE, HAITI | CARIBBEAN

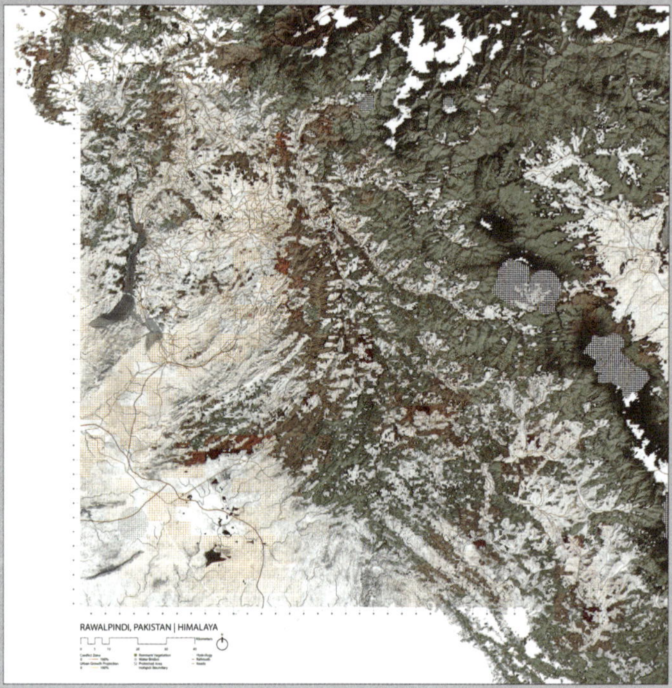
RAWALPINDI, PAKISTAN | HIMALAYA

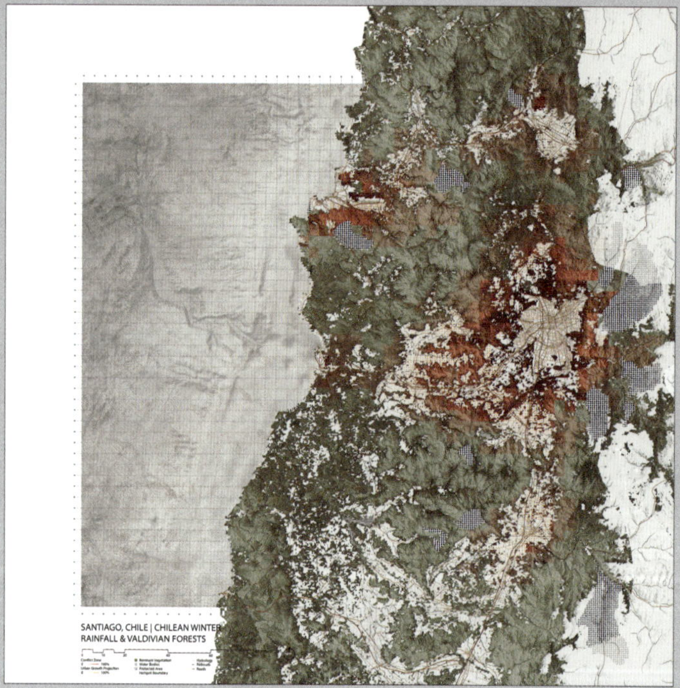
SANTIAGO, CHILE | CHILEAN WINTER
RAINFALL & VALDIVIAN FORESTS

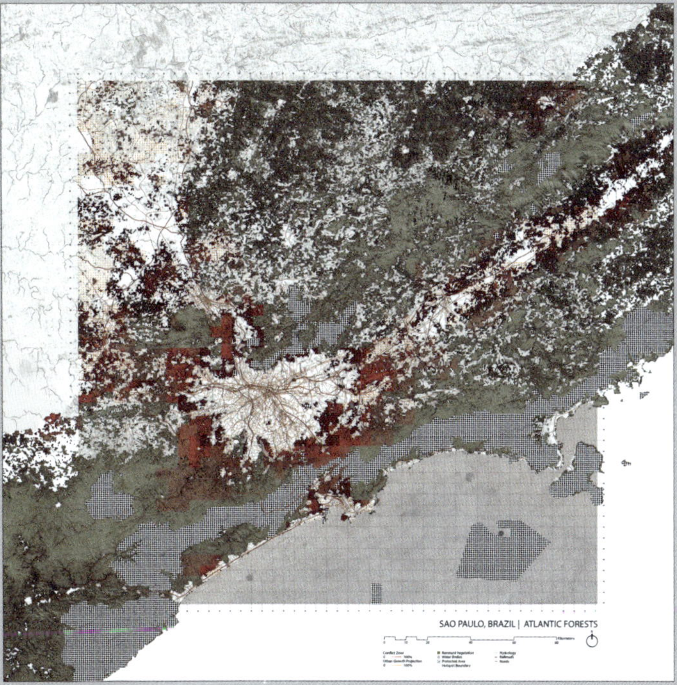
SAO PAULO, BRAZIL | ATLANTIC FORESTS

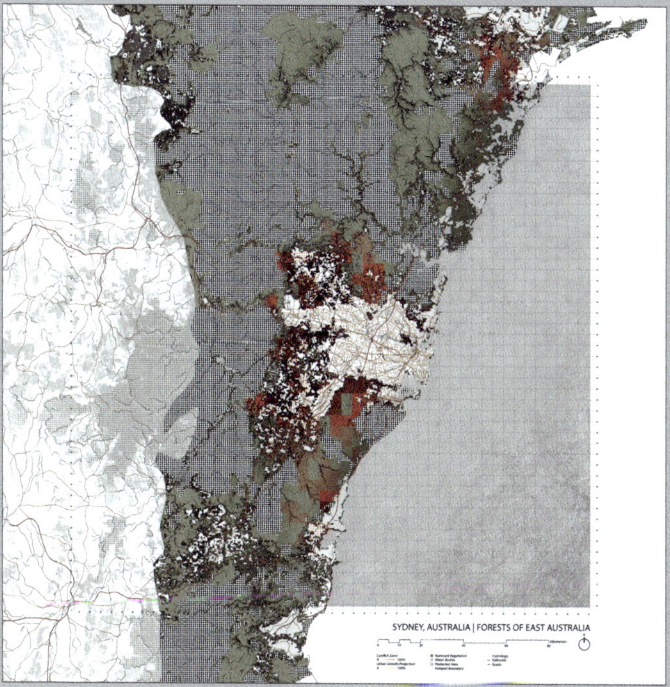
SYDNEY, AUSTRALIA | FORESTS OF EAST AUSTRALIA

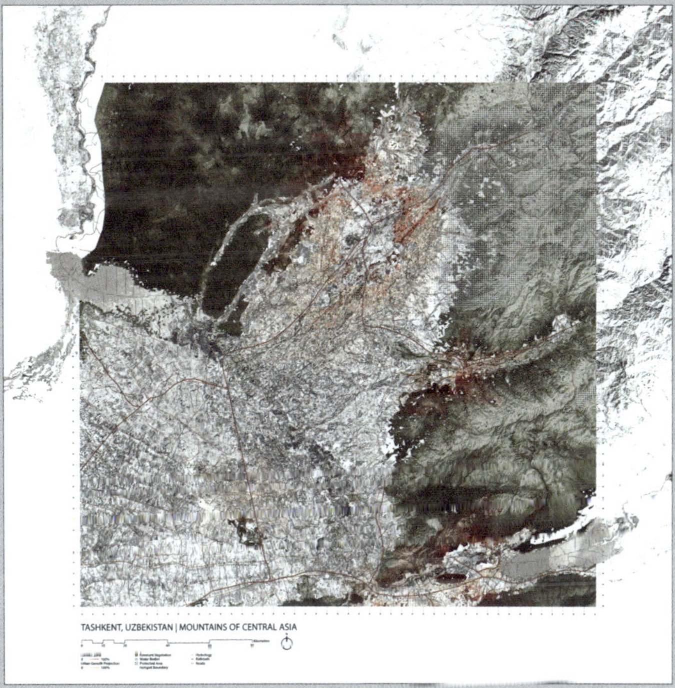
TASHKENT, UZBEKISTAN | MOUNTAINS OF CENTRAL ASIA

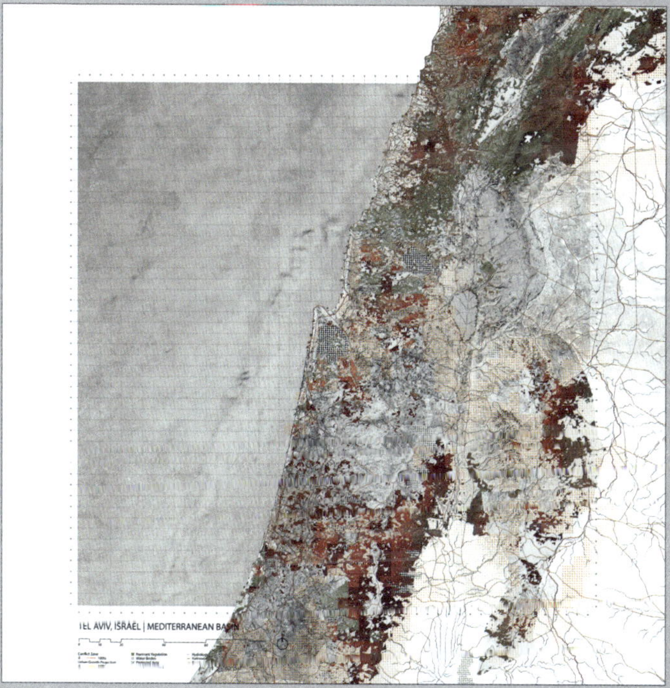
TEL AVIV, ISRAEL | MEDITERRANEAN BA

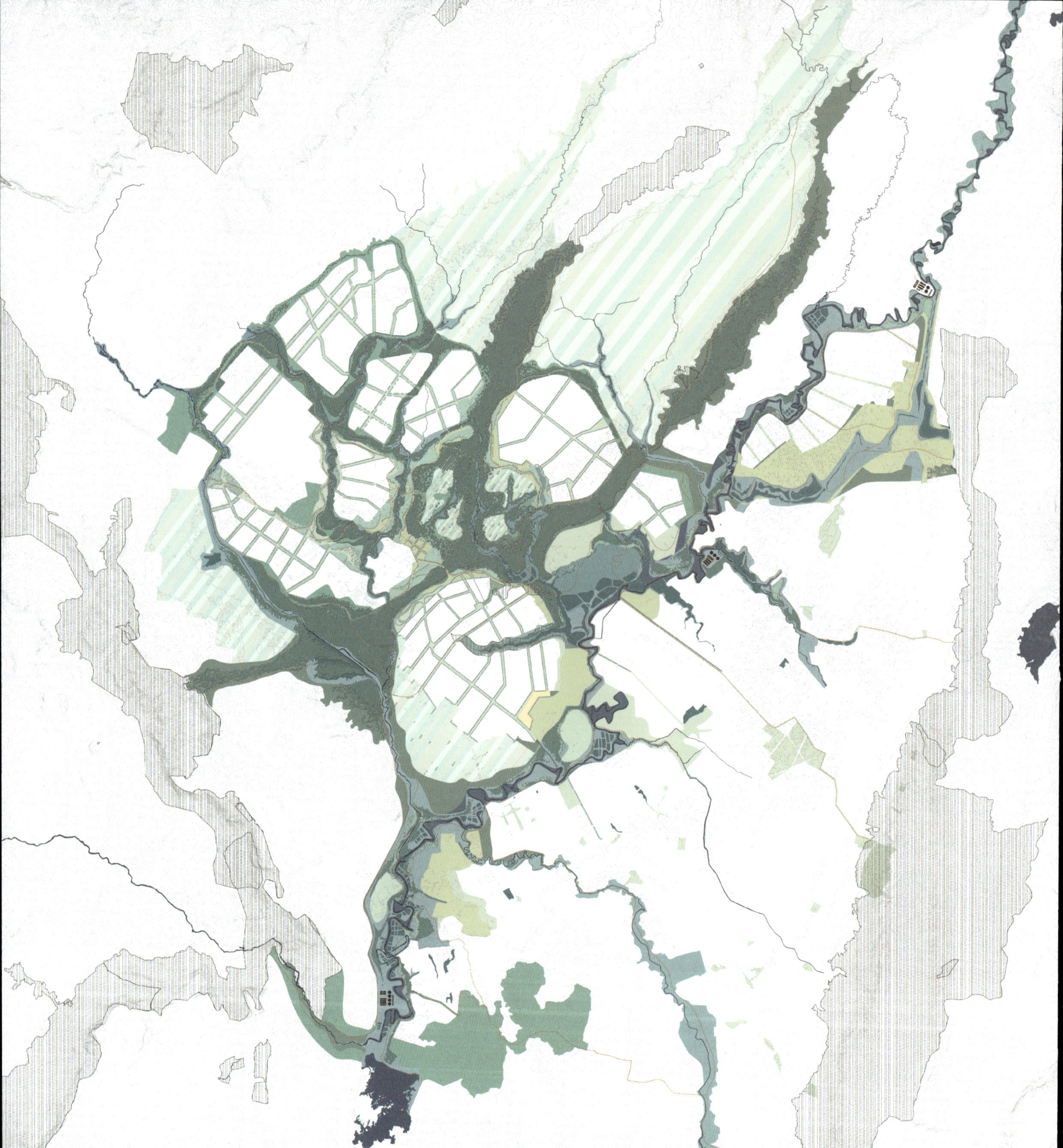

Master planning concept for the 2050 urban growth of Bogotá, Columbia, which seeks to reconcile an ideal ecological framework (*left*) with an ideal urban framework (*right*) and accommodate both formal and informal development [149].

Combined master plan concept for the 2050 urban growth of Bogotá, Colombia, from the "Bogotá – La Sabana 2050" studio (2018). At the heart of the new city is a biodiversity research park and wetland system eight times as large as Central Park. [149].

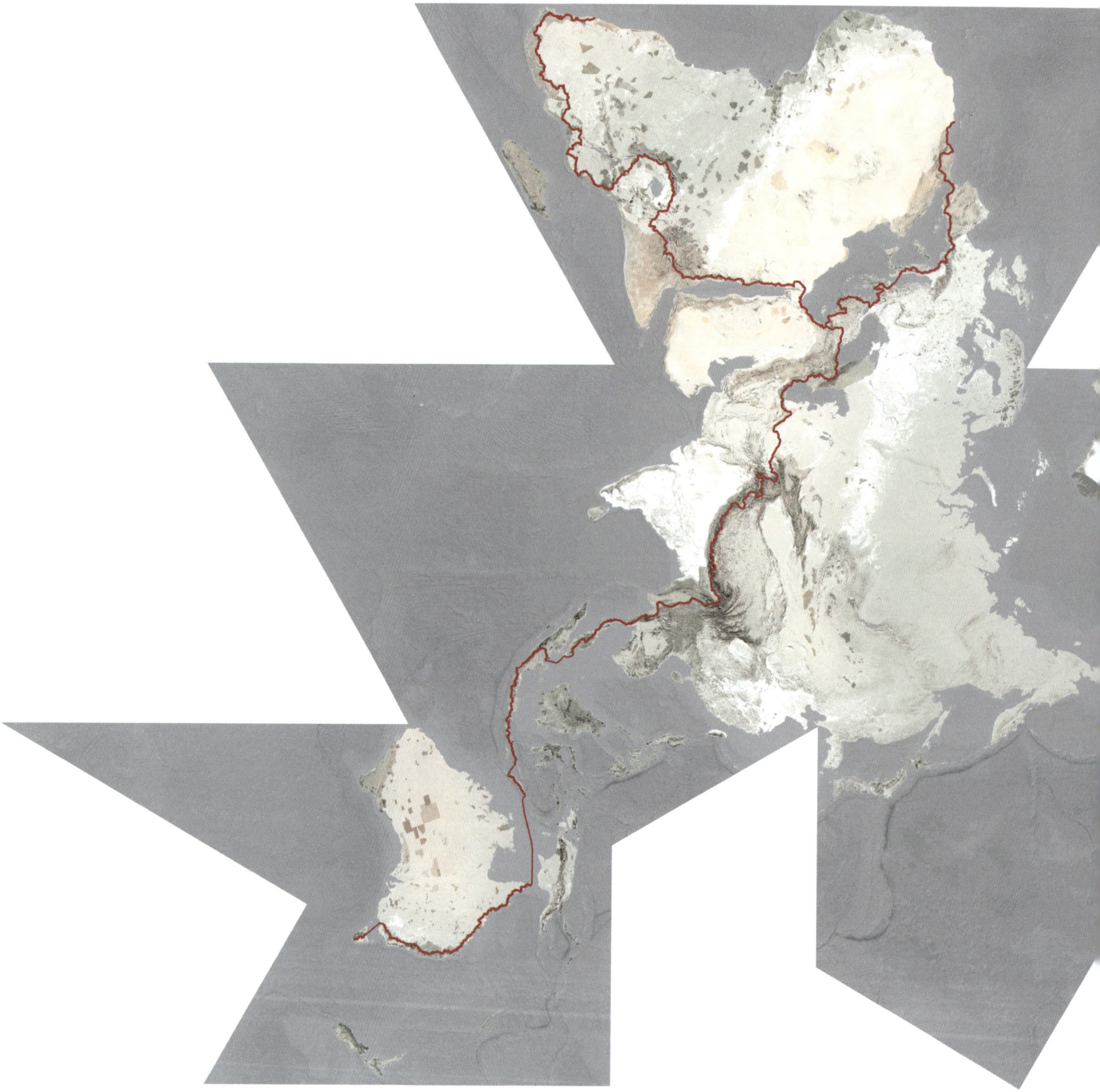

Overview of "The World Park Project" (2015–). The concept of creating a World Park begins with three global walking and cycling trails connecting protected areas through 19 biodiversity hotspots across 55 nations, and serving as catalysts for a globally coordinated landscape restoration program [150].

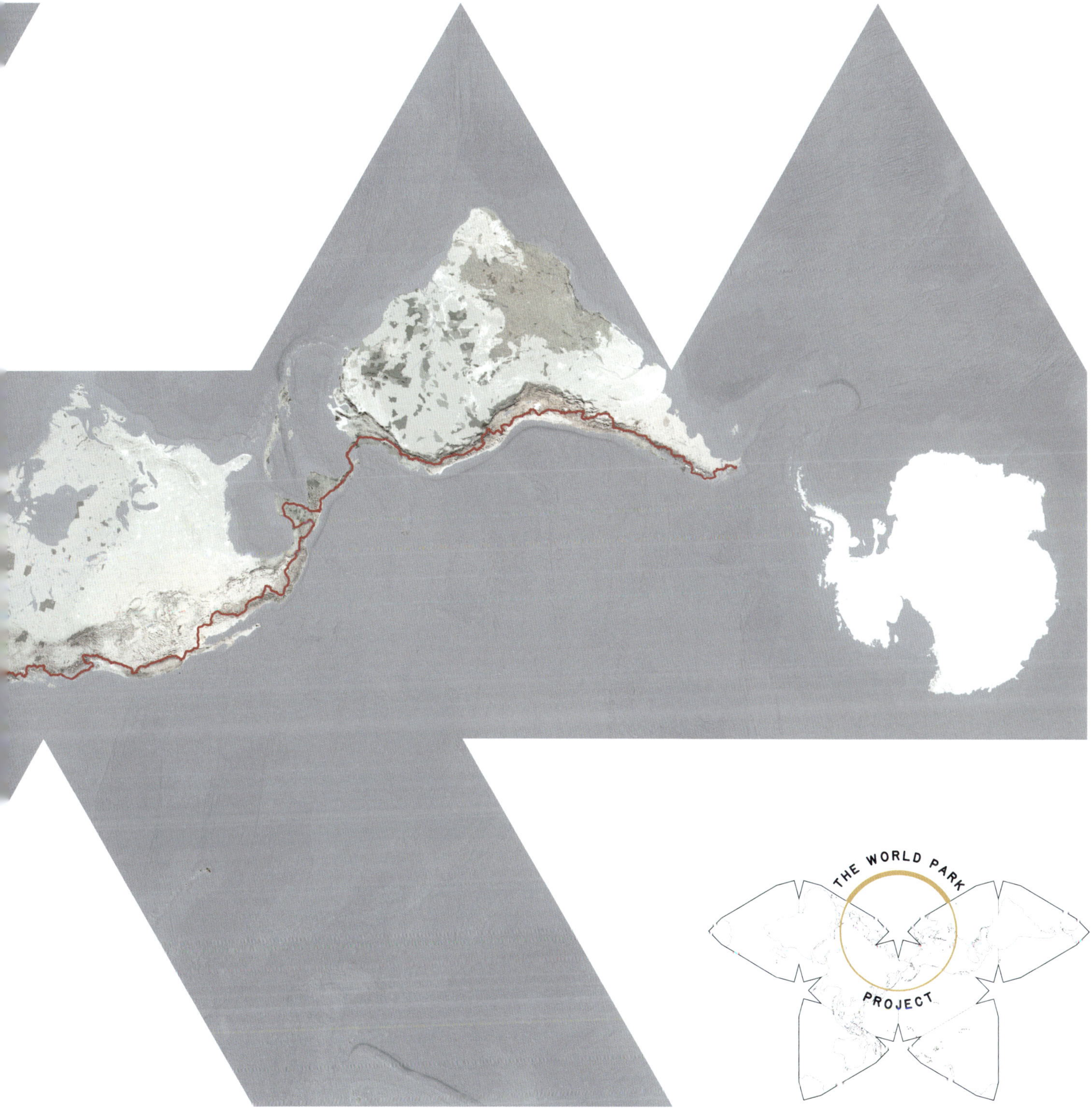

THE WORLD PARK PROJECT

The Aus-roc trail from "The World Park Project," a cycling and walking trail from southeastern Australia to Morocco, linking protected areas through biodiversity hotspots. As well as recreational value, the trail catalyzes landscape restoration projects to engage visitors in meaningful work, restore ecosystem function, and achieve habitat connectivity [150].

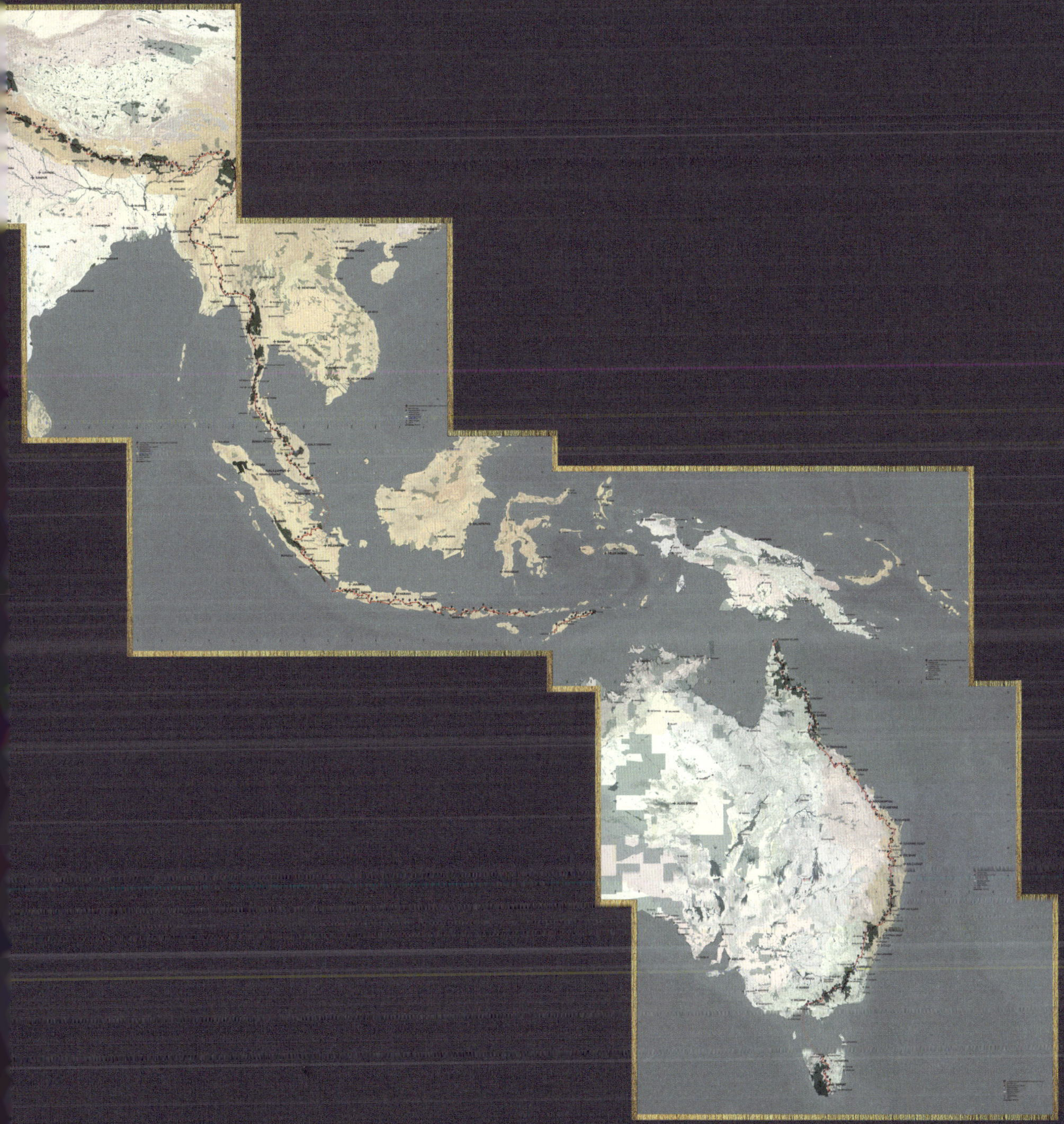

The Tur-ibia trail from "The World Park Project," linking protected areas through biodiversity hotspots from southeastern Turkey to Namibia [150].

The Pat-aska trail from "The World Park Project," linking protected areas through biodiversity hotspots from Patagonia to Alaska [150].

An example of mapping of the World Park trails from "The World Park Project" website: https://theworldpark.com.

TURIBIA
FRAME 29
+ Existing trail 115 km
Proposed trail 207 km
+ Countries 2
+ Cities 8
+ World Heritage Sites 1
+ Ecoregions 4
+ Threatened Species 252
LEGEND
Mercator Auxilary Sphere
Campsites
Cities
World Heritage Site
Existing Trail
Proposed Trail
Ferry Rides
Rohengeri
Goma
Gisenyi
Byumba
Kigali
Gitarama

TURIBIA
FRAME 30
+ Existing trail 31 km
Proposed trail 282 km
+ Countries 3
+ Cities 18
+ World Heritage Sites 1
+ Ecoregions 5
+ Threatened Species 225
LEGEND
Mercator Auxilary Sphere
Campsites
Cities
World Heritage Site
Existing Trail
Proposed Trail
Ferry Rides
Goma
Gisenyi
Kigali
Gitarama
Nyanza
Bukavu
Butare
Muyinga
Uvira
Bujumbura

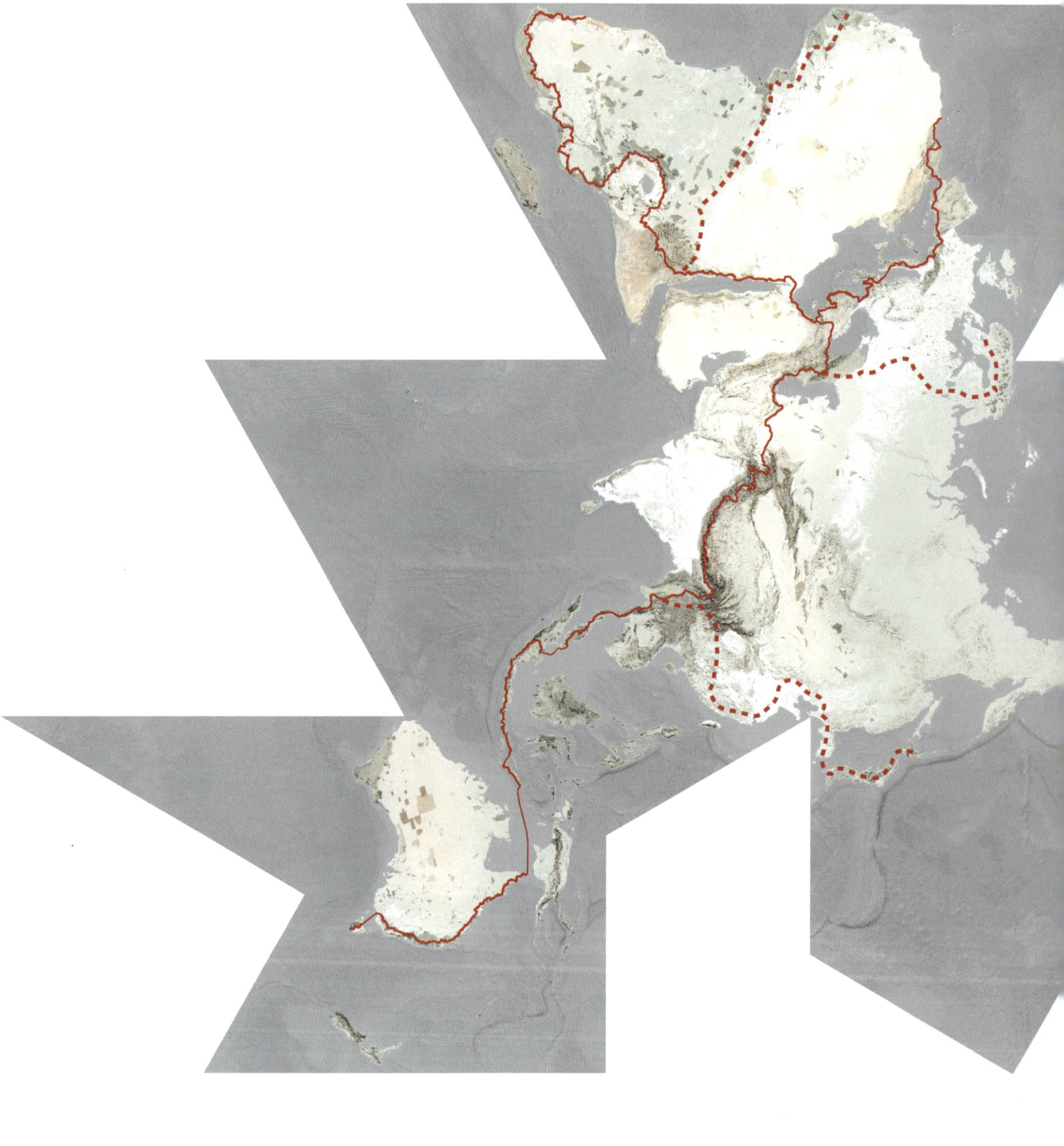

The geographic range of the concept of a World Park can be expanded beyond its initial phase with the addition of further trails (indicated here in dashed lines) to connect with and incorporate additional nations and biodiversity hotspots [150].

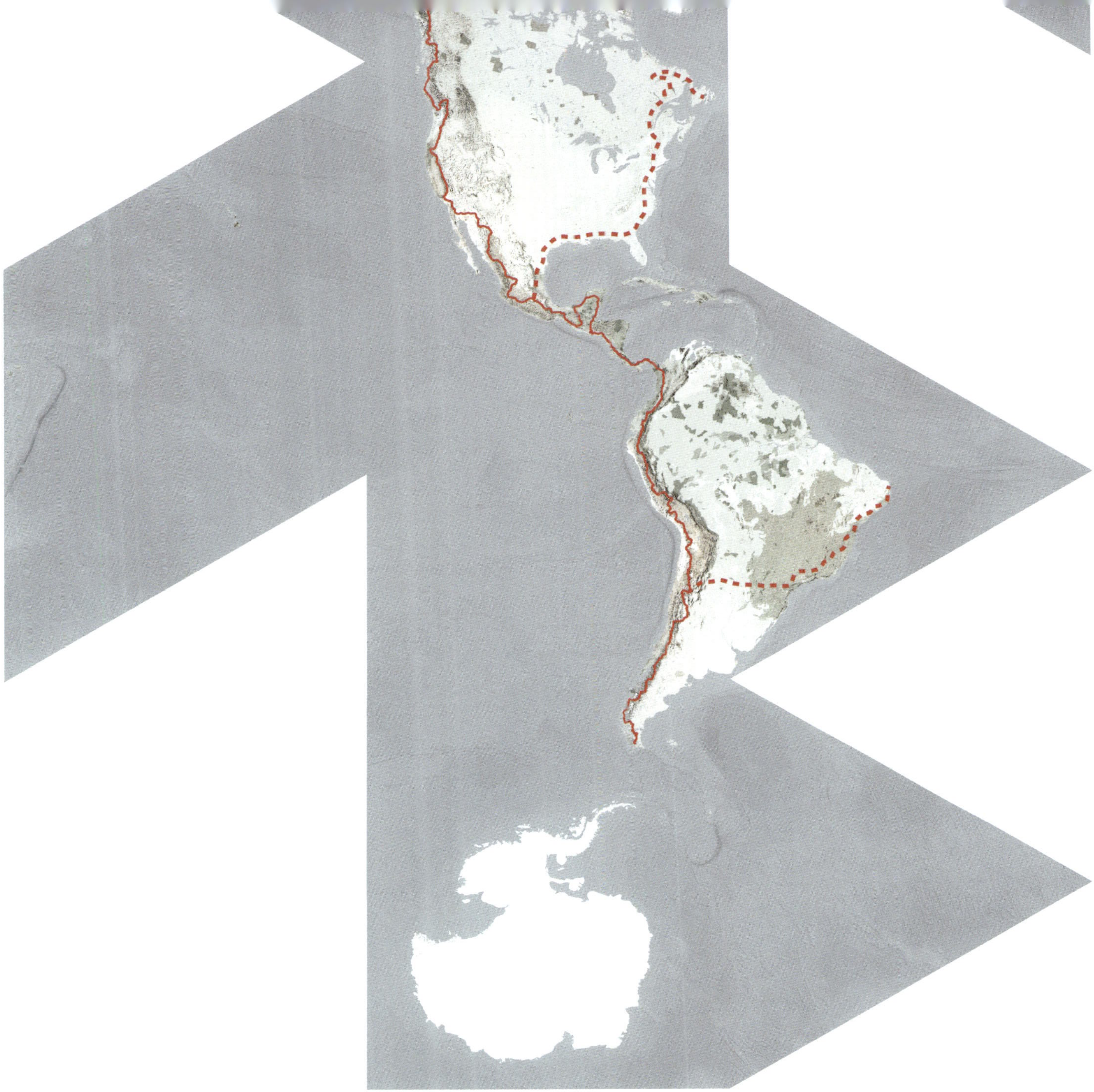

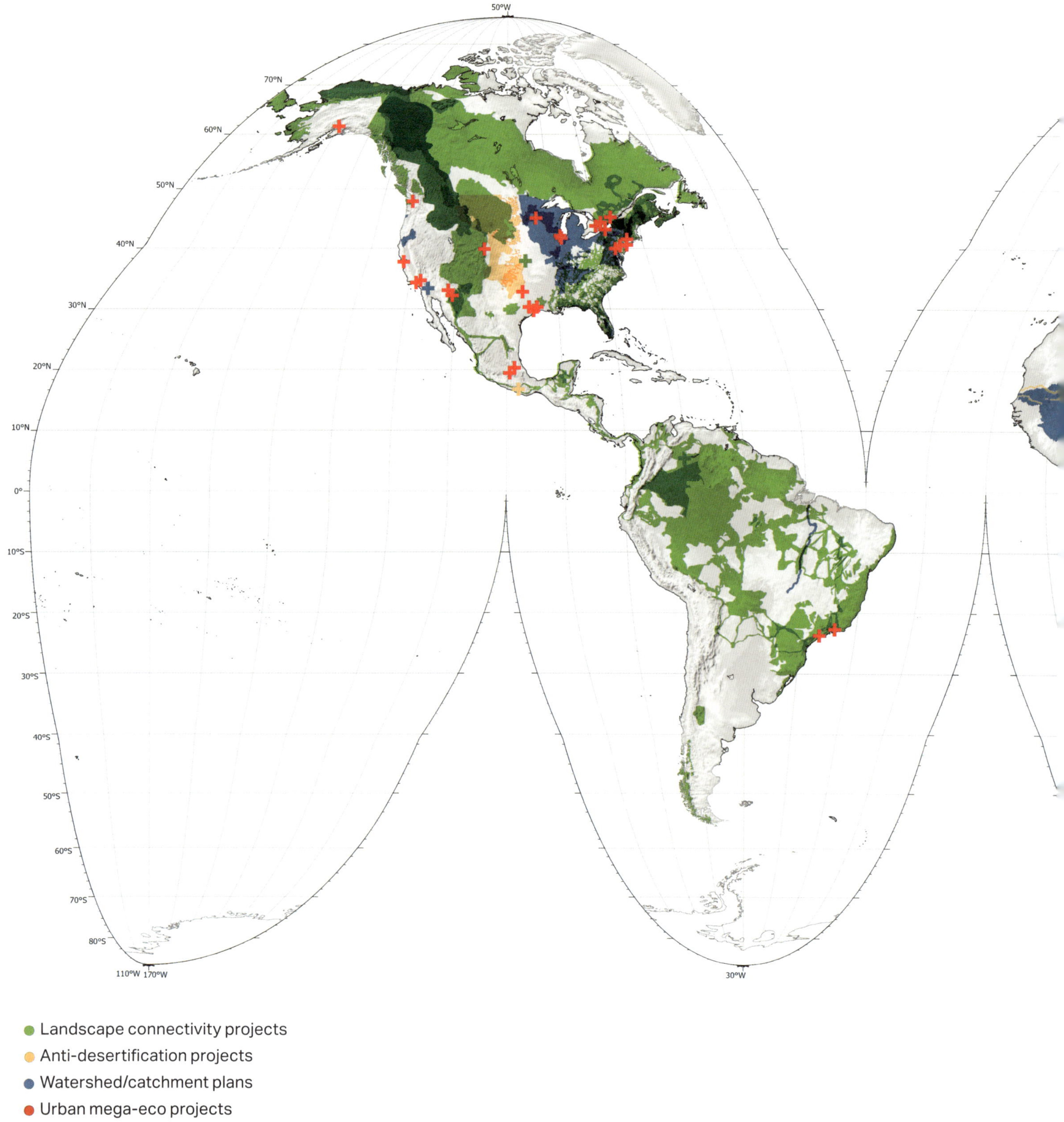

There are over 200 active mega-eco projects around the world today. The projects fall into four categories: landscape connectivity projects, watershed plans, antidesertification initiatives, and metropolitan projects [151].

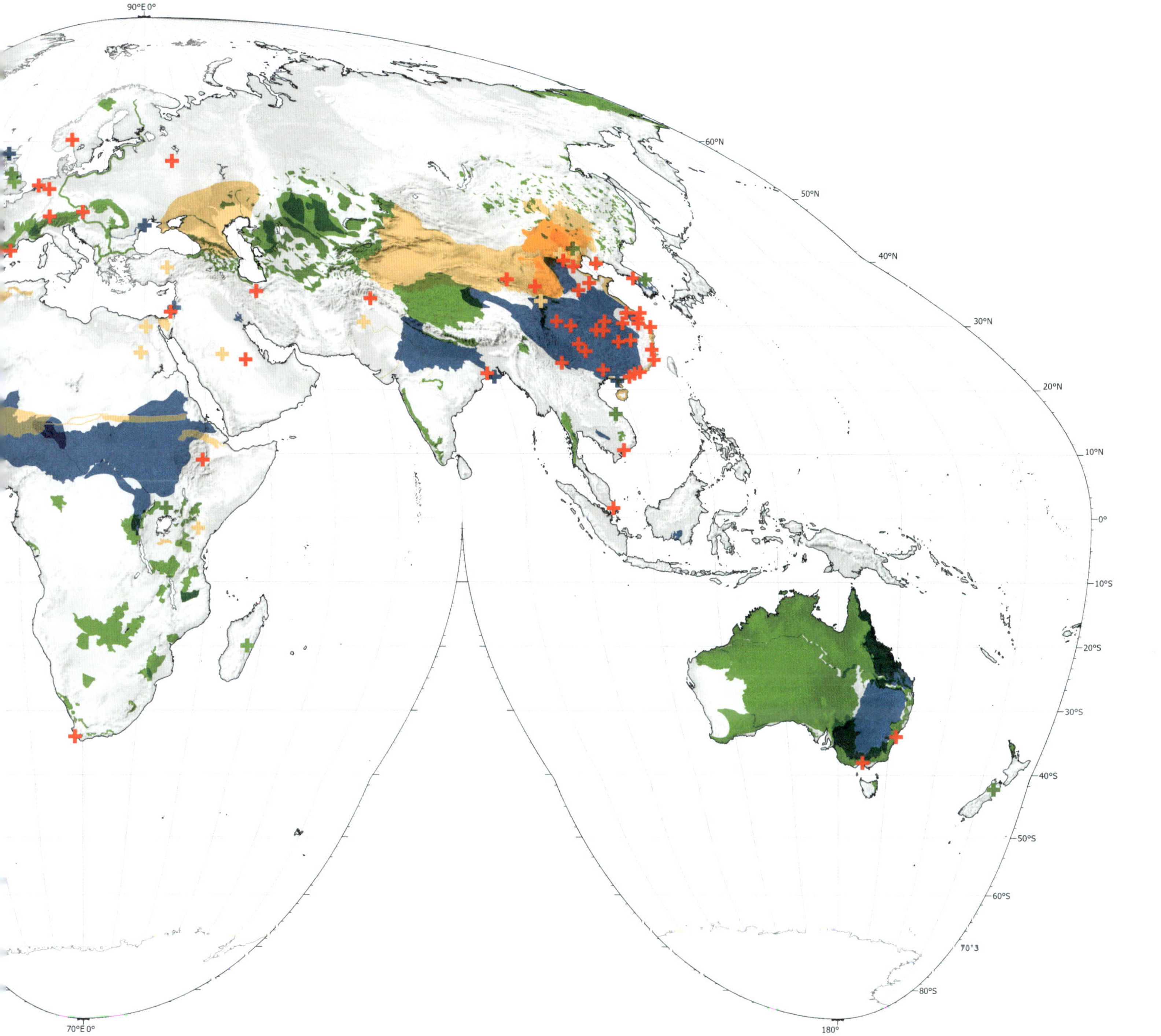
90°E 0°
60°N
50°N
40°N
30°N
20°N
10°N
0°
10°S
20°S
30°S
40°S
50°S
60°S
80°S
70°E 0°
180°

Installation image of "The Hotspot Cities Project" from *What We Can't Live Without* (Venice Biennale, 2021). Maps indicating conflict zones between biodiversity and urban growth in 33 cities in biodiversity hotspots, accompanied by wooden panels engraved with IUCN red-listed species related to each city [153].

Yellowstone National Park • Ten Deserts • Arctic Beringia • Northern Great Plains • Patagonia and Andean Steppe • Kavango Zambezi Transfrontier Conservation Area (TCA) • Changtang • Emerald Edge • 2 Countries 1 Forest • Caucasus Ecoregion • Habitat 141 Alliance • Tsa Tue Biosphere Reserve • Sky Island Alliance • Roundtable at the Crown of the Continent • Dawna Tenasserim Landscape • Alpine Network of Protected Areas • Heart of the Amazon Colombia • Coast to Cascades Grizzly Bear Initiative • Hill County Alliance • Great Gila Bioregion • Niassa National Reserve Co-Management Arrangements • Maiko-Tayna Kahuzi- Biega Landscape • Sacred • Himalayan Landscape • Kgalagadi Transfrontier Park • Carpathian • Network of Protected Areas • Mayombe Transboundary Protected Area • Great Limpopo TCA • Malawi- Zambia TCA • Northern Rangelands Trust • Northern Forest Complex • Northern Tanzania • Rangelands Initiative • Giant Panda National Park • Gorongosa-Marromeu Landscape Complex • Kruger to Canyons • Kimberley to Cape • Central Asia Econet • Ustyurt Plateau Conservation Initiative • Central India Tiger Landscape • Wildlands, Woodlands, Farmlands & Communities • Western Ghats • Amur Green Belt • Pilbara Corridors • Eastern Plains Landscape • Waterton Glacier International Peace Park • Lower Zambezi- Mana Pools TCA • Maloti- Drakensberg TCA • Greater Virunga Transboundary Area • Big Bend Rio Bravo International Peace Park • Eastern Wildway Network • Western Wildway Network • Pacific Wildway Network • Boreal Songbird Initiative • Jaguar Corridor 2030 • European Greenbelt • Yellowstone to Yukon • Great Eastern Ranges Kanangra • Boyd to Wyangala Link • Florida Ecological Greenways Network • Gondwana Link • Zambian Carnivore Programme • Terai Arc Landscape • Algonquin to Adirondacks • Reconnecting Northland • Tasmania East Coast Conservation Corridor • Kaeng Krachan Forest Complex • Wild Eyre Corridor • Eden to Addo • Kariba Wildlife Corridor • Ocala to Osceola • Murchison-Semliki Landscape • Selous-Niassa Corridor • Southern Highlands and Ruaha-Katavi Landscape • Strong Roots Gorilla Corridor • Trinational De La Sangha • The Greater Mountain Corridor • Civilian Conservation Corps • America's Longleaf Restoration Initiative • Succulent Karoo Ecosystem Programme • The Restoration Initiative: China • The Restoration Initiative: Tanzania • Rewilding Europe: Swedish Lapland • Rewilding Europe: Southern Carpathians • Rewilding Europe: Affric Highlands • Rewilding the American West • Five Million Hectare Reforestation Program (Vietnam) • Republic of Korea's National Reforestation Program • Community and Government Planting Project (Uganda) • The Fandriana Marolambo FLR Project • Vichada Climate Reforestation • The National Forest SOS Mata Atlantica • New Zealand Billion Tree Programme • USA's Plant 1 Billion Trees • Ireland Climate Action Plan • England Trees Action Plan • ROOTS (Uganda) • Northern Forest • Yucatan Reforestation Project • Amazon Reforestation Project, Inc • Forest Ontario's 50 Million Tree Program • Trillion Tree Campaign • Costa Rica Conservation and Reforestation • 20x20 National Campaigns • Great Hedge of India • Great Green Wall Initiative • Three North Shelter Forest Program • Coastal Shelterbelt Development Program (SDP) • PRC's (6) Forest Shelterbelts (Green Great Walls) • Great Plan for the Transformation of Nature • Great Plains Shelterbelt • Algerian Green Dam (1970) • Algerian Green Dam (2021) • SDP - along the Middle Reaches of the Yellow River • Integrated SDP in Liaohe River Valley • Great Green Wall of India • Middle East Green Initiative • Saudi Green Initiative • Regreen the Sinai • Grain for Green (China) • Kubuqi Ecological Restoration Project • Shinyanga Soil Conservation Programme • Buffalo Commons • Plain Afforestation Programme (China) • The Sandification Control Program (Beijing and Tianjin) • The National Afforestation and Erosion Control (Türkiye) • National Programme to Combat Desertification (China) • Saihanba Afforestation Community • Chocho - Mixtecas Community Alliance • Ten Billion Tree Tsunami (Pakistan) • Billion Tree Tsunami • KKL-JNF Israeli Forest Program • Greenbelt Movement (Kenya) • Egypt Sustainable Agriculture Initiative • 100 Million Trees (Egypt) • Tennessee Valley Authority • Comprehensiv¬¬e Everglades Restoration Project • Four Major Rivers Project • Great Lakes Restoration Initiative (GLRI) • Room for the River • Murray Darling Basin Plan • Upper Mississippi River Restoration Program • Reef 2050 • Kissimmee River Restoration Project • Border Meuse • Elwha River Restoration • Klamath River Renewal Project • Tonle Sap Lake and Inundation Zone Corridor • Lower Danube Green Corridor • Protection of the Free-Flowing Bita River • Penobscot River Restoration Project • Salmon SuperHWY • SDP - Upper and Middle Reaches of the Yangtze River • Taihang Mountains Afforestation Programme • SDP - Huaihe River and Taihu Lake Basin Area • SDP - in the Pearl River Valley • Agenda 21 - Mangrove Restoration in Southern China • Iraqi Marshlands Restoration Project • Central Kalimantan Peatlands Restoration Project • Peatland Restoration (Scotland) • Humberhead Levels Partnership • Mangrove Afforestation Programme of the National Forest Department (Bangladesh) • Katingan Peatland Restoration and Conservation Project • Rewilding Europe: Danube Delta • Blue Lifelines for a Secure Sahel • The National Water Carrier • Transaqua Project • [Unnamed] Salton Sea Replenishment Project • Red Sea-Dead Sea Conveyance • Araguaia Biodiversity Corridor • Chesapeake Bay Program • River Dee Trust • Regional Flyway Initiative • Resilient Asian Deltas (World Wildlife Fund) • Medina Edict • Barcelona Greenbelt • Sao Paulo Greenbelt and Biosphere Reserve • San Francisco Bay Area Greenbelt / Greenprint • Ontario Greenbelt • Melbourne Green Wedges • Metropolitan • Greenbelt (London) • Green Heart (Netherlands) • Seoul Metropolitan Greenbelt • Forterra – The Cascade Agenda • Chugach State Park • Biosphere Park Wienerwald • Hunan East Dongting Lake National Nature Reserve • Gatineau Park • Addis-Bah Development Forestry • Project + Ethiopian Forest Action Program • The Forest Preserves of Cook County • Table Mountain National Park • Margalla Hills Nat ional Park • Texcoco Lake Ecological Park • Pedra Branca State Park • McDowell Sonoran Preserve • Losiny Ostrov National Park • Greater • Sydney Parklands • Chicago Wilderness† • Emscher Landscape Park • Tehran Greenbelt† • Emerald Necklace • Sponge City Initiative • LA River Plan • Green City Clean Water • Croton and Catskill Reservoir Areas • Galveston Bay Park Plan • East Kolkata Wetlands • Mangrove Restoration in Can Gio • The Zurich Stream Day-Lighting Program • Oslo Reopening Waterways • Rio la Piedad Project • Guangzhou Ecological Belt • Singapore Park Connector Network • Houston Bayou Greenways • The Grand Rounds National Scenic Byway • Greenbelt Vitoria Gasteiz • Freshkills Park • Hariya Landfill • Green Riyadh • Houston Climate Action Plan • Plant 1 Million Philadelphia • Million Trees NYC • Million Trees LA • One Million Tree Initiative (Amherst, NY) • One Million Trees Mississauga • Mile High Million (Denver) • The Shanghai Roots and Shoots Million Tree Project • Tucson Million Trees

Installation image of The Butterfly and the Locust, from the Eco-Vision exhibition (Chinese Academy of Fine Art, Beijing, 2023), comprising aerial photographs of 200 mega-eco projects printed on wood-framed acetate and mounted like insects in a natural history museum [153].

A swimmer from the NASA Underwater Demolition Team 11 opens the hatch of the Apollo 11 Command Module following splashdown on July 24, 1969. Image: NASA, public domain [153].

CABIN DEPRESS

1. CLOSE HATCH
2. CABIN FAN (2) – OFF
3. REPRESS PKG 02 VIV – FILL
4. REPRESS. 02 VIV – CLOSE (VERF)
5. CAB REPRESS REL VIV – OPEN
6. (O2) FLOW HI WARNING LT MAY COME ON
7. PRIOR TO CABIN PRESS REG LOCK UP
8. AT 3.25 PSIA, SIDE HATCH DUMP VIV – CLOSE
9. O2 FLOW IND – LESS THAN 0.5 LB/HR
10. SUIT CKT PRESS STABLE 3.5-4.0
11. SIDE HATCH DUMP VIV – OPEN
12. SET TERRESTRIAL CO-ORDS

LANDING PROCEDURE

1. INSTALL EARTH SYSTEM COMMAND
2. SHUT DOWN FUEL LINES
3. RE-ROUTE PO3/NO3 FLOWS
4. CH4 EXHAUST OFF
5. OPEN SOLAR SURFACES
6. LAUNCH SEED DISPERSERS
7. RELEASE MICROBES (1- 14)
8. BOOST CO2 FILTERS
9. OPEN H2O VALVES
10. OPEN SEED DISPERSERS
11. LAUNCH INCUBATORS (1-8)
12. OPEN HATCH

Installation image of "Not the Blue Marble" from *What We Can't Live Without* (Venice Biennale, 2021). This artwork is a 1:1 copy of the Apollo 11 command module hatch with a simulated view to a climate-changed Earth in the distant future [153].

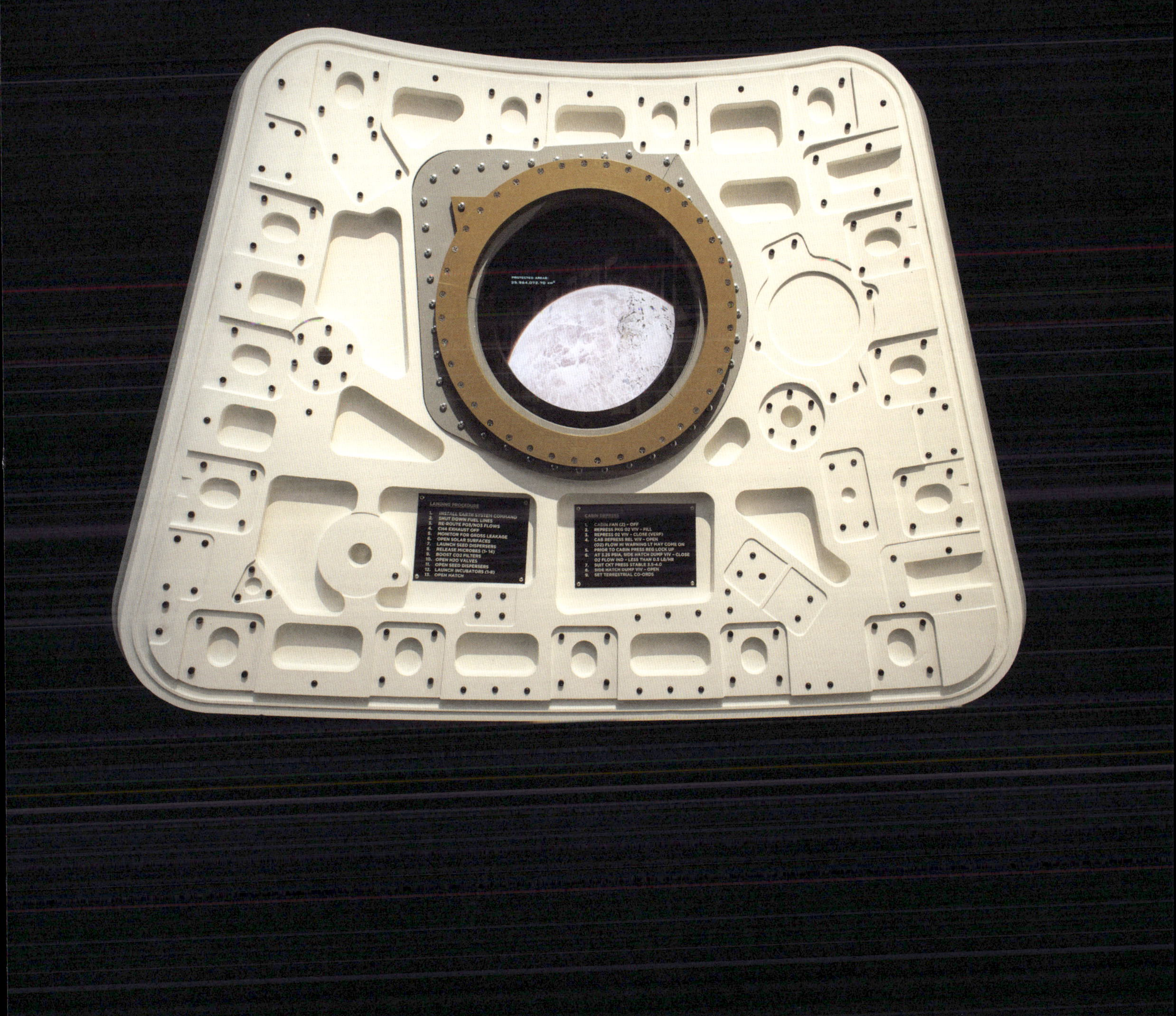
LANDING PROCEDURE
1. INSTALL EARTH SYSTEM COMMAND
2. SHUT DOWN FUEL LINES
3. RE-ROUTE PO3/NO3 FLOWS
4. CH4 EXHAUST OFF
5. MONITOR FOR GROSS LEAKAGE
6. OPEN SOLAR SURFACES
7. LAUNCH SEED DISPERSERS
8. RELEASE MICROBES (1- 14)
9. BOOST CO2 FILTERS
10. OPEN H2O VALVES
11. OPEN SEED DISPERSERS
12. LAUNCH INCUBATORS (1-8)
13. OPEN HATCH
CABIN REPRESS
1. CABIN FAN (2) - OFF
2. REPRESS PKG O2 VIV - FILL
3. REPRESS O2 VIV - CLOSE (VERF)
4. CAB REPRESS REL VIV - OPEN
(O2) FLOW HI WARNING LT MAY COME ON
5. PRIOR TO CABIN PRESS REG LOCK UP
6. AT 3.25 PSIA, SIDE HATCH DUMP VIV - CLOSE
O2 FLOW IND - LESS THAN 0.5 LB/HR
7. SUIT CKT PRESS STABLE 3.5-4.0
8. SIDE HATCH DUMP VIV - OPEN
9. SET TERRESTRIAL CO-ORDS

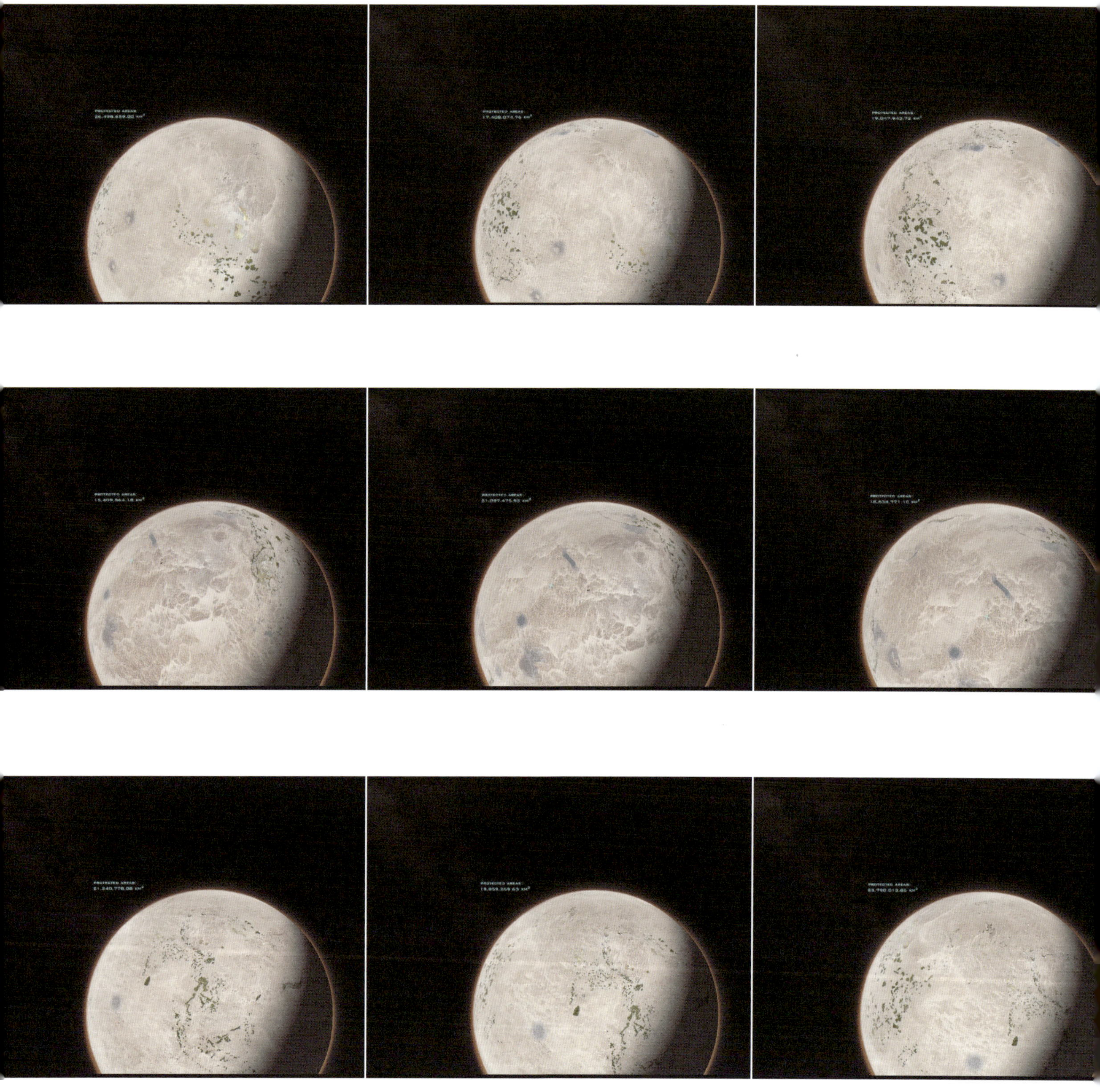

Animation of a future Earth, rendered arid by global warming, except for patches of vegetation and water coinciding with today's protected areas: "Not the Blue Marble" from *What We Can't Live Without* (Venice Biennale (Italy, 2021) [153].

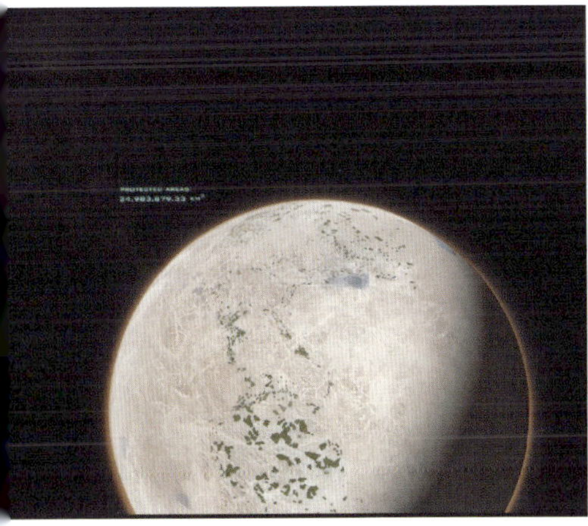
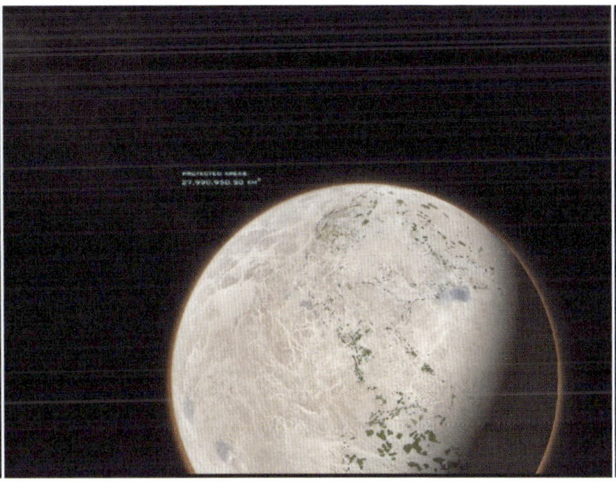

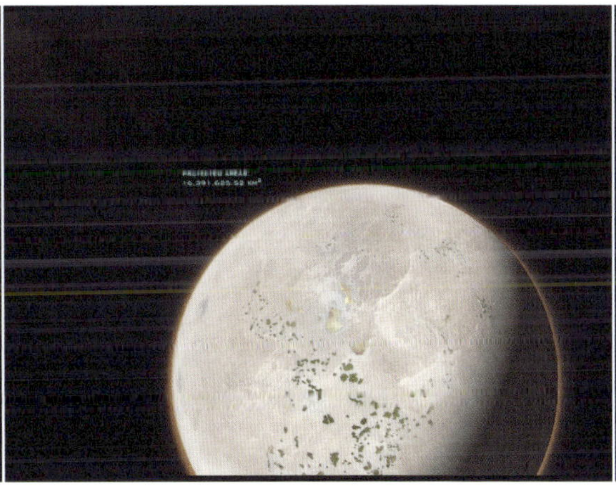

Methane vent at Fresh Kills Park in Staten Island (*left*). Image: Virginia Hanusik (2016); the Sand Motor, The Netherlands (*right*). Image courtesy of the Ministry of Infrastructure and Water Management and Province of South Holland (2016) [154–55].

AFTERWORD BY DIRK SIJMONDS

AN ART OF INSTRUMENTALITY?

An atlas for the end of the world, mega-eco projects, plans to redesign the earth's land use, and different scenarios for a planet where astronauts return after eons. As Richard Weller describes it, "this recultivated earth is not some boring, sanctimonious, doctrinaire, new age ecotopia: it is a highly scientific, aesthetic, inventive, diverse, and experimental project. It is a landscape architectural project." Before the stunned reader closes the book, gasping for breath in the face of such hubris, we take a moment to ask ourselves: what are we actually looking at?

To call Weller's bluff, let's take a closer look at the case of the World Park project. It involves a proposal to connect the most important biomes of the planet in a project of ongoing landscape restoration starting with a walking and cycling route from Australia to Morocco, a second from Turkey to Namibia, and the last through the Americas from Patagonia to Alaska. These would connect the most important biodiversity hotspots, UNESCO World Heritage sites, and biosphere reserves.

Isn't this a dangerous form of overreaching? Haven't we learned from the era of spatial determinism that not all the problems in the world can be solved by spatial means? That may be true, but the problem of rapidly eroding biodiversity—by far the most serious environmental problem we are struggling with—has a dominant spatial component. Due to exploitation for agriculture, urbanization, fragmentation by infrastructure, and large-scale extraction of minerals, there is less and less territory left for nonhuman life. The planetary dominance of our species has taken on bewildering forms. Vaclav Smil calculates in his book *Harvesting the Biosphere* that of the total biomass production of our planet, humans directly and indirectly appropriate 23.8%, about one-quarter.[1] If we were able to weigh all the terrestrial vertebrates on our planet, 95% of that weight would be ourselves with our domesticated herds of cows, goats, sheep, chickens, etc. Only 5% of the total weight consists of wild animals. An article in *Nature* in 2020 showed that the weight of our built environment has surpassed that of the planet's total biomass, and adds alarmingly that this mass, and everything we've built over the past 7,000 years, will double, maybe even triple, by 2050.[2] Weller's research project the "Atlas for the End of the World," shows where this viral urbanization threatens to collide head-on with the main hotspots of biodiversity.

Mapped and monitored from above by satellites, this great acceleration of everything, from extraction, to energy, agriculture, and urbanization, looks like the work of a plague organism. The closer we gnaw our way to the edge of the petri dish, the clearer it becomes that the most erosive industries—agriculture, mining, fishing, and construction—have the end of their business model in sight. One would expect this to lead to reflection and repentance, but nothing could be further from the truth. The more eroding the industry, the more government subsidy and government protection these sectors seem to be able to count on. There is a merciless war of clashing interests precisely because they see the end approaching. There were more fossil fuel industry lobbyists at COP27, in Sharm El-Sheikh, than the biggest national delegations.

Recent research shows that the fossil fuel industry can count on $64 billion in direct government subsidies annually, as well as $531 billion in further subsidies to keep fuel costs low. Agriculture receives about $500 billion, and fishing receives approximately $35 billion annually to increase engine power to ply the oceans even more effectively.[3] Globalism is crashing against its planetary boundaries, but in this final act, vested interests unleash formidable resistance that opposes real change. In light of this battle for the last space and the ever-rarer resources, it is a radical, but not crazy idea to bet high in terms of making spatial claims for the preservation of a living planet. Is it too expensive? On the wave of the effective altruism movement, the richest billionaires in the world are better off putting their dishonestly earned money into the first phase of the World Park project—the trails and cycling routes—than aiming for a hopeless mission to other planets after having made the earth untenable.

At the end of his illustrious career, the authoritative ecologist and Pulitzer Prize winner E.O. Wilson argued for reserving 50% of the planet's surface as a biodiversity reserve.[4] This of course sounds ridiculously unrealistic to today's economists and resource managers. As Weller points out, globally we are now close to 17% more or less protected areas on land and 8% of the oceans. Wilson's plea for more is based on the observation that only with sufficient functional surface can natural processes such as predation and herbivory, and abiotic processes such as erosion and sedimentation really develop. In the Anthropocene, Wilson argues that we need to think not only at the scale of landscapes or ecosystems but at the scale level of the biosphere as a whole. It is not just about protecting life as we know it, it is about protecting evolution itself, it is about maintaining the fundamental ecological processes that underpin all life on earth.[5] In this regard, Weller is right to imagine a project that tries to forge large contiguous surfaces. As a majority of the world's nations now agree, protection of 30% of the earth's terrestrial surface should be the long-term target. Weller's plan for a World Park is timely.

But is it a plan? Yes and no. It looks suspiciously like a plan and it is structured as a plan, but not in the usual sense of the word. The World Park project does not seem to be intended as a foundation for direct execution. It's an idea, a concept that makes people think. It is the product of what we call research-by-design, a specific form of future-oriented research.[6] This happens mainly in the creative space of biennales and competitions, or within universities, where problems can be addressed that will never get a paying customer. In the case of the World Park project, the world's biodiversity is the client.

As a polemical work, the World Park can be compared to earlier examples of alternative realities from architectural history. Archizoom's alarming continuation of trends, for example, in the dystopian "The Endless Grid of Consumption" (1968)[7] and in Archigram's attractive, light technological architecture of indeterminacy as an attempt to recover the thrill of modernism's pioneering phase.[8] Or, from the same period, "The Twelve Ideal Cities" (1970) of Superstudio, in which a kind of anthropological-architectural research is carried out into society and visionary myths are sketched in their "Supersurface: An Alternative Model for Life on Earth," where the fundamental acts (education, love, death, ceremony) are captured in still intriguing otherworldly architecture collages (1972).[9] These works all provide, from different angles, stinging commentary on society, and criticize the position of architecture in it. They do this, very plastically and evocatively, by conjuring up the spatial expression of other worldviews. Another pioneer in this field, the Situationist artist and architect Constant Nieuwenhuijs, prophesied in his long-term project *New Babylon* (1956–1974) what the world would look like if *Homo faber* were gradually replaced by *Homo ludens*. The playing man would soon throw off the yoke of obligatory and mind-numbing work.[10] Where Constant's New Babylon is characterized as the "Hyper-Architecture of Desire," Weller's World Park project could be called the "Hyper-Landscape-Architecture of Biophilia." These kinds of exercises are desperately needed to help explore the possibilities of escaping the form of modernity that has caused the environmental conundrum we are in, and in which our thinking is trapped.

And so, the big question behind this type of work is whether it helps us escape modernity's suicidal tendencies? In answering this question, I will limit myself to four possibilities as originally developed by the Australian philosopher Clive Hamilton.[11] Hamilton's fourfold approach to the Anthropocene is constructed around two sets of opposing concepts. On the vertical axis, humankind is represented as a species unable to change the course of natural history, or alternatively, a species that considers itself an omnipotent force free of nature's limits. On the horizontal axis, the world is presented as a passive backdrop to human affairs or alternatively, as an independent, vital entity of immense force.

This quadrant sets out four positions that can be characterized as Denialism (passive species x passive earth), Ecomodernism (omnipotent species x passive earth), Posthumanism (passive species x vital planet), and Anthropocentrism 2.0 (omnipotent species x vital planet).[12] Denialism rejects the idea that humans could have a far-reaching influence on nature, let alone the planet. On the sociopolitical plane, this worldview tends to translate into a denial of climate change. Paradoxically, denialism escapes modernity by failing to even recognize it as a problem in the first place.

No less paradoxical is the ecomodernist approach. That is, ecomodernism upholds modernity's central tenet that technological progress can yet solve the problems that modern technology has itself created. Ecomodernists also argue that economic growth can go hand in hand with reducing humanity's ecological footprint, and climate change can be tackled with new energy sources and geoengineering. Acidification of the oceans can be turned around with the addition of Fe+ particles. There are technical solutions for all side effects. Overcoming all these problems will be the ultimate triumph of mankind: the Good Anthropocene. The escape route here is simply to stick the prefix eco- onto modernism and thus modernize modernism. Ecomodernism is therefore the hope of The System for continuation.

In posthumanism, the climate crisis is thought to be at root a spiritual problem as much as a physical problem. In this worldview, humanity realizes it is not the crowning glory of creation, and through artistic, philosophical, and scientific paths seeks communion with all nonhuman life forms. What has no voice is given rights in legislation and is represented in a "parliament of things," and our appreciation of existence expands from the human-centric to the eco-centric. In this way, modernity is transcended.

The new Anthropocentrism 2.0 is based on the realization that humans are a geological force and not just a small part of the ecological network. We are a conscious force now in direct conflict with our powerful planet. In this worldview, humanity must now take responsibility for the havoc and destruction it has caused and for preventing further catastrophe. In this view, neither technical innovation nor spiritual reformation can bring back the calm of the Holocene. For Anthropocentrism 2.0, only the worst may still be prevented through healing, restoring, undoing, reverse engineering, reconnecting, and, as McHarg put it, "designing with nature."

It is not hard to guess which worldview underpins the World Park project. As an imagination construct it shows what it would take to repair the catastrophic fragmentation of wildlife areas—to heal, and to partially repair, the damage we have caused. It is a "healing" project in all respects. It is unique in its size and span, but it is not alone in its ambition. Examples of healing projects can be found on all continents. In China, the tremendous effort spearheaded by Kongjian Yu to prevent viral urbanization from becoming a hydrological nightmare by making the Sponge City concept the standard.[13] In Africa, the Great Green Wall Initiative to green the Sahel and stop desertification has evolved from its initial focus on tree planting toward a comprehensive rural development initiative aiming to transform the lives of Sahelian populations by creating a mosaic of green and productive landscapes across the continent.[14] Sergey and Nikita Zimov, father and son ecologists, with their Pleistocene Park in Siberia are trying to restore the Arctic taiga by reintroducing megafauna and thus dismantling the methane bomb that would go off with the melting of the permafrost.[15] The photographer-couple Sebastião and Lélia Salgado embody perhaps the finest example in South America with their initiative for reforestation of the clear-cut family hacienda with local tree species of the Atlantic rainforest, an initiative that went viral in the region and was institutionalized at the Instituto Terra.[16] In Europe, the Dam Removal Europe Foundation is a good example of this responsible Anthropocentrism. Here, with the unbridled commitment of volunteers and successful crowdfunding actions, work is being done to demolish the thousands of dams, culverts, sluices, and other barriers that have become superfluous, to restore fish migration.[17] In the US, the epicenter of capitalism, the founder of the outdoor clothing brand Patagonia, Yvon Chouinard, donated 98% of his shares, worth some $3 billion, to the specially founded nonprofit organization The Holdfast Collective, to finance climate and nature projects where the only shareholder is the earth.[18] All these large-scale healing plans require a synergy and balance between top-down and bottom-up forces.

The quadrant I have described charts the ideological fault lines of the environmental debate without getting bogged down in crippling left-right partisanship. None of the four extremes is completely right or wrong. This means that in the environmental debate we must prepare ourselves for cooperation and discussion. Planning will remain the science of muddling through, and design will stumble forward, intelligently. The quadrant can also be helpful in another way—for example, for constructing design narratives where the assets of all four stances are combined: the casual detachment from denialism, the joy of making from ecomodernism, the empathy for the nonhuman from posthumanism, and the power of healing from Anthropocentrism 2.0.

But none of this is a reason not to take sides. For landscape architecture, a choice for posthumanism or the new Anthropocentrism seems obvious. There will then be dispute between proponents of these views. I can think of many interesting posthumanist artistic projects that would result in individual enlightenment and new forms of empathy for the nonhuman, but beyond that, they would prove a dead-end street when it comes to solving real world problems.

Weller opens this book by describing landscape architecture as an instrumental art, or as an art of instrumentality, and in that vein we must not let posthumanism be relegated to representation, or for Anthropocentrism 2.0 to become mere instrumentality led by ecologists. Our ambition should be to bring art forms to the healing projects of Anthropocentrism 2.0 and greater instrumentality to posthumanism, and this is what we find in Weller's significant body of work.

END NOTES

1. Vaclav Smil, *Harvesting the Biosphere: What We Have Taken from Nature* (MIT Press, 2013).
2. Emily Elhacham, et al., "Global Human-Made Mass Exceeds All Living Biomass," *Nature* 588 (2020): 442–44.
3. George Monbiot, "From the Amazon to Australia, Why Is Your Money Funding Earth's Destruction?" *The Guardian* (November 30, 2022).
4. Edward O. Wilson, *Half-Earth: Our Planet's Fight for Life* (Liveright Publishing, 2016).
5. In terms of scientific underpinning, the World Park Project scores a triple Wilson rating: the older Wilson of *Half-Earth* (2016) meets the young Wilson of the influential McArthur-Wilson Island Biogeographical theory (1967) and the mid-career Wilson that introduced the term biophilia (1984). All three concepts are building blocks of the WPP.
6. Dirk Sijmons, "When Research-By-Design Takes Politics on a Sabbatical Detour," in *The Next Economy*, catalogue to the International Architecture Biennale Rotterdam, eds. George Brugmans, Jolanda Strien & Maarten Hajer (2016).
7. Lara Schrijver, *Radical Games: Popping the Bubble of 1960s' Architecture* (NAi Publishers, 2009).
8. Simon Sadler, *Archigram: Architecture without Architecture* (MIT Press, 2005).
9. Emanuelle Chiappone-Piriou, *Superstudio Migrazione* C I.II.III.IV., A Verlag der Buchhandlung Walther und Franz König Köln Catalogue (2021).
10. Mark Wigley, *Constant's New Babylon: The Hyper-Architecture of Desire* (010 Publishers, 1998).
11. Clive Hamilton, *Defiant Earth: The Fate of Humans in the Anthropocene* (Polity Press, 2017).
12. See for an elaboration of this typology: Dirk Sijmons, "In the Anthropocene, Site Matters in Four Ways" in *Site Matters: Strategies for Uncertainty through Planning and Design*, eds. Andrea Kahn & Carol J. Burns, (Routledge, 2021).
13. Kongjian Yu, *Letters to the Leaders of China* (Terreform Publishers, 2018).
14. African Union, Great Green Wall Initiative (2007), see www.unccd.int.
15. Pleistocene Park, see, www.pleistocenepark.ru.
16. See *The Salt of the Earth* (2018), a documentary by Wim Wenders & Juliano Ribeiro Salgado.
17. Dam Removal Europe, #Dambusters, www.damremoval.eu.
18. Patagonia, www.patagonia.com.

Richard Weller is the Meyerson Chair of Urbanism and Professor and Chair of Landscape Architecture at The University of Pennsylvania, where he teaches advanced design studios and subjects in the history and theory of landscape architecture and urbanism. Weller also serves as Executive Director of the McHarg Center for Urbanism and Ecology, and Creative Director of *LA+ Interdisciplinary Journal of Landscape Architecture*. He also holds adjunct positions at the University of New South Wales and the University of Western Australia. He was founding director (with Vladimir Sitta) of Room 4.1.3, an Australian design firm honored with a Penn Press monograph in 2005. Weller's work has been frequently awarded in international design competitions and exhibited in galleries such as the Guggenheim in New York, the Venice and Rotterdam Biennales, the Museum of Contemporary Art in Sydney, the Isabella Stewart Gardner Museum in Boston, the MAXXI Gallery in Rome, the Canadian Design Museum in Toronto, and the Central Academy of Fine Arts in Beijing. His publications include *Room 4.1.3: Innovations in Landscape Architecture* (2005), *Boomtown 2050: Scenarios for a Rapidly Growing City* (2009), *Made in Australia: The Future of Australian Cities* (2013), *Transects* (2014), *Design with Nature Now* (2019), *Beautiful China: Reflections on Landscape Architecture in Contemporary China* (2020), *The Landscape Project* (2023), and *To the Ends of the Earth: A Grand Tour for the 21st Century* (forthcoming), as well as over one hundred single-authored academic papers, book chapters, and articles on the theory and practice of landscape architecture and urban design. The *Atlas for the End of the World*, Weller's recent research work on biodiversity and cities, has been published in *National Geographic* and *Scientific American*, while his related research and design project to establish a World Park is currently being considered for implementation by UNESCO.

Jillian Walliss is an associate professor of landscape architecture at the University of Melbourne. Her work focuses on the intersection of theory, technology, culture, and contemporary design practice. Through research, curating, writing, and design teaching Jillian has contributed significantly to the intellectual advancement of landscape architecture. She has collaborated with Heike Rahmann on two books: the award-winning *Digital Technologies and Landscape Architecture: Reconceptualising Design and Making* (2016), and *The Big Asian Book of Landscape Architecture* (2020). In 2019 she was co-creative director of the International Festival of Landscape Architecture in Australia, which featured the *Future Park Design Ideas* competition, exploring new open space futures for Melbourne 2050. This was documented in *Future Park & Beyond* (2021). She was also part of the Yalinguth project (2021), which produced an innovative immersive audio app showcasing the Indigenous stories of Melbourne's Gertrude Street.

Dirk Sijmons is a founder of H+N+S Landscape Architects where he is mostly involved in regional plans and research-by-design commissions. In 2002 Sijmons received the Maaskant award, and in 2007 the Edgar Doncker award for his contribution to Dutch culture. His books include *Landscape* (1998), *Greetings from Europe* (2008), *Landscape and Energy* (2014), *Moved Movement: Landscape Under the Hood* (2015), and *Room for the River* (2017). Sijmons was appointed the first State Landscape Architect of the Netherlands (2004–2008), and held, at TU-Delft, the chair of environmental design (2008–2011) and the chair of landscape architecture (2011–2015). He was curator of IABR—2014 "Urban-by-Nature," and has lectured around the world. In 2017 at the World Design Summit in Montreal, Sijmons received the IFLA Sir Geoffrey Jellicoe Award, recognizing "a living landscape architect whose lifetime achievements and contributions have had a unique and lasting impact on the welfare of society and the environment and on the promotion of the profession of landscape architecture."

PROJECT CREDITS

Projects mentioned in this book but not listed below are credited solely to Richard Weller.

Landscape Painting
Installation, Museum of Contemporary Art, Sydney, 1998. In association with Vladimir Sitta (Room 4.1.3). Assistants: Lizzie Burt, Daniel Firns, Karl Kullmann, Maren Parry, Oleg Putilin.

The Berlin Room
Competition entry, Berlin, 1995. Fifth Prize. In association with Müller, Knippschild, Wehberg. Assistant: Constanza Bitzageio.

Future Generations University
Competition entry, New South Wales, 1996. Finalist. In association with Vladimir Sitta (Room 4.1.3), Rosemary King, Robert King, Des Smith, Ian Weir, Simeon Glasson, Tatum Hands, Craig Burton, Oui Chantarachota, Nigel Westbrook, Peter England, Shaun Tan, Paul Collins, Victor Bossell, Kevin Williams, Marni Shepherd, Anne Davis, Andrew Marsch, Bob Sinclair, Elwyn Dennis, Anne Davis, Rosanna Blackett.

The Women's Rooms
Competition entry, Berlin, 1993. Second Prize. In association with Müller, Knippschild, Wehberg. Assistant: Frank Kiessling.

Decomposition
Competition entry, Berlin, 1995. First Prize. In association with Studio Libeskind and Müller, Knippschild, Wehberg. Assistant: Kamel Louafi.

Deutsches Institut für Normung (German Institute of Standards)
Built work, Berlin, 1991–1993. In association with Müller, Knippschild, Wehberg.

The National Museum of Australia and Garden of Australian Dreams
Competition entry and built work, Canberra, 1996–2001. First Prize. In association with Vladimir Sitta (Room 4.1.3) and Ashton Raggatt McDougall. Assistants: Maren Parry, Lizzie Burt, Daniel Firns, Kioshi Furuno, Luca Ginoulhiac, Scott Hawken, Silvia Krizova, Paul Moravcik.

The Pentagon Memorial
Competition entry, Virginia, 2002. Finalist. In association with Vladimir Sitta (Room 4.1.3), Peter England, and Jacky Bowring. Assistants: Martin Musiatowicz, Maren Parry, Robert Faber, Tom Griffiths, Sid Thoo, Andrew Nugent.

The Tsunami Memorial
Competition entry, Thailand, 2005. Finalist. In association with Vladimir Sitta (Room 4.1.3) and Gary Marinko. Assistant: Mike Rowlands.

Wungong
Built work, Perth, 2004–2007. In association with Tinka Sack. Advisors: Sharni Howe, Patric de Villiers. Assistants: Andrew Nugent, Julia Robinson, Alexandra Farrington.

Boomtown 2050: Scenarios for a Rapidly Growing City
Funded research (Australian Research Council), 2006–2009. Project coordinator: Donna Broun. Assistants: Karl Kullmann, Julia Robinson, Phivo Geogiou.

Made in Australia: The Future of Australian Cities
Funded research (Australian Urban Design Research Center), 2011–2013. In association with Julian Bolleter. Assistants: Rebecca Giggs, Rebecca Lewis.

The Atlas for the End of the World
Self-funded research, 2014–2017. Assistants: Claire Hoch, Chieh Huang, Darcy van Buskirk.

The Hotspots Cities Project
Funded research (Penn Global), 2018–2020. Project coordinator: Zuzanna Drozdz. Assistants: Nangxi Dong, Chieh Huang, Tone Chu, Josh Ketchum, Thomas Delahouliere, Claudia Silver, Nicole Leonard, Chris Proctor.

Bogotá 2050
Studio project, Weitzman School of Design, 2018. In association with David Gouverneur. Assistants: Zuzanna Drozdz, Boya Ye. Student Team: Yifan Cai, Yu-Te Chi-ang, Mariela Hernandez, Terence Hogan, Ruobing Huang, Yichao Jia, Mei-chun Jia, Hong Li, Xuanang Li, Zhiyu Wcio.

The World Park Project
Self-funded research, 2015–ongoing. Assistants: Claire Hoch, Oliver Atwood, Elliot Bullen, Alice Bell, Chieh Huang, Tone Chu, Misako Murata, Emily Bunker, Rob Levinthal, Shannon Rafferty, Lucy Whitacre, Lujian Zhang, Allison Nkwocha, Madeleine Ghillany-Lehar.

The Mega-Eco Project
Funded research (Penn Global and Penn Environment Innovation Initiative), 2020–ongoing. In association with Rob Levinthal, Carolyne Kousky, and Matthijs Bouw. Assistants: Charlotte Stewart, Tristan Grupp, Weijing Wang, Xinge Zhang, Kelvin Vu, Priyanjali Sinha.

The Butterfly and the Locust
Installation, China Central Academy of Arts, 2023. In association with Rob Levinthal. Assistants: Siyang Jing, Erlu Ni, Jessica Wu, Lu Wang, Hanyu Hu.

Not the Blue Marble
Installation, Venice Biennale, 2021. Assistants: Tone Chu, Francesca Garzilli.

Richard J. Weller & Tatum L. Hands (eds.), *The Landscape Project* (San Francisco: AR+D Publishing, 2022).

Richard J. Weller, "Green Stuff," *LA+ Interdisciplinary Journal of Landscape Architecture* 15 (2022) 116–23.

Richard J. Weller, "The Hype of Representation: Some Thoughts on the Roles of the Hyperreal and the Hyperobject in Contemporary Landscape Architecture" *Ri-Vista: Research for Landscape Architecture* 18(2) (2021), 30–39.

Richard J. Weller, "The World Park Project," *International Journal of Protected Areas and Conservation* 27, no.2 (2021), 75–78.

Richard J. Weller, Zuzanna Drozdz, David Gouverneur & Boya Ye, "The Hotspot Cities Project: The Case Study of Bogotá 2050," *JoLA: Journal of Landscape Architecture* 16, no. 1 (2021), 44–57.

Richard J. Weller, Zuzanna Drozdz & Sara Padgett Kjaersgaard, "Hotspot Cities: Identifying Peri-Urban Conflict Zones in the World's Biodiversity Hotspots," *JoLA: Journal of Landscape Architecture* 14, no. 1 (2019), 36–47.

Richard J. Weller, Frederick Steiner, Karen M'Closkey & William Fleming, *Design with Nature Now* (New York: Lincoln Institute of Land Policy & Columbia University Press, 2019).

Richard J. Weller, "Landscape Genres: Towards a Taxonomy of Landscape Architecture in the 21st Century," *Landscape Architecture Frontiers* 26, no. 8 (July 2019).

Richard J. Weller, "Terrarium: The Ultimate Design Experiment, *LA+ Interdisciplinary Journal of Landscape Architecture* 9 (2019) 102–109.

Richard J. Weller, "Our Time?" in *The New Landscape Declaration: A Call to Action for the 21st Century* (Los Angeles: Rare Bird Books, 2017).

Richard J. Weller, "Acts of Gods: Geoengineering Risk" *LA+ Interdisciplinary Journal of Landscape Architecture* 6 (2017) 16–25.

Richard J. Weller, "The City Is Not an Egg," in *Cities and Nature*, eds. Frederick Steiner & George Thompson (New York: Lincoln Institute of Land Policy, 2016).

Richard J. Weller, "Stewardship Now? Reflections on Landscape Architecture's Raison d'être in the 21st Century," *Landscape Journal* 33, no. 2 (2015), 85–108.

Richard J. Weller & Julian Bolleter, *Made in Australia: The Future of Australian Cities* (Perth: UWA Publishing, 2013).

Richard J. Weller, *Boomtown 2050: Scenarios for a Rapidly Growing City* (Perth: UWA Publishing, 2009).

Richard J. Weller, "Landscape Sub-urbanism: Towards a Theory and Practice of Landscape Architecture in Contemporary Suburban Conditions," *Landscape Journal* 27, no. 2 (2008), 255–70.

Richard J. Weller, "Planning by Design: Scenarios for a City of Three Million People," *JoLA: Journal of Landscape Architecture* 6 (2008), 6–17.

Richard J. Weller, "An Art of Instrumentality: Thinking Through Landscape Urbanism" in *The Landscape Urbanism Reader*, ed. Charles Waldheim (New York: Princeton Architectural Press, 2006).

Richard J. Weller, *Room 4.1.3: Innovations in Landscape Architecture* (Philadelphia: University of Pennsylvania Press, 2005).

Richard J. Weller, "Between Hermeneutics and Datascapes: A Critical Appreciation of Emergent Landscape Design Theory and Praxis through the Writings of James Corner 1990–2000 – Part I and Part II," *Landscape Review* 7, no. 1 (2002), 3–24; 25–44.

Richard J. Weller, "The National Museum and Its Garden of Australian Dreams," *Studies in the History of Gardens and Designed Landscapes* 21, no. 1 (2001), 66–85.

http://richardweller.net
https://atlas-for-the-end-of-the-world.com
https://theworldpark.com
https://hotspotcitiesproject.com

"The World Park Project" (2015-). Triptychs containing the World Park's territory exhibited in Meyerson Hall at the University of Pennsylvania. Etched into the surface of the closed triptychs are the names of endangered species related to the territory of each map within (see page 4–5). Image by Gordon Stillman.

ACKNOWLEDGMENTS

Until now I have never stopped work to really acknowledge the importance of the friends, family, and colleagues who have variously enabled and contributed to my career. I'm grateful to my parents, Robin and Sam, for a childhood full of freedom and imagination. Contrary to the negative stereotype, suburbia for me was full of eccentric characters conducting backyard experiments. I was also fortunate to have always had wildly intelligent and creative friends. Chris and Steve Packer, Jay Balbi, Peter Beasley, and the Bossell family loom large in my memory. Academically, I was lucky to study under two inspirational design professors, Helen Armstrong and Craig Burton, and philosophy professor Graham Pont. Later, academic colleagues such as Simon Anderson, Geoffrey London, Patrick Beale, Clarissa Ball, Leon van Schaik, John Dixon Hunt, Laurie Olin, Marilyn Jordan Taylor, and Fritz Steiner have all been supportive and generous at different times. Professionally, I was fortunate to have been given significant opportunities by Luqman Keale, Jan Wehburg and Cornelia Müller, and architects Ashton Raggatt McDougall. Thank you also to the Landscape Architecture Foundation and the Australian Institute of Landscape Architects for involving me in the curation of legacy events. Over the years I have had talented research assistants and collaborators such as Lizzie Burt, Daniel Firns, Karl Kullmann, Julian Bolleter, Tom Griffiths, Mike Rowlands, Donna Broun, Claire Hoch, Shuo Yan, Chieh Huang, Tone Chu, Zuzanna Drozdz, Nanxi Dong, Oliver Atwood, Madeleine Ghillany-Lehar, Alice Bell, Shannon Rafferty, Elliot Bullen, Emily Bunker, Jiacheng Chen, and Rob Levinthal. Of this group I especially want to acknowledge Donna Broun whose research underpinned the Boomtown 2050 project and Julian Bolleter who partnered with me on the Made in Australia project. I want to also thank Jiachen Sun, Andreina Sojo, Yining Zhu, and Elliot Bullen for helping me pull together the manuscript and refine the images and layout for this book. I am also particularly thankful that Jillian Walliss and Dirk Sijmons—two landscape architects whom I admire—agreed to contribute essays.

Finally, I would especially like to single out four people. First, Vladimir Sitta, a master craftsman and relentless experimentalist from Brno in Czech, who has served as a co-conspirator pretty much from the beginning. On all the projects we did together over many years, while I could think a project to life, it was Vladimir who could refine it and build it. Second, I raise a very big glass to my best mate, the landscape architect and set designer Peter England with whom I've shared many sleepless nights arguing about art and earth spirits. Third, James Corner, whose writings in the early 1990s confirmed my own ramblings and who entrusted me to succeed him as Chair of Landscape Architecture at Penn. Finally, and above all, I thank my partner Tatum Hands who has not only put up with my constant over-indulgence in all this work, but contributed to it in myriad ways.